When should I travel to get the best airfare?

Where do I go for answers to my travel questions?

What's the best and easiest way to plan and book my trip?

frommers.travelocity.com

Frommer's, the travel guide leader, has teamed up with **Travelocity.com,** the leader in online travel, to bring you an in-depth, easy-to-use resource designed to help you plan and book your trip online.

At **frommers.travelocity.com**, you'll find free online updates about your destination from the experts at Frommer's plus the outstanding travel planning and purchasing features of Travelocity.com. Travelocity.com provides reservations capabilities for 95 percent of all airline seats sold, more than 47,000 hotels, and over 50 car rental companies. In addition, Travelocity.com offers more than 2,000 exciting vacation and cruise packages. Travelocity.com puts you in complete control of your travel planning with these and other great features:

> **Expert travel guidance from Frommer's** - over 150 writers reporting from around the world!
>
> **Best Fare Finder** - an interactive calendar tells you when to travel to get the best airfare
>
> **Fare Watcher** - we'll track airfare changes to your favorite destinations
>
> **Dream Maps** - a mapping feature that suggests travel opportunities based on your budget
>
> **Shop Safe Guarantee** - 24 hours a day / 7 days a week live customer service, and more!

Whether traveling on a tight budget, looking for a quick weekend getaway, or planning the trip of a lifetime, Frommer's guides and Travelocity.com will make your travel dreams a reality. You've bought the book, now book the trip!

Here's what the critics say about Frommer's:

"Amazingly easy to use. Very portable, very complete."

—*Booklist*

"The only mainstream guide to list specific prices. The Walter Cronkite of guidebooks—with all that implies."

—*Travel & Leisure*

"Complete, concise, and filled with useful information."

—*New York Daily News*

♦

"Hotel information is close to encyclopedic."
—*Des Moines Sunday Register*

♦

"The best series for travelers who want one easy-to-use guidebook."

—*U.S. Air Magazine*

P O R T A B L E

Las Vegas
2001

by Mary Herczog

IDG Books Worldwide, Inc.
An International Data Group Company
Foster City, CA • Chicago, IL • Indianapolis, IN • New York, NY

ABOUT THE AUTHOR

Mary Herczog lives in Los Angeles and works in the film industry. She is the author of *Frommer's New Orleans, Frommer's Las Vegas,* and *Las Vegas for Dummies.* She still isn't sure when to hold and when to hit in blackjack.

IDG BOOKS WORLDWIDE, INC.

An International Data Group Company
909 Third Ave.
New York, NY 10022

Find us online at **www.frommers.com**

ISBN: 0-02-863876-X
ISSN: 1090-5472

Editor: Lisa Renaud/Dog-Eared Pages
Production Editor: Tammy Ahrens
Photo Editor: Richard Fox
Design by Michele Laseau
Cartographer: Elizabeth Puhl
Production by IDG Books Indianapolis Production Department

SPECIAL SALES

For general information on IDG Books Worldwide's books in the U.S., please call our Consumer Customer Service department at 1-800-762-2974. For reseller information, including discounts, bulk sales, customized editions, and premium sales, please call our Reseller Customer Service department at 1-800-434-3422.

Manufactured in the United States of America

5 4 3 2 1

Contents

List of Maps

AN INVITATION TO THE READER

In researching this book, we discovered many wonderful places—hotels, restaurants, shops, and more. We're sure you'll find others. Please tell us about them, so that we can share the information with your fellow travelers in upcoming editions. If you were disappointed with a recommendation, we'd love to know that, too. Please write to:

Frommer's Portable Las Vegas 2001
IDG Books Worldwide, Inc.
909 Third Ave.
New York, NY 10022

AN ADDITIONAL NOTE

Please be advised that travel information is subject to change at any time, and this is especially true of prices. We therefore suggest that you write or call ahead for confirmation when making your travel plans. The authors, editors, and publishers cannot be held responsible for the experiences of readers while traveling. Your safety is important to us, however, so we encourage you to stay alert and be aware of your surroundings. Keep a close eye on cameras, purses, and wallets, all favorite targets of thieves and pickpockets.

WHAT THE SYMBOLS MEAN

✪ Frommer's Favorites

Our favorite places and experiences—outstanding for quality, value, or both.

The following abbreviations are used for credit cards:

AE	American Express	ER	EnRoute
CB	Carte Blanche	JCB	Japan Credit Bank
DC	Diners Club	MC	MasterCard
DISC	Discover	V	Visa
EC	Eurocard		

FIND FROMMER'S ONLINE

www.frommers.com offers up-to-the-minute listings on almost 200 cities around the globe—including the latest bargains and candid, personal articles updated daily by Arthur Frommer himself. No other Web site offers such comprehensive and timely coverage of the world of travel.

Planning a Trip to Las Vegas

*I*n the pages that follow, you'll find everything you need to know to handle the practical details of planning your trip in advance: airlines and area airports, a list of major conventions you may want to avoid, details on package deals, resources for those of you with special needs, and much more.

We also suggest that you check out chapter 8, "Las Vegas After Dark," before you leave home; if you want to see the most popular shows, it's a good idea to order tickets well in advance to avoid disappointment. (Ditto if you want to dine in one of the city's top restaurants; head to chapter 4, "Dining," for full reviews and contact information.)

1 Visitor Information

For advance information, call or write the **Las Vegas Convention and Visitors Authority,** 3150 Paradise Rd., Las Vegas, NV 89109 (☎ 800/332-5333 or 702/892-7575; www.lasvegas24hours. com). They can send you a comprehensive packet of brochures, a map, a show guide, an events calendar, and an attractions list; help you find a hotel that meets your specifications (and even make reservations); and tell you if a major convention is scheduled during the time you would like to visit Las Vegas. Or stop by when you're in town. They're open Monday to Friday 7am to 5pm and Saturday and Sunday 8:30am to 5pm.

Another excellent information source is the **Las Vegas Chamber of Commerce,** 3720 Howard Hughes Pkwy., #100, Las Vegas, NV 89109 (☎ 702/735-1616). Ask them to send you their *Visitor's Guide,* which contains extensive information about accommodations, attractions, excursions, children's activities, and more. They can answer all your Las Vegas questions, including those about weddings and divorces. They're open Monday to Friday 8:30am to 5pm.

2   When to Go

Since most of a Las Vegas vacation is usually spent indoors, you can have a good time here year-round. The most pleasant seasons are spring and fall, especially if you want to experience the great outdoors.

Weekdays are slightly less crowded than weekends. Holidays are always a mob scene and come accompanied by high hotel prices. Hotel prices also skyrocket when big conventions and special events are taking place. The slowest times of year are June and July, the week before Christmas, and the week after New Year's.

If a major convention is to be held during your trip, you might want to change your date. Check the box later in this section, and contact the **Las Vegas Convention and Visitors Authority** (☎ **800/332-5333** or 702/892-7575; www.lasvegas24hours. com), since convention schedules often change.

THE WEATHER

First of all, Vegas isn't always hot, but when it is, it's *really* hot. One thing you'll hear again and again is that even though Las Vegas gets very hot, the dry desert heat is not unbearable. This is true, except in the hotel pool areas; they are surrounded by massive hotels covered in mirrored glass, which acts like a giant magnifying glass on the antlike people below. Still, generally the humidity averages a low 22%, and even on very hot days, there's apt to be a breeze. Also, except on the hottest summer days, there's relief at night when temperatures often drop by as much as 20°F.

Las Vegas's Average Temperatures (°F)

	Jan	Feb	Mar	Apr	May	June	July	Aug	Sept	Oct	Nov	Dec
Average	44	50	57	66	74	84	91	88	81	67	54	47
Avg. High	55	62	69	79	88	99	105	103	96	82	67	58
Avg. Low	33	39	44	53	60	68	76	74	65	53	41	36

But this is the desert, and it's not hot all year-round. It can get quite cold, especially in the winter, when at night it can drop to 30°F and lower. The breeze can also become a cold, biting, strong wind of up to 40 m.p.h. and more. So there are entire portions of the year when you won't be using that hotel swimming pool at all (even if you want to—be aware that most of the hotels close huge chunks of those fabulous swimming pool areas for "the season,"

Major Convention Dates for 2001

Listed below are Las Vegas's major annual conventions with projected attendance figures for 2001; believe us, you probably want to avoid the biggies. Contact the **Las Vegas Convention and Visitors Authority** (☎ **800/332-5333** or 702/892-7575; www.lasvegas24hours.com) to double-check the latest info before you commit to your travel dates, since convention schedules frequently change.

Event	Dates	Expected Attendance
Consumer Electronics Show	Jan 7–10	100,000
Sporting Goods Manufacturers Association	Jan 21–24	90,000
Men's Apparel Guild in California (MAGIC)	Feb 13–16	90,000
Western Shoe Associates	Feb 23–27	30,000
World of Concrete Exposition	Feb 27–Mar 2	70,000
Associated Surplus Dealers	Mar 4–8	51,000
National Association of Broadcasters (NAB)	Apr 23–26	125,000
Networld/Interop	May 7–11	60,000
Western Shoe Associates	Aug 2–5	30,000
Men's Apparel Guild in California (MAGIC)	Aug 27–30	90,000
Softbank Comdex	Nov 12–16	225,000

which can be as long as from Labor Day to Memorial Day). If you aren't traveling in the height of summer, bring a wrap. Also, remember your sunscreen and hat—even if it's not all that hot, you can burn very easily and very fast. (You should see all the lobster-red people glowing in the casinos at night.)

3 Money-Saving Package Deals

Package tours are not the same as escorted tours. They are simply a way to buy airfare and accommodations (and sometimes extras like sightseeing tours and hard-to-get show tickets) at the same time. When you're visiting Las Vegas, a package can be a smart way to go. In many cases, a package that includes airfare, hotel, and a rental car will cost you less than your hotel bill alone would have had you booked it yourself.

Packages, however, vary widely. Some offer a better class of hotels than others. Some offer the same hotels for lower prices. Prices vary according to the season, seat availability, hotel choice, whether you travel midweek or on the weekend, and other factors. But since even an advance-purchase round-trip fare between New York and Las Vegas can easily be $100 or $200 more than the figures quoted below, it seems almost insane *not* to book a less expensive package that includes so many extras.

So how do you find a package deal?

Perhaps the best place to start is with the airlines themselves, which often package their flights together with accommodations. **National Airlines** (☎ 888/757-5387; nationalairlines.com), a new low-cost carrier based in Las Vegas, offers discount packages that include hotel stays at either Harrah's or the Rio Suites. Other airlines that offer some excellent packages to Las Vegas include **American Airlines FlyAway Vacations** (☎ 800/321-2121), **America West Vacations** (☎ 800/442-5013), **Delta Dream Vacations** (☎ 800/872-7786), **Southwest Airline Vacations** (☎ 800/423-5683), and **US Airways Vacations** (☎ 800/455-0123).

Reservations Plus (☎ 800/805-9528; fax 702/795-3999) runs a free room-reservation service, but they can also arrange packages (including meals, transportation, tours, show tickets, car rentals, and other features) and group rates.

One of the biggest packagers in the Northeast, **Liberty Travel** (☎ 888/271-1584; www.libertytravel.com) boasts a full-page ad in many Sunday papers. You won't get much in the way of service, but you will get a good deal. **American Express Vacations** (☎ 800/241-1700; www.leisureweb.com) is another option.

For one-stop shopping on the Web, go to **www.vacationpackager. com**, a search engine that will link you to many different package-tour operators offering Vegas vacations, often with a company profile summarizing the company's basic booking and cancellation terms.

4 Getting There

BY PLANE

The following airlines have regularly scheduled flights into Las Vegas (some of these are regional carriers, so they may not all fly from your point of origin): **Air Canada** (☎ 888/247-2262;

www.aircanada.ca; does not offer direct service but will book on partner airlines, usually with a change in San Francisco), **Alaska Airlines** (☎ 800/426-0333; www.alaskaair.com), **Allegiant Air** (☎ 877/202-6444; www.allegiantair.com; service only from Long Beach and Fresno, CA), **America West** (☎ 800/235-9292; www.americawest.com), **American/American Eagle** (☎ 800/433-7300; www.americanair.com or www.aa.com), **American Trans Air** (☎ 800/543-3708; www.ata.com; currently only has service to Vegas through Chicago or Indianapolis), **Continental** (☎ 800/525-0280; www.flycontinental.com), **Delta/Skywest** (☎ 800/221-1212; www.delta-air.com), **Frontier Airlines** (☎ 800/432-1359; www.frontierairlines.com), **Hawaiian Airlines** (☎ 800/367-5320; www.hawaiianair.com), **Japan Airlines** (☎ 800/525-3663), **Legend Airlines** (☎ 800/452-2022; www.legendairlines.com; a small start-up airline that currently only offers service from Dallas, Los Angeles, and Washington, D.C.), **National Airlines** (☎ 888/757-5387; www.nationalairlines.com), **Northwest** (☎ 800/225-2525; www.nwa.com), **Reno Air** (☎ 800/736-6247), **Southwest** (☎ 800/435-9792; www.iflyswa.com), **Sun Country** (☎ 800/752-1218; www.suncountry.com), **TWA** (☎ 800/221-2000; www.twa.com), **United** (☎ 800/241-6522; www.ual.com), and **US Airways** (☎ 800/428-4322; www.usair.com).

Consolidators, also known as bucket shops, are a good place to find low fares, often below even the airlines' discounted rates. Basically, they're just big travel agents that get discounts for buying in bulk and pass some of the savings on to you. We've gotten great deals from **Cheap Tickets** (☎ 800/377-1000; www. cheaptickets.com). Other reliable consolidators include **Lowestfare.com** (☎ 888/278-8830; www.lowestfare.com); **1-800-AIRFARE** (www.1800airfare.com); **Cheap Seats** (☎ 800/451-7200; www.cheapseatstravel.com); and **1-800-FLY-CHEAP** (www.flycheap.com).

You can also search the Internet for cheap fares. A few of the better-respected virtual travel agents are **Travelocity** (**www.travelocity.com**), **Microsoft Expedia** (**www.expedia.com**), and **Yahoo! Travel** (**www.yahoo.com**).

BY CAR

The main highway connecting Las Vegas with the rest of the country is I-15; it links Montana, Idaho, and Utah with southern California. The drive from Los Angeles is quite popular, and thanks to the narrow two-lane highway, can get very crowded on Friday and Sunday afternoons with hopeful weekend gamblers making their way to and from Vegas.

From the east, take I-70 or I-80 west to Kingman, Arizona, and then U.S. 93 north to Downtown Las Vegas (Fremont Street). From the south, take I-10 west to Phoenix and then U.S. 93 north to Las Vegas. From San Francisco, take I-80 east to Reno and then U.S. 95 south to Las Vegas.

Vegas is 286 miles from Phoenix, 759 miles from Denver, 421 miles from Salt Lake City, 269 miles from Los Angeles, and 586 miles from San Francisco.

Since driving on the outskirts of Las Vegas—for example, coming from California—involves desert driving, you must take certain precautions. It's a good idea to check your tires, water, and oil before leaving. Take at least 5 gallons of water in a clean container that can be used for either drinking or the radiator. Pay attention to road signs that suggest when to turn off your car's air conditioner. And don't push your luck with gas—it may be 35 miles, or more, between stations. If your car overheats, do not remove the radiator cap until the engine has cooled, and then remove it very slowly. Add water to within an inch of the top of the radiator.

BY TRAIN

It's about 2 years behind schedule, but **Amtrak** (☎ **800/ USA-RAIL;** www.amtrak.com) plans to restore passenger service to Las Vegas in late 2000 using the TALGO. This European-designed "Casino Train" completes the trip from Los Angeles in about 5½ hours, with a wholesale seat price of $99 round-trip. (There's some talk that the train's route may continue on to Salt Lake City, but this had not been finalized at press time.) Much of the train will be pre-sold to various hotels, so the final price to the traveler will depend on how you get the ticket. High rollers will probably end up with freebies, but the ticket will most likely be in three figures purchased at the counter. A different higher-speed "Maglev" train is several years away from construction, if it happens at all.

2

Getting to Know Las Vegas

*L*ocated in the southernmost precincts of a wide, pancake-flat valley, Las Vegas is the biggest city in the state of Nevada. Treeless mountains form a scenic backdrop to hotels awash in neon glitter. For tourism purposes, the city is quite compact.

1 Orientation

VISITOR INFORMATION

All major Las Vegas hotels provide comprehensive tourist information at their reception and/or sightseeing and show desks.

Other good information sources are: the **Las Vegas Convention and Visitors Authority,** 3150 Paradise Rd., Las Vegas, NV 89109 (☎ **800/332-5333** or 702/892-7575; www.lasvegas24hours.com), open Monday to Friday 8am to 6pm, Saturday and Sunday 8am to 5pm; the **Las Vegas Chamber of Commerce,** 711 E. Desert Inn Rd., Las Vegas, NV 89109 (☎ **702/735-1616**), open Monday to Friday 8am to 5pm; and, for information on all of Nevada, including Las Vegas, the **Nevada Commission on Tourism** (☎ **800/638-2328**), open 24 hours.

CITY LAYOUT

There are two main areas of Las Vegas: the **Strip** and **Downtown.** For many people, that's all there is to Las Vegas. But there is actually more to the town than that; maybe not as glitzy and glamorous—okay, definitely not—but you will find still more casino action on Paradise Road and in east Las Vegas, mainstream and alternative culture shopping on Maryland Parkway, and different restaurant choices all over the city. Confining yourself to the Strip and Downtown is fine for the first-time visitor, but repeat customers (and you will be) should get out there and explore. Las Vegas Boulevard South (the Strip) is Ground Zero for addresses; anything crossing it will start with 1 East and 1 West (and go up from there) at that point.

THE STRIP

The Strip is probably the most famous 4-mile stretch of highway in the nation. Officially called Las Vegas Boulevard South, it contains most of the top hotels in town and offers almost all of the major showroom entertainment. First-time visitors will, and probably should, spend the bulk of their time on the Strip. If mobility is a problem, then we suggest basing yourself in a South or Mid-Strip location.

For the purposes of organizing this book, we've divided the Strip into three sections. The **South Strip** can be roughly defined as the portion of the Strip south of Harmon Avenue, including the MGM Grand, the Monte Carlo, New York–New York, and the Luxor hotels.

Mid-Strip is a long stretch of the street between Harmon Avenue and Spring Mountain Road, including Caesars, the Mirage and Treasure Island, Bally's, the Flamingo Hilton, and Harrah's.

North Strip stretches north from Spring Mountain Road all the way to the Stratosphere Tower and includes the Stardust, Sahara, Riviera, Desert Inn, and Circus Circus.

EAST OF THE STRIP/CONVENTION CENTER

This area has grown up around the Las Vegas Convention Center. Las Vegas is one of the nation's top convention cities, attracting more than 2.9 million conventioneers each year. The major hotel in this section is the Las Vegas Hilton, but in recent years, Marriott has built Residence Inn and Courtyard properties here, and the Hard Rock Hotel has opened. You'll find many excellent smaller hotels and motels southward along Paradise Road. All of these offer close proximity to the Strip.

DOWNTOWN

Also known as **"Glitter Gulch"** (narrower streets make the neon seem brighter), downtown Las Vegas, which is centered on Fremont Street between Main and 9th streets, was the first section of the city to develop hotels and casinos. With the exception of the Golden Nugget, which looks like it belongs in Monte Carlo, this area has traditionally been more casual than the Strip. But with the advent of the **Fremont Street Experience** (see chapter 5 for details), Downtown has experienced a revitalization. The area is clean, the crowds are low-key and friendly, and the light show

Las Vegas at a Glance

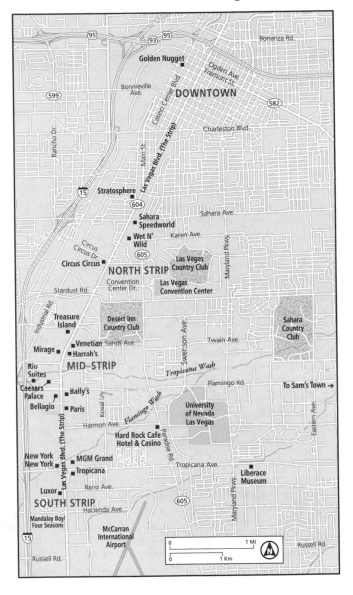

overhead is as silly as anything on the Strip. Don't overlook it. Las Vegas Boulevard runs all the way into Fremont Street Downtown.

2   Getting Around

BY CAR

We highly recommend that visitors rent a car. The Strip is too spread out for walking (and is often too hot or too cold to make strolls pleasant), Downtown is too far away for a cheap cab ride, and public transportation is ineffective at best. Plus, further visits call for exploration in still more parts of the city, and a car brings freedom (especially if you want to do any side trips—bus tours are available, but a car lets you explore at your own pace rather than according to a tour schedule).

You should note that places with addresses some 60 blocks east or west from the Strip are actually less than a 10-minute drive—provided there is no traffic.

However, if you plan to confine yourself to one part of the Strip (or one cruise down to it) or to Downtown, your feet will suffice.

Having said that you should rent a car, however, we should warn you that the growing population means a proportionate increase in the number of cars. Traffic is getting worse, and it's harder and harder to get around town with any certain swiftness. A general rule of thumb is to avoid driving on the Strip whenever you can, and avoid driving at all during peak rush hours, especially if you have to make a show curtain.

Parking is usually a pleasure, since all casino hotels offer valet service. That means that for a mere $1 tip you can park right at the door (though the valet usually fills up on busy nights).

RENTING A CAR

All of the major car-rental companies are represented in Las Vegas. We like **Allstate** (☎ **800/634-6186** or 702/736-6147), the least expensive of the airport-based car-rental agencies. We've found this local family-owned company (the largest independent operator in Las Vegas) friendly and competent, with an invariably charming staff at the airport. They're open 24 hours. And they've agreed to offer our readers a **20% discount off regular rental rates** at any Allstate location (just show the agent your copy of this book). In addition to McCarran Airport, there are Allstate car desks at the Riviera and Jackie Gaughan's Plaza hotels, and the company offers free pickup anywhere in Las Vegas.

National companies with outlets in Las Vegas include **Alamo** (☎ 800/327-9633; www.goalamo.com), **Avis** (☎ 800/367-2847; www.avis.com), **Budget** (☎ 800/922-2899; www.budgetrentacar.com), **Dollar** (☎ 800/842-2054; www.dollarcar.com), **Enterprise** (☎ 800/325/8007; www.pickenterprise.com), **Hertz** (☎ 800/654-3131; www.hertz.com), **National** (☎ 800/227-7368; www.nationalcar.com), and **Thrifty** (☎ 800/367-2277; www.thrifty.com).

BY TAXI

Since cabs line up in front of all major hotels, an easy way to get around town is by taxi. Cabs charge $2.20 at the meter drop and 30¢ for each additional ⅕ mile. A taxi from the airport to the Strip will run you $8 to $12, from the airport to Downtown $15 to $18, and between the Strip and Downtown about $7 to $10. You can often save money by sharing a cab with someone going to the same destination (up to five people can ride for the same fare).

If you want to call a taxi, any of the following companies can provide one: **Desert Cab Company** (☎ 702/376-2688), **Whittlesea Blue Cab** (☎ 702/384-6111), and **Yellow/Checker Cab/Star Company** (☎ 702/873-2000).

FAST FACTS: Las Vegas

American Express There are about a dozen offices in town, but the closest one to the Strip is at 3504 S. Maryland Pkwy. (in the Boulevard Mall; ☎ 702/794-2811).

Baby-sitters Contact **Around the Clock Child Care** (☎ 800/798-6768 or 702/365-1040). In business since 1987, this reputable company clears its sitters with the health department, the sheriff, and the FBI, and carefully screens references. Charges are $45 for 4 hours for one or two children, $10 for each additional hour, with surcharges for additional children and on holidays. Sitters are on call 7 days a week, 24 hours a day, and they will come to your hotel. Call at least 3 hours in advance.

Car Rentals See "Getting Around," earlier in this chapter.

Cash & Credit   It's extremely easy, too easy, to obtain cash in Las Vegas. Most casino cashiers will cash personal checks and can exchange foreign currency, and just about every casino has a machine that will provide cash on a wide variety of credit cards.

Conventions   Las Vegas is one of America's top convention destinations. Much of the action takes place at the **Las Vegas Convention Center,** 3150 Paradise Rd., Las Vegas, NV 89109 (☎ **702/892-7575**), which is the largest single-level convention center in the world. Its 1.3-million square feet includes 89 meeting rooms. And this immense facility is augmented by the **Cashman Field Center,** 850 Las Vegas Blvd. N., Las Vegas, NV 89101 (☎ **702/386-7100**). Under the same auspices, Cashman provides another 98,100 square feet of convention space.

Dentists & Doctors   See also "Hospitals," below.

For dentist referrals, you can call the **Clark County Dental Society** (☎ **702/255-7873**), weekdays 9am to noon and 1 to 5pm; when the office is closed, a recording will tell you who to call for emergency service.

For physician referrals, call the **Desert Springs Hospital** (☎ **800/842-5439** or 702/733-6875). Hours are Monday to Friday 8am to 5pm.

Hospitals   Emergency services are available 24 hours a day at **University Medical Center,** 1800 W. Charleston Blvd., at Shadow Lane (☎ **702/383-2000**); the emergency room entrance is on the corner of Hastings and Rose streets. **Sunrise Hospital and Medical Center,** 3186 Maryland Pkwy., between Desert Inn Road and Sahara Avenue (☎ **702/731-8080**), also has a 24-hour emergency room.

For more minor problems, if you are on the Strip, the Imperial Palace has a 24-hour urgent care facility, the **Nevada Resort Medical Center,** an independently run facility on the 8th floor, with doctors and X-ray machines; it's located at 3535 Las Vegas Blvd. S., between the Sands and Flamingo (☎ **702/893-6767**).

Hotlines   Emergency hotlines include the **Rape Crisis Center** (☎ **702/366-1640**), **Suicide Prevention** (☎ **702/731-2990**), and **Poison Emergencies** (☎ **800/446-6179**).

Liquor & Gambling Laws   You must be 21 to drink or gamble; proof of age is required and often requested at bars, nightclubs, and restaurants, so it's always a good idea to bring ID when you go out if you look young. There are no closing hours in Las Vegas for the sale or consumption of alcohol, even on Sunday. Don't even think about driving while you're under the influence or having an open container of alcohol in your car. Beer, wine, and liquor are all sold in all kinds of stores pretty much round the clock; trust us, you won't have a hard time finding a drink in this town. It's even legal to have an open container on the Strip.

Newspapers & Periodicals   There are two Las Vegas dailies: the *Las Vegas Review Journal* and the *Las Vegas Sun.* The *Review Journal*'s Friday edition has a helpful "Weekend" section with a comprehensive guide to shows and buffets. There are two free alternative papers, with club listings and many unbiased restaurant and bar reviews. Both *City Life* and *Las Vegas Weekly* are weekly. And at every hotel desk, you'll find dozens of free local magazines, such as *Vegas Visitor, What's On in Las Vegas, Showbiz Weekly,* and *Where to Go in Las Vegas,* that are chock-full of helpful information—although probably of the sort that comes from paid advertising.

Parking   Valet parking is one of the great pleasures of Las Vegas and well worth the dollar tip (given when the car is returned) to save walking a city block from the far reaches of a hotel parking lot, particularly when the temperature is over 100°. Another summer plus: The valet will turn on your air-conditioning so that you don't have to get into an "oven on wheels."

Pharmacies   There's a 24-hour **Walgreens** (which also has a 1-hour photo) at 3765 Las Vegas Blvd. S. (☎ **702/895-6878**) almost directly across from the Monte Carlo. **Sav-On** is a large 24-hour drugstore and pharmacy close to the Strip at 1360 E. Flamingo Rd., at Maryland Parkway (☎ **702/731-5373** for the pharmacy, 702/737-0595 for general merchandise). **White Cross Drugs,** 1700 Las Vegas Blvd. S. (☎ **702/382-1733**), open daily 7am to 1am, will make pharmacy deliveries to your hotel during the day.

Police   For non-emergencies, call ☎ **702/795-3111.** For emergencies, call ☎ **911.**

Safety   In Las Vegas, vast amounts of money are always on display, and criminals find many easy marks. Don't be one of them. At gaming tables and slot machines, men should keep wallets well-concealed and out of the reach of pickpockets, and women should keep handbags in plain sight (on laps). Outside casinos, popular spots for pickpockets and thieves are restaurants and outdoor shows, such as the volcano at the Mirage or at the Treasure Island pirate battle. Stay alert. Unless your hotel room has an in-room safe, check your valuables in a safe-deposit box at the front desk. The area northeast of Harmon and Koval has had increased gang activity of late and should be avoided or at least approached with caution.

Show Tickets   See chapter 8 for details on obtaining show tickets.

Taxes   Clark County hotel room tax is 9%; the sales tax is 7%.

Time Zone   Las Vegas is in the Pacific time zone, 3 hours earlier than the East Coast, 2 hours earlier than the Midwest. For exact local time, call ☎ **702/248-4800.**

3

Accommodations

*I*f there's one thing Vegas has, it's hotels. Big hotels. Here you'll find the 10 largest hotels in the United States, if not in the world. And rooms: 125,000 rooms, to be exact—or at least exact at this writing. Every 5 minutes, or so it seems, someone is putting up a new giant hotel, or adding another 1,000 rooms to an already existing one. So finding a place to stay in Vegas should be the least of your worries.

Or is it?

When a convention, a fight, or some other big event is happening—and these things are always happening—darn near all of those 120,000 rooms are going to be sold out. (Over the course of last year, the occupancy rate for hotel rooms in Las Vegas ran at about 90%.) A last-minute Vegas vacation can turn into a housing nightmare. If possible, plan in advance so that you can have your choice: Ancient Egypt or Ancient Rome? New York or New Orleans? Strip or Downtown? Luxury or economy? Vegas has all that and way too much more.

The bottom line is that with a few, sometimes subtle, differences, a hotel room is a hotel room is a hotel room. After you factor in location, price, and whether you have a pirate-loving kid, there isn't that much difference between rooms, except for perhaps size and the quality of their surprisingly similar furnishings.

Prices in Vegas are anything but fixed, so you will notice wild ranges (the same room can routinely go for anywhere from $60 to $250, depending on demand), and even that range is negotiable if it's a slow time (though such times are less and less common thanks to the influx of conventions).

Reservations Services

If you get harried when you have to haggle, use a free service offered by **Reservations Plus**, 2275 A Renaissance Dr., Las Vegas, NV 89119 (☎ **800/805-9528;** fax 702/795-3999). They'll find you a hotel room in your price range that meets your specific requirements. Because they book rooms in volume, they are able to get discounted rates. Not only can they book rooms, but they can arrange packages (including meals, transportation, tours, show tickets, car rentals, and other features) and group rates.

The **Las Vegas Convention and Visitors Authority** also runs a room reservations hotline (☎ **800/332-5334**) that can be helpful. They can apprise you of room availability, quote rates, contact a hotel for you, and tell you when major conventions will be in town.

A couple of words of warning: Make sure they don't try to book you into a hotel you've never heard of. Try to stick with the big names or ones listed in this book. Always get your information in writing and then make some phone calls just to confirm that you really have the reservations that they say they've made for you.

1 South Strip

VERY EXPENSIVE

✪ **The Four Seasons.** 3960 Las Vegas Blvd. S., Las Vegas, NV 89119. ☎ **877/632-5200** or 702/632-5000. Fax 702/632-5195. www.fourseasons. com. 424 units. A/C MINIBAR TV TEL. $200–$500 double; from $400 suite. Free parking.

As various mammoth Vegas hotels attempt to position themselves as luxury resorts, insisting that service and fine cotton sheets can be done on a mass scale, a true luxury resort—in some people's eyes, *the* luxury resort—has very quietly moved in. The Four Seasons is located on the top five floors of Mandalay Bay, but in many ways, it's light-years away. A separate driveway and portico entrance, plus entire registration area, sets you up immediately. This is the one fancy hotel in town where you are not greeted, even at a distance, with the clash and clang of slots, and the general hubbub that is the soundtrack to Vegas.

Inside the Four Seasons, all is calm and quiet. But it's really the best of both worlds—all you have to do is walk through a door and instantly you are in Mandalay Bay, with access to a casino, nightlife and, yes, general hubbub. The difference is quite shocking, and frankly, once you've experienced Vegas this way, it's kind of hard to go back to the sensory overload. So let's scurry quickly back to the womblike comfort of the Four Seasons.

The rooms don't look like much at first—slightly bland but in good taste—but when you sink down into the furniture, you appreciate the fine quality. The beds have feather pillows and down comforters, robes are plush, and amenities (such as safes, irons, voice-mail, hair dryers, and VCRs) are really, really nice. Since the Four Seasons has the southernmost location on the Strip, its Strip-view rooms (the most expensive units) give you the whole incredible panorama.

Service is superb. Your needs are anticipated so quickly that you're tempted to sink to the floor in the lobby because you know someone will have a chair under your rear before you land. Children are encouraged and spoiled—welcome gifts of toys and goodies, and the list of comforts available for the asking is a yard long—and rooms are childproofed in advance. Once you factor in all the freebies (gym/spa access, pool cabanas, various other amenities), not to mention the service and the blessed peace, the difference in price between the Four Seasons and Bellagio (with all its hidden charges) is nothing.

Dining: Two restaurants and two lounges; afternoon tea is available.

Amenities: The Four Seasons has its own pool, with free cabanas, chilled spritzer bottles, fruit slices, and iced towels (you also have access to Mandalay Bay's pool). The gym is small but well-stocked (use of the gym is free, unlike those at most other hotels in town). Also available are 24-hour room service, concierge, daily newspaper, laundry, dry cleaning, complimentary children's amenities and services, business center, and a lounge area for late departure.

EXPENSIVE

Aladdin Resort & Casino. 3667 Las Vegas Blvd. S., Las Vegas, NV 89109. ☎ **877/333-WISH (333-9474).** www.aladdincasino.com. 2,600 units. A/C TV TEL. $119–$149 double. AE, DC, DISC, MC, V. Free self- and valet parking.

Die-hard sentimentalists that we are, we felt serious pangs of nostalgia when the old Aladdin was destroyed—because after all,

Elvis married Priscilla there and that counts for a lot. But sentiment carries us only so far, and so we have to admit that the old Aladdin was, in its waning years, a dump we didn't even bother listing in this book.

The new Aladdin promises to be an entirely different case. Though not yet open at press time, the building appears handsome indeed, and the plans for this newest resort are similarly ambitious. It's designed to be very smart-looking, and management brags that guests need never pass through the multistory casino in order to go to other hotel destinations (the lobby is on a different level entirely), and that you'll never be more than seven doors away from an elevator. It plans to offer more dining (21 restaurants total) and shopping (130 stores) than any resort on the Strip, plus a fun Middle Eastern theme.

Dining/Diversions: 21 restaurants, including a branch of New Orleans's famous **Commander's Palace,** lauded by the James Beard Foundation as the best restaurant in America. The **London Club at Aladdin** promises to be Vegas's first "European gaming club," a casino within a casino offering Monte Carlo gambling. The **Theater for the Performing Arts,** a 7,000-seat venue, was completely gutted and renovated, with plans to host touring productions and concert acts. There is also a showroom with a show still unannounced at press time.

Amenities: Facilities will include two swimming pools on the sixth-floor pool deck overlooking the Strip, a large health club and spa, and much more.

✪ **Mandalay Bay.** 3950 Las Vegas Blvd. S. (at Hacienda Ave.), Las Vegas, NV 89119. ☎ **877/632-7000** or 702/632-7000. Fax 702/632-7228. www. mandalaybay.com. 3,309 units. A/C TV TEL. From $99 standard double; from $149 suite; from $149 for House of Blues Signature Rooms. Extra person $35. AE, CB, DC, DISC, JCB, MC, V. Free self- and valet parking.

The Mandalay Bay may well prove to be our favorite new hotel. Why? Well, we love the elegant lobby and the fact that the other public areas really do seem more like an actual resort hotel than just a Vegas version of one. You don't have to walk through the casino to get to any of these public areas or the guest room elevators, the pool area is spiffy, and the whole thing is less confusing and overwhelming than some of the neighboring behemoths. We also find a place whose theme doesn't bop you over the head refreshing.

South Strip Accommodations

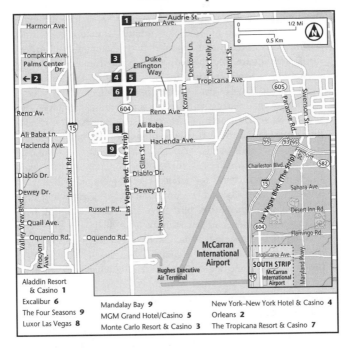

Aladdin Resort & Casino **1**	Mandalay Bay **9**	New York–New York Hotel & Casino **4**
Excalibur **6**	MGM Grand Hotel/Casino **5**	Orleans **2**
The Four Seasons **9**	Monte Carlo Resort & Casino **3**	The Tropicana Resort & Casino **7**
Luxor Las Vegas **8**		

The rooms are perhaps the best on the Strip (king rooms are more attractive than doubles), spacious and subdued in decor, with extras like irons, data ports, hair dryers, and more. King beds have large carved headboard posts and firm mattresses. Sheets are slightly scratchy and pillows too firm for those with neck problems. The bathrooms are the crowning glory. Certainly the best on the Strip and maybe the best in Vegas, they're downright large, with impressive, slightly sunken tubs, glassed-in showers, double sinks, and separate water closets, plus fab amenities and lots of them.

Service overall is pretty good, and those pool-area employees are the best in Vegas, though there were no security guards at the guest elevators. A monorail system connects the hotel with Luxor and Excalibur, by which time you are well into Strip action, and this should more than help you get over any feelings of isolation.

Dining/Diversions: The numerous restaurants in Mandalay Bay feature some of the most innovative interiors in Vegas, each one more whimsical and imaginative than the last. Even if you don't eat there, drop in and poke around. **Aureole,** a branch of Charlie Palmer's renowned New York City restaurant, the **Border Grill, Red Square,** and the **buffet** are reviewed in chapter 4.

And then there's **rumjungle,** which features a dramatically skewered, all-you-can-eat, multicourse Brazilian feast, which you'll enjoy while listening to world beat drums, surrounded by fire and water walls and other striking visual features. More casual food can be found at the **House of Blues,** probably the best place in town to see rock bands. Mandalay Bay has a showroom and a separate arena, which was inaugurated by none other than Pavarotti. See chapter 8 for details on the hotel's major nightlife offerings. There's also a big, comfortable casino, airier and less claustrophobic than most, plus three bars, often featuring live music (including rock impersonator acts) at night.

Amenities: Concierge, 24-hour room service, dry cleaning and laundry, foreign-currency exchange, boutiques, baby-sitting, business center, safe-deposit boxes, wedding chapel, salon, and 12,000-seat sports and entertainment complex. They also have a "museum," an overpriced room full of rare coins and only worthwhile for the dedicated numismatist.

There are no fewer than four pools, including the touted wave pool, which is unfortunately a classic example of Vegas bait-and-switch. It's supposed to feature waves of various size, from Barely There to Stun, breaking on a sand-covered beach. But it turned out the waves couldn't be turned on full force, as the pool was too short and surfers went crashing into the concrete lip at the end. As of this writing, surfing still isn't happening. Plan instead to bob gently in miniwaves, or better still, float happily in the lazy river (boogie and surf board rentals are available).

The health club is sufficiently stocked to give you a good workout (it should be, since they charge guests $22 per day to use it). The spa area proper—featuring hot and warm pools, plus a cold plunge—is exotically designed.

✪ **MGM Grand Hotel/Casino.** 3799 Las Vegas Blvd. S. (at Tropicana Ave.), Las Vegas, NV 89109. ☎ **800/929-1111** or 702/891-7777. Fax 702/891-1030. www.mgmgrand.com. 5,034 units. A/C TV TEL. $69–$329 standard double; $99–$2,500 suite. Extra person $25. Children under 12 stay free in parents' room. AE, DC, DISC, MC, V. Free self- and valet parking.

When the MGM Grand first opened, the massive glaring green "Wizard of Oz"–themed behemoth was the largest hotel in town, with a casino to match—and they were mighty proud of it, boasting still further of their family-friendliness. But times change, and with every other hotel in town trying to be a luxury resort, the MGM Grand had no choice but to follow. And while the result is somewhere in the middle of these two choices, it's surprisingly successful.

The place is still big—really, really big and more on that in a moment—to be sure, and its new "City of Entertainment" theme (which means all MGM movies are fair game for decorating purposes) is a bit nebulous, but there is a great deal to like here. The outside is still green, but gone is the Oz attraction (though it may reappear at a later date in a different, less prominent part of the hotel), now replaced by a Rain Forest Cafe and Studio 54, both of which are accessed through an ornate circular domed room, full of replicated '30s glamour, glitz, and gilded statues. Obviously, this is all more appealing to adults. But the place's size is still daunting. Despite plenty of signage, it is still a lengthy, confusing schlep from anywhere to anywhere.

On the absolute plus side, we are just knocked out by the newly redone rooms. They're a modern-day homage to 1930s moderne, all clean, curvy lines, good wood, and a fun palette of colors, plus black-and-white movie-star glamour photos. They are the best choice in town in their price range. The expanded pool area is another victory, with several choices for dunking, including a lazy river (though we wish portions of it weren't closed off for non-summer months). Overall, report guests, the staff couldn't be more friendly and helpful, and the place is still popular with families who must not mind that they are no longer openly catered to.

Dining/Diversions: MGM houses a prestigious assemblage of dining rooms, among them the **Wolfgang Puck Café,** Emeril Lagasse's **New Orleans Fish House, Gatsby's,** and Mark Miller's **Coyote Café** (see chapter 4 for reviews of these). In addition, there's a **Rain Forest Cafe,** a **Brown Derby** (modeled after the legendary Los Angeles celebrity haunt), buffet offerings, a 24-hour coffee shop, a food court, and much more. Several of these places are reviewed in chapter 4.

As befits a behemoth of this size, there's an appropriately gigantic casino. The MGM is also home to ✪ *EFX,* a lavish show that's full of special effects and elaborate sets, plus a headliner showroom and a larger events arena that hosts sporting events and bigger concerts. See chapter 8 for details on all the nightlife options.

The **Lion Habitat** is reviewed in chapter 5, as is the **MGM Grand Adventures** theme park.

Amenities: 24-hour room service, 30,000-square-foot video arcade (including virtual-reality games), carnival midway with 33 games of skill, foreign-currency exchange, guest relations desk, shoe shine (in the men's rooms), full-service beauty salon, business center, florist, shopping arcade, two wedding chapels (in the theme park), show/sports event ticket desks, car-rental desk; sightseeing/tour desks, monorail to Bally's (runs 9am to 1am). A new shopping center will include high-ticket stores like DKNY.

The MGM G.and recently redid their spa, and it's now a Zen-Asian minimalist wonder. The services offered are quite marvelous. The health club is state-of-the-art and larger than most, with some serious machines, including ones equipped with fancy computer video monitors (it'll cost you $20 to work up a sweat here most of the day, but you can use the gym facilities only, without the whirlpools and other amenities of the spa, for only $10 after 6pm).

The swimming pool area was also recently completely redone and is a rousing success. The 6.6 acres of landscaped grounds feature five pools, including the longest lazy river in town.

The **MGM Grand Youth Center,** a first-rate facility for children ages 3 to 16, has separate areas for different age groups. The center has a playhouse and tumbling mats for toddlers, a game room, extensive arts-and-crafts equipment, video games, a dining area, and a large-screen TV/VCR for children's movies. Accompanied by professional counselors, youngsters can visit the theme park or the swimming pool, take excursions to nearby attractions, have meals, and participate in all sorts of entertainment and activities (☎ **702/891-3200** for details and prices).

Monte Carlo Resort & Casino. 3770 Las Vegas Blvd. S. (between Flamingo Rd. and Tropicana Ave.), Las Vegas, NV 89109. ☎ **800/311-8999** or 702/730-7777. Fax 702/730-7250. www.monte-carlo.com. 3,002 units. A/C TV TEL. Sun–Thurs $49–$179 double, Fri–Sat $109–$269 double; $149–$339 suite. Extra person $15. Children under 12 stay free in parents' room. AE, CB, DC, DISC, MC, V. Free self- and valet parking.

When it was built, the massive Monte Carlo was the world's seventh largest hotel. It's now somewhat overshadowed by its more high-profile, more theme-intensive brethren, but guests who stay here come away quite pleased with the experience. It comes off as a European casino hotel, fronted by Corinthian colonnades, triumphal arches, splashing fountains, and allegorical (and slightly naughty) statuary, with an entranceway opening onto a bustling casino. A separate entrance in the rear of the hotel leads to a splendid marble-floored, crystal-chandeliered lobby. Palladian windows behind the registration desk overlook the hotel's vast swimming pool area and extensive water attractions. Spacious rooms with big marble baths exude a warmly traditional European feel. Cable TVs are equipped with hotel information channels, keno, and pay-movie options.

Dining/Diversions: The Monte Carlo's **Pub & Brewery** and **Dragon Noodle Co.** are described in chapter 4. In addition, there is now a branch of the classic Downtown French restaurant **Andre's,** and a recommended Italian restaurant.

There's a large and overly ornate casino, plus a lavish showroom that currently hosts the recommended show by magician ✪ **Lance Burton** (see chapter 8).

Amenities: 24-hour room service, foreign-currency exchange, limo rental, casino, car-rental desk, four tennis courts, sightseeing/tour/show desk, barber/beauty salon, wedding chapel, full business center, large video-game arcade, large shopping arcade. The numerous water attractions include a 20,000-square-foot pool area, a lushly landscaped miniature water park with a 4,800-foot wave pool, a surf pond, waterfalls, and a "river" for tubing. Also notable is the Monte Carlo's spa ($14 for 1 day's access, which is cheaper than the fee at most other hotels), offering extensive workout facilities, hot and cool whirlpools, steam and sauna, and numerous treatments. Workout clothing and toiletries are provided.

✪ **New York–New York Hotel & Casino.** 3790 Las Vegas Blvd. S. (at Tropicana Ave.), Las Vegas, NV 89109. ☎ **800/693-6763** or 702/740-6969. Fax 702/740-6920. www.nynyhotelcasino.com. 2,033 units. A/C TV TEL. Sun–Thurs from $59 double, Fri–Sat from $109 double. Extra person $20. AE, CB, DC, DISC, JCB, MC, V. Free self- and valet parking.

Just when you think Las Vegas has done it all, they go and do something like this. New York–New York is just plain spectacular. Even the jaded and horrified have to admit it. You can't miss the hotel; it's that little (hah!) building on the corner of the Strip and Tropicana that looks like the New York City skyline: the Empire State Building, the Chrysler Building, the Public Library, right down to the 150-foot Statue of Liberty and Ellis Island, all built to approximately one-third scale. And as if that weren't enough, they threw in a roller coaster running around the outside and into the hotel and casino itself.

And inside, it all gets better. There are details everywhere—so many, in fact, that the typical expression on the face of casino-goers is slack-jawed wonder. If you enter the casino via the Brooklyn Bridge (the walkway from the Strip), you find yourself in a replica of Greenwich Village, down to the cobblestones, the manhole covers, the tenement buildings, and the graffiti. (Yes, they even re-created that. You should see the subway station.) The reception area and lobby are done in an art deco, golden-age-of-Manhattan style; you feel like breaking out into a 1930s musical number while standing there. It really is impossible to adequately describe the sheer mind-blowing enormity of the thing. So we are just going to leave it at *Wow!*

Upstairs—oh, yes, there's much more—is the arcade, which is Coney Island–themed (naturally), and just as crowded as the real thing, where kids play boardwalk games in the hopes of winning tickets redeemable for cheap prizes. (You're never too young to start learning about gambling.) The line for the roller coaster (lengthy at this writing) is here.

Rooms are housed in different towers, each with a New York–inspired name. Truthfully, the place is so massive and maze-like that finding your way to your room can take a while. There are 64 different styles of rooms, and they are all smashing. Each essentially is done up in a hard-core art deco style. However, some of the rooms are downright tiny (just like New York again!), and in those rooms, all this massively detailed decoration could be overwhelming, if not suffocating. The bathrooms are also small, but have black-marble-topped sinks, which again lend a glamorous '20s image.

Cranks would have us note that coming here is not like going to the real New York. On the other hand, given how crowded it is (everyone wants to come check it out and stays to play) and how noisy, it kind of is just like being in New York. Especially with the all-too-realistic traffic and parking nightmares. But those who do stay here come away as pleased as if they had enjoyed a visit to the real Big Apple.

Dining/Diversions: New York–New York gets packed, particularly within 2 hours (in either direction) of mealtimes. This translates to long lines and waits for restaurants, and occasionally less-than-terrific service. The choices include the **Motown Café; Il Fornaio,** a reliable chain featuring nouvelle Italian cuisine; **Chin-Chin,** a less reliable chain Szechuan and Cantonese cuisine; plus pizza, a deli, **Nathan's** hot dogs, **Schraft's Ice Cream,** and more.

There are several festive and beautifully decorated bars throughout the property, including the **Bar at Times Square** (see chapter 8). The main casino area is done as Central Park, complete with trees, babbling brooks, streetlamps, and footbridges. The change carts are little Yellow Cabs. The production show *Lord of the Dance* is described in chapter 8.

Amenities: Concierge, room service, courtesy limo, foreign-currency exchange, dry cleaning, express checkout, laundry, newspaper delivery, safe-deposit boxes, video rentals, beauty salon, car rental, arcade, pool, and tour desk. The spa is smaller than average and merely adequate, and there's a $20 fee to use the facilities for 1 day. The march to the pool will in some cases trot you right down the Central Park bridge—wave to all the restaurant patrons as you parade in your swimsuit. The pool is the only disappointment; though fairly large with a waterfall, it's shallow and ringed on one side by the parking garage. The roller coaster regularly screams by overhead.

The Tropicana Resort & Casino. 3801 Las Vegas Blvd. S. (at Tropicana Ave.), Las Vegas, NV 89109. ☎ **800/634-4000** or 702/739-2222. Fax 702/739-2469. www.tropicanalv.com. 1,877 units. A/C TV TEL. $79–$229 double. Extra person $15. Children under 18 stay free in parents' room. AE, CB, DC, DISC, MC, V. Free self- and valet parking.

This hotel was once known for its lavish tropical resort stylings, but it's beginning to look more than a little worn around the edges, especially when compared with its splashy neighbors. Gone are all the birds and other wildlife, which makes things a little less messy, but still around are the tacky "Garden rooms," which really ought to be demolished ASAP. Gone also is the outside light show. Island tower rooms have "tropical" themed furniture, including gaudy mirror-and-bamboo headboards and (egads!) mirrors on the ceiling. Think a clean '70s motel room, but a little bit nicer. Unless you're a Jimmy Buffet fan, you are better off staying in the Paradise tower, where the rooms are slightly bigger and much easier on the eyes—it all appears less shabby and more fresh. Bathrooms are also bigger here, but dull, except for the ones with Jacuzzi tubs. Even without the wildlife, the pool area is among the best around and is the biggest draw of

ⓑ Family-Friendly Hotels

We've said it before, and we'll say it again: Vegas is simply not the best place to bring your kids along. Most of the major hotels are backing away from being perceived as places for families. But if you have to make it a family trip, here are our recommendations. In addition to the suggestions below, you might consider choosing a non-casino hotel, particularly a reliable chain (like any of the several Marriotts in town), and a place with kitchenettes. See especially section 4 of this chapter, "East of the Strip," for details on several such choices.

Circus Circus Hotel/Casino (*see p. 52*)   Centrally located on the Strip, this is our first choice if you're traveling with the kids. The hotel's mezzanine level offers ongoing circus acts daily from 11am to midnight, dozens of carnival games, and an arcade with more than 300 video and pinball games. And behind the hotel is a full amusement park.

Excalibur (*see p. 27*)   Also owned by Circus Circus, Excalibur features a whole floor of midway games, a large video-game arcade, crafts demonstrations, free shows for kids (puppets, jugglers, and magicians), and thrill cinemas. It has child-oriented restaurants and shows (details in chapter 8).

The Four Seasons (*see p. 16*)   For free goodies, service, and general child-pampering, the costly Four Seasons is probably worth the dough (your kid will be spoiled!).

Luxor Las Vegas (*see p. 28*)   Another Circus Circus property. Kids will enjoy VirtuaLand, an 18,000-square-foot video-game arcade that showcases Sega's latest game technologies. Another big attraction here is the "Secrets of the Luxor Pyramid," a high-tech adventure/thrill ride using motion simulators and IMAX film.

MGM Grand Hotel/Casino (*see p. 20*)   This resort is backed by a 33-acre theme park and houses a state-of-the-art video-game arcade and carnival midway. A unique offering here is a youth center for hotel guests ages 3 to 16, with separate sections for different age groups. Its facilities range from a playhouse and tumbling mats for toddlers to extensive arts-and-crafts equipment for the older kids. They also have a terrific new pool area and the whole property still seems popular with families.

the place. Note, however, that their touted swim-up blackjack is seasonal (read: summer only).

Dining/Diversions: There are a number of restaurants, providing a range of cuisines, including a good buffet (see chapter 4). There's a good-looking casino, and the Casino Legends Hall of Fame will charge you $6 to see the largest collection of gaming chips in the world and other gambling doodads and trivia. The showroom currently hosts the **Folies Bergère** revue (see chapter 8).

Amenities: 24-hour room service, health club (limited but adequately stocked; $16-per-day fee), video-game arcade, tour and show desks, wedding chapel, car-rental desk, beauty salon and barbershop, business center, travel agent, shops, shoe shine, and foreign-currency exchange. Three swimming pools (one Olympic-size) and three whirlpool spas are located in a 5-acre garden with 30 splashing waterfalls, lagoons, and lush tropical plantings. One pool has a swim-up bar/blackjack table.

MODERATE

Excalibur. 3850 Las Vegas Blvd. S. (at Tropicana Ave.), Las Vegas, NV 89109. ☎ **800/937-7777** or 702/597-7777. Fax 702/597-7009. www.excalibur-casino.com. 4,008 units. A/C TV TEL. $49–$119 for up to 4 people. Children under 17 stay free in parents' room; children over 17 pay $12. Rates are higher during holidays and convention periods. AE, CB, DC, DISC, MC, V. Free self- and valet parking.

Now, *this* is kitsch. One of the largest resort hotels in the world, Excalibur (a.k.a. "the Realm") is a gleaming white, turreted castle complete with moat, drawbridge, battlements, and lofty towers. And it's huger than huge, with the chaotic feel that implies.

Rooms are freshly and successfully redecorated. Given the price, they're perhaps the best bet on the Strip for the budget-minded. Note that none of the bathrooms have tubs, just showers. Guests who have stayed in Tower 2 have complained about the noise from the roller coaster across the street at New York–New York. (It runs till 11pm, so early birds should probably stay in a different part of the hotel.)

The second floor holds the recently refurbished Medieval Village site of Excalibur's restaurants and quaint shops along winding streets and alleyways, a sort of permanent Renaissance Faire, which could be reason enough to stay away. On the Village's Jester's Stage, jugglers, puppeteers, and magicians amuse guests with free 20-minute performances throughout the day. Up here you can access the newly enclosed, air-conditioned, moving sidewalk that connects with the Luxor.

Dining/Diversions: There are plenty of restaurants, including a good buffet (reviewed in chapter 4); **Sir Galahad's,** a dinner-only prime rib restaurant; the kid-friendly **Sherwood Forest Café;** and a branch of **Krispy Kreme** donuts. The *Tournament of Kings* is a medieval dinner/show that's reviewed in chapter 8, and there's a very loud, claustrophobic casino.

Amenities: 24-hour room service, free gaming lessons, tour and show desks, state-of-the-art video-game arcade, wedding chapel (you can marry in medieval attire), shoe shine, foreign-currency exchange, unisex hairdresser, car-rental desk, a parking lot that can accommodate RVs, and shops. The pool area is large, with front and back pools, the latter of which has waterslides. Below the casino level is the Fantasy Faire, housing a very dark and large video-game arcade, dozens of medieval-themed carnival games, and two "magic motion machine" theaters featuring high-tech visual thrills. Note that there's no health club.

✪ Luxor Las Vegas. 3900 Las Vegas Blvd. S. (between Reno and Hacienda aves.), Las Vegas, NV 81119. ☎ **800/288-1000** or 702/262-4000. Fax 702/262-4452. www.luxor.com. 4,400 units. A/C TV TEL. Sun–Thurs $49–$259 double, Fri–Sat $99 and up; $149 and up for a whirlpool suite, $249–$800 for other suites. Extra person $15. Children under 12 stay free in parents' room. AE, CB, DC, DISC, JCB, MC, V. Free self- and valet parking.

After a $300-million renovation and expansion, the Egyptian fantasma that set the pace for all others isn't all that tacky anymore. Oh sure, the main hotel is still a 30-story bronze pyramid, complete with a really tall 315,000-watt light beam at the top. Sure, replicas of Cleopatra's Needle and the Sphinx still grace the outside, but the redesign has made the interior much more inviting, classier and functional.

Rooms in the pyramid open into the vast center that contains the casino—indeed, ground level rooms open more or less right onto the action, so if you want only a short drunken stumble back to your room, these are for you. Otherwise, ask for ones higher up. By mid-2001, all the pyramid rooms will have new furnishings, a marvelous redecoration that crosses Egyptian kitsch with deco stylings, including gleaming inlaid wood furniture and a hilarious hieroglyphic bedspread. Marvelous views are found through the slanted windows (the higher up the better, of course), but there are showers in the bathrooms only, no tubs. High-speed "inclinator" elevators run on a 39° angle, making the ride up to your room a bit of a thrill—check out that sensation as the mechanisms grind to a halt! Tower rooms are even heavier on the Egyptian motif, pleasing in a campy way but not as aesthetically successful, and some can be dark, though the bathrooms, including deep tubs, are better, so it might be a worthwhile tradeoff. All units have hair dryers. Regardless of which room you get, these are some of the few rooms in Las Vegas that stand out.

Dining/Diversions: The Luxor's **Pharaoh's Pheast** buffet is discussed in chapter 4. **Isis,** their dinner-only gourmet dining room, has gotten high praise. You'll also find steak and seafood places, fast-food joints, plus the 24-hour **Pyramid Café.**

The hotel's high-tech nightclub **Ra** is reviewed in chapter 8. The plush **Nefertiti's Lounge** features live bands for dancing nightly; off-hours sporting events are aired on a large-screen TV. And there are plenty of other bars besides, not to mention the huge casino.

King Tut's Tomb & Museum is a cute if silly attraction; the **Luxor IMAX Theater** is described in chapter 5.

Amenities: 24-hour room service; VirtuaLand, an 18,000-square-foot video arcade that showcases Sega's latest game technologies; car-rental desk; tour/show/sightseeing desks; foreign-currency exchange; shoe shine; and full-service unisex hair salon. The Luxor's 24-hour full-service spa and health club (closed only Tuesday nights) features a complete array of machines, services, and beauty treatments; it's $20 for 1 day's access. The hotel has five swimming pools. The main one is an immense palm-fringed pool (palms even grow right *in* the pool) with outdoor whirlpool, kiddie pool, pool-accessories shop, and luxurious cabanas that rent for a whopping $75 a day (cooled by misting systems, they're equipped with rafts, cable TVs, phones, ceiling fans, tables and chairs, chaise longues, and refrigerators stocked with juices and bottled water).

INEXPENSIVE

✪ **Orleans.** 4500 W. Tropicana Ave. (west of the Strip and I-15), Las Vegas, NV 89103. ☎ **800/ORLEANS (675-3267)** or 702/365-7111. Fax 702/365-7505. www.orleanscasino.com. 840 units. A/C TV TEL. $39–$89 standard double; $175–$225 1-bedroom suite. AE, DC, DISC, MC, V. Free self- and valet parking.

The Orleans is owned by the same company that owns the Barbary and Gold Coast casinos. It's a little out of the way, and there is virtually nothing around it, but with a 12-screen movie complex, complete with food court and day-care center, this is an attractive option to staying on the hectic Strip. Plus, there is a shuttle that runs continuously to the Barbary Coast on the Strip. Its facade is aggressively fake New Orleans, more reminiscent of Disneyland than the actual Big Easy. Inside it's much the same. But a bright casino (complete with Cajun and zydeco music over the loud speakers) and a policy of handing out Mardi Gras beads at all the restaurants and bars (ask if you haven't gotten yours) make for a pleasantly festive atmosphere. However, we could do without those scary mannequins simulating Mardi Gras fun leaning over French Quarter–style railings above the casino.

If the prices hold true (as always, they can vary), this hotel is one of the best bargains in town, despite the location. The rooms are particularly nice, all with a definite New Orleans–French feel, even if some feel crowded with too many furnishings and a busy floral theme. The medium-size bathrooms are also nice, but there is no closet, only a rod for hanging clothes.

Dining/Diversions: The hotel has your basic Vegas-type places to eat. Worth noting is **Don Miguel's,** a basic but satisfying Mexican restaurant that makes its own tortillas. There are several bars, including one with live music at night. The **Branson Theater** is a 827-seat theater featuring live entertainment, and of course, there's a casino.

Amenities: Room service, courtesy bus to/from airport and the Strip, health club (only a $2 fee for use), beauty salon, business center, game room, 70-lane bowling alley, wedding chapel, two medium-size pools with grass and cabanas, and safe-deposit boxes.

2 Mid-Strip

VERY EXPENSIVE

Bally's Las Vegas. 3645 Las Vegas Blvd. S. (at Flamingo Rd.), Las Vegas, NV 89109. ☎ **800/634-3434** or 702/739-4111. Fax 702/967-3890. www. ballyslv.com. 2,814 units. A/C TV TEL. $69 and up, $35–$60 more for concierge floor (including breakfast); $300 and up suite. Extra person $15. Children 17 and under stay free in parents' room. AE, CB, DC, JCB, MC, V. Free self- and valet parking.

Despite a $72-million renovation, which included the construction of a monorail that whisks passengers from its downstairs shopping level (a bit of a hike from the casino) to the MGM Grand, Bally's is beginning to suffer by comparison with its swank new neighbors, particular its sister property, Paris–Las Vegas. Bally's casino adjoins the Paris property, and its gaudy neon contrasts badly with the charms of this mock City of Lights. Mind you, it's not a bad place, and those who prefer their Vegas hotels honestly glitzy, rather than pretending that quiet good taste can be achieved on a massive level, will feel much better here. Rooms are large and forgettable.

Dining/Diversions: Bally's has the usual range of dining choices. Of particular note is **Chang's,** which offers very good quality high-end Chinese food (try the ginger steamed lobster) in a hushed environment. Food outlets in the shopping mall include a branch of New York's **Stage Deli.** Be sure to read "Buffets & Sunday Brunches" in chapter 4. The casino is large, well-lit, and colorful, and there's also a headliner showroom and the splashy *Jubilee!* revue (see chapter 8).

Amenities: State-of-the-art health spa and fitness center ($20 fee for 1 day's use), eight night-lit tennis courts and pro shop (lessons available), 24-hour room service, guest-services desk, foreign-currency exchange, tour and show desks, car-rental desk, small video-game arcade, shopping arcade, wedding chapel, and men's and women's hair salons. A very fine, palm-fringed sundeck surrounds an Olympic-size swimming pool. There's a whirlpool, and guests can rent private cabanas with stocked refrigerators, TVs, ceiling fans, rafts, and private phones for $70 to $95 a day.

✪ **Bellagio.** 3600 Las Vegas Blvd. S. (at the corner of Flamingo Rd.), Las Vegas, NV 89109. ☎ **888/987-6667** or 702/693-7444. Fax 702/693-8346. www.bellagiolasvegas.com. 3,270 units. A/C TV TEL. $129–$499 double. Extra person $30. AE, CB, DC, DISC, MC, V. Free self- and valet parking.

Steve Wynn ushered in the new post-Vegas-is-for-families elegance epoch with his $1.6-billion luxury resort. What did he—and you—get for that money? Well, for starters, though it is named for a charming Lake Como village, Bellagio is not, thankfully, as theme-intensive as some of its nearest competition. There is an 8-acre Lake Como stand-in out front, complete with a dazzling choreographed water ballet extravaganza, plus the simulated front of an Italian lakeside village, while the pool area is sort of Hearst Castle Romanesque, but that's about it. Just as well. This is not much like a getaway to a peaceful, romantic Italian village. But it is exactly like going to a big, grand, state-of-the-art Vegas hotel. To expect more probably isn't fair, but then again, they tried to set the tone with those dreamy, soft-focus TV ads.

Nothing with a casino stuck in the middle of it can be that serene and restful.

But does it work as a luxury hotel? Sort of. It certainly is much closer to a European casino hotel than a Vegas one. Fabulous touches abound, including a lobby that's unlike any other in Vegas. It's not just grand, with marble and a gaudy blown-glass flower sculpture on the ceiling (the largest of its kind in the world), but it's also brave, with plants, natural lighting, and actual seating. There's a downright lovely conservatory, complete with a 100-year-old fountain and stuffed full of gorgeous, brightly colored flowers and plants. The classical Italian garden has six swimming pools, plus a Grand Patio that seems right off a movie set. There's also the best collection of restaurants in town, and an art gallery that hosts traveling exhibits.

However, you still can't avoid a walk through the casino to get just about anywhere (at least it's laid out in an easy-to-navigate grid with wide aisles), and there are hidden charges galore. The rooms are nice—oh, very nice, nicer than the Mirage even, but maybe just not quite nice enough for the price. Furnishings are plush (good beds with quality linens), the roomy bathrooms even more so, but it's all still just a slightly more luxurious, and busy, variation on what's found over at the Mirage. Stripside rooms, while featuring a much-desired view of the water fountains, don't quite muffle the booms said fountains make as they explode. Still, service is top-notch, despite the size of the place; the staff is eager to please and non-patronizing.

Dining/Diversions: Just about all the best new restaurants are found in Bellagio. Full reviews of **Picasso, Le Cirque, Circo, Aqua,** and **Olives** are found in chapter 4, as well as a review of the buffet. But there is also ✪ **Prime,** Bellagio's knock-out elegant steakhouse. There are other decent choices, plus several very nice lounges, one of which serves high tea in the afternoon.

The man who brought us a free pirate show and a volcano explosion now brings us a ✪ **water ballet,** courtesy of a dancing fountain with jets timed to a rotating list of nine songs. This sounds cheesy, but it absolutely is not. It's really quite delightful and even witty (no, really), and is the best free show in Vegas.

Bellagio also features an upscale casino, and *O,* the latest and most incredible show from Cirque du Soleil (see review in chapter 8).

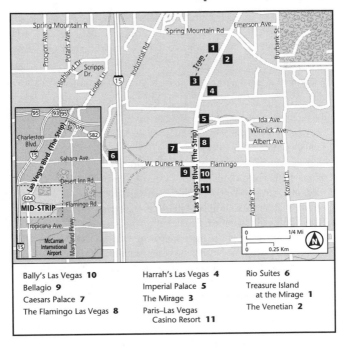

Bally's Las Vegas **10**
Bellagio **9**
Caesars Palace **7**
The Flamingo Las Vegas **8**

Harrah's Las Vegas **4**
Imperial Palace **5**
The Mirage **3**
Paris–Las Vegas
   Casino Resort **11**

Rio Suites **6**
Treasure Island
   at the Mirage **1**
The Venetian **2**

Amenities: 24-hour room service, concierge, shoe shine, laundry and dry cleaning, video arcade, twice-daily maid service, business center, and beauty salon. Free monorail travels between Bellagio and Monte Carlo nearly around the clock.

The pool area skidded to the top of our favorites list; six swimming pools (two heated year-round and two with fountains) geometrically set in a neoclassical Roman garden, with flowered, trellised archways and Italian opera over the sound system.

The spa and health club are marvelous, but at $25 a pop, it's pretty pricey if all you want is a simple session on a treadmill (though with your fee, you are allowed to return throughout the day for additional soaking/steaming/workouts). The busy gym has the latest in cardio and weight machines, but can be crowded, with waits for all of it. Attendants ply you with iced towels and drinks. The spa has a serene soaking area, with sumptuous plunge pools ranging in temperature from icy to boiling. In addition to drinks and snacks, smoothies are often offered. They do a full range of spa services, though again these are costly.

The shopping area called **Via Bellagio** features all the stores that advertise in color in glossy magazines. You know, the kind where you can't even afford to breathe their oxygen: Tiffany, Armani, Gucci, Prada, Hermès, and the like.

☉ Caesars Palace. 3570 Las Vegas Blvd. S. (just north of Flamingo Rd.), Las Vegas, NV 89109. ☎ **800/634-6661** or 702/731-7110. Fax 702/731-6636. www.caesars.com. 2,471 units. A/C TV TEL. From $99 standard double, $109–$500 "run of house deluxe" double; $549–$1,000 suite. Extra person $20. Children under 12 stay free in parents' room. AE, CB, DC, DISC, MC, V. Free self- and valet parking.

Since 1966, Caesars has stood as simultaneously the ultimate in Vegas luxury and the nadir (or pinnacle, depending on your values) of Las Vegas cheese. It's the most Vegas-style hotel you'll find. Or at least it was. A couple of years ago, Caesars completed a massive $300 million renovation, inside and out. Don't worry, the Roman theme remains. But as with everything else in Vegas, it has been upgraded to, let's say, a nicer neighborhood in Rome. It's all generally lighter, brighter, and perhaps closer to the elegance Caesars originally sought to evoke. But never fear, the Roman statues still remain, as do the toga-clad cocktail waitresses, and so does Caesars' giggle factor.

Past or future, Caesars remains spectacular. From the Roman temples, heroic arches, golden charioteers, and 50-foot Italian cypresses of its entrance, to the overwhelming interiors, it's the spectacle a good Vegas hotel should be. However, all of this makes for a very haphazard layout; this is one of the more confusing and hard to navigate hotels in town. Sometimes you feel like just surrendering and staying in, which isn't necessarily a bad thing. Caesars is also known for its luxurious rooms and service.

Accommodations occupy four towers. Art in the rooms keeps to the Greco-Roman theme (some have classical sculptures in niches); furnishings tend to neoclassic styles; Roman columns, pilasters, and pediments are common. Many rooms have four-poster beds with mirrored ceilings, and all are equipped with three phones, hair dryers, irons, safes, and cable TVs with HBO and a gaming instruction channel. The newest rooms are handsome, if not as giggle-tastic as the classic ones, and have floor-to-ceiling windows that offer a hypnotizing panorama view. You'll likely enjoy a lavish bath with marble floor, European fixtures, and oversize marble tubs (about half are whirlpools). Some of the rooms have lavish tubs in the middle of the room, which can be uncomfortable if you wish to shower and don't want this to turn into a spectator sport.

Dining/Diversions: Caesars has a well-deserved reputation for superior in-house restaurants. There's a good sushi restaurant, **Hyakumi,** along with the hotel's food court and buffets. Restaurants in the Forum Shops arcade include **Spago, Chinois** (both Wolfgang Puck's famed establishments), **The Palm, Planet Hollywood,** and the **Stage Deli.** In the new Atlantis section, there is a **Caviartorium,** and a **Cheesecake Factory.**

In the three fabulously luxurious and kitschy casinos, there are several lounges, among them the **Olympic Lounge** and **La Piazza Lounge,** offering nightly live entertainment in the Olympic Casino. There's also the **Cleopatra's Barge Nightclub.**

Still more things to take advantage of are the **OMNIMAX Theatre** and the **Race for Atlantis IMAX 3-D Ride** (described in chapter 5).

Amenities: 24-hour room service, state-of-the-art video arcade, American Express office, show desks, car-rental desk, foreign-currency exchange, complimentary gaming lessons, valet/dry cleaning, and extensive meeting space.

Having spent over $100 million renovating its **Garden of the Gods,** Caesars has created a tasteful, although undeniably Caesars, masterpiece. With three pools measuring a total of 22,000 square feet, there is plenty of space for frolicking in the hot sun. Inspired by the healing Baths of Caracalla in Rome, each of the pools is adorned with griffins or sea horses and inlaid with classic granite and marble mosaics. To feel even more regal, there are also 16 shaded cabanas that offer phones, TV, and air-conditioning for $150 a day. (Reserve them early.) Several amenities are also available by the pool area including Caribbean massage, two whirlpools, three tennis courts, the Neptune Bar, and of course, a Snackus Maximus.

The ✪ **Caesars Spa** is another gorgeous facility, offering full salon services (a large range of facials, massages, wraps, and other beauty treatments). The spa also offers saunas, steam rooms, and whirlpool tubs, plus an incredibly well-supplied health club with state-of-the-art machinery, a rock-climbing wall, personal trainers, and more (it's a whopping $24 per day just to work out, though).

The ✪ **Forum Shops** (see chapter 7) are in the grandest mall you can imagine (think of the *La Dolce Vita* walk on the Via

Veneto), covered by a sky that is supposed to change during the day to reflect the passing of time. These high-rent boutiques (Armani, Versace, and so on) lead to a group of Animatronic Roman statues that come to life every hour to mumble something about bacchanals and the good life. Another hall leads to more expensive shops and a fountain that performs another show with somewhat better production values, during which Atlantis literally rises from the deep and the room is transformed into a sound, light, and fire extravaganza. It runs every 1½ hours. And still another massive addition to the shops should be finished by the time you read this—it should roughly double the size of the existing shopping areas.

Paris–Las Vegas Casino Resort. 3655 Las Vegas Blvd. S., Las Vegas, NV 89109. ☎ **888/BONJOUR (266-5687)** or 702/964-7000. Fax 702/946-4405. www.paris-lv.com. 2,916 units. A/C MINIBAR TV TEL. $119–$269 double; $350 and way up for suites. AE, CB, DC, DISC, JCB, MC. V.

Sacre bleu! The City of Light comes to Sin City in this, the latest fantasy hotel to hit the Strip. It's theme-run-amok time again. The outside reproduces various Parisian landmarks, complete with a half-scale perfect replica of the Eiffel tower. The interior puts you in the middle of a dollhouse version of the city. You can stroll down a mini–Rue de la Paix, ride an elevator to the top of the Eiffel Tower, stop at an over-priced bakery for a baguette, take your photo by several very nice fountains.

Everywhere is signage employing the kind of dubious use of the language that makes genuine Frenchmen really cross ("le car rental" and so forth), while all the employees are forced to dust off their high school French ("Bonjour, Madame! Merci beaucoup!") when dealing with the public. Don't worry, it's all not quite enough to make you sick to "le stomach."

Quelle dommage, this attention to detail does not extend to the rooms, which are nice enough but disappointingly uninteresting, with furniture that only hints at mock French Regency and extras like in-room safes, irons, two-line phones, voice-mail, and dataports. Bathrooms are small but pretty, with deep tubs and hair dryers. Try to get a Strip-facing room so you can see the Bellagio fountains across the street. Overall, not a bad place to stay but a great place to visit—*quelle hoot!*

Dining/Diversions: The hotel has eight more-or-less French-themed restaurants, including a highly lauded **buffet,** the **Eiffel Tower restaurant** (located guess where), and bistro **Mon Ami**

Gabi. Bread for all these restaurants is made fresh on-site at the bakery; you can buy delicious, if pricey, loaves of same there yourself. There are also five lounges, including the clubby and oh-so-darkly-French **Napoleon's.**

The **Eiffel Tower** attraction is covered in chapter 5, and there's a big casino.

Amenities: Concierge, 24-hour room service, business center, beauty salon, tour and travel desk, car rental, two wedding chapels, ballrooms, retail shops, and foreign-currency exchange. The spa, operated by Mandara Spa, is aesthetically pleasing but doesn't do much with the space, which includes a somewhat understocked gym ($20 fee for 1 day's access). The casino-top swimming pool area uses the space well but is ultimately sterile, prettier to look down on from a room than to actually be in (the actual pool is so shallow it's more like a glorified kiddie wading pool).

✪ **The Venetian.** 3355 Las Vegas Blvd. S., Las Vegas, NV 89109. ☎ **888/ 2-VENICE (283-6423)** or 702/414-1000. Fax 702/414-1100. www.venetian. com. 3,354 units. A/C MINIBAR TV TEL. $125–$399 double. AE, CB, DC, DISC, JCB, MC, V. Free self- and valet parking.

One of the newest hotel spectacles in town, the Venetian falls squarely between an outright adult Disneyland experience and the luxury resort sensibility of the other recent hotels. Its front, which re-creates most of the top landmarks of Venice (the Campanile, a portion of St. Mark's Square, part of the Doge's Palace, a canal or two), ranks right up there with New York–New York as a must-see, and since you can wander freely through the "sights," it even has a slight edge. The attention to detail here is impressive indeed. Stone is aged for that weathered look, statues and tiles exactly copy their Italian counterparts, security guards wear Venetian police uniforms—all that's missing is the smell from the canals, but we are happy to let that one slide.

Inside, ceilings are covered with hand-painted re-creations of Venetian art. With plenty of marble, soaring ceilings, and impressive pillars and archways, it's less kitschy than Caesars but more theme park than Bellagio. The lobby, casino, and shops can all be accessed from outside through individual entrances, which helps avoid that irritating circuitous maneuvering required by most other locations. This is all the more appreciated because the casino seems to have a most confusing layout, with poor signage.

The rooms are the largest and probably the most handsome in town, with a flair more European than Vegas. They are all "suites," with a good-size bedroom giving way to steps down to a sunken living area, complete with pullout sofa bed. The decor has just one too many patterns, but it manages to work, and nice touches abound. Rooms have somewhat stately furniture; half canopies over the beds; two TVs; hair dryers; safes; three dual-line phones with modem access; and fax machines that double as printers. The marbled bathrooms rocketed to virtually the top of our list of favorites, in a tie for second place with those at Bellagio. (Mandalay Bay's are the best.) Glassed showers, deep soaking tubs, double sinks, fluffy towels, and lots of space—that does it for us every time. Stripside rooms have a nice view of Treasure Island's pirate battle, but sounds from said battle also bleed in. (It stops at midnight.)

But there is a certain amount of price gouging at this hotel that unpleasantly reminds one of the real Venice. There is a charge for that in-room faxing and printing, and the minibar is automated so if you so much as rearrange items inside you are charged for it. We hope these are all things that will settle down in time, as there is so much here to like.

Dining/Diversions: There are many celebrity chefs and high-profile restaurants in residence at the Venetian, including **Star Canyon, Delmonico Steakhouse, Canneletto, Valentino, Lutèce,** and **Pinot Brasserie.** See chapter 4. **Postrio** is another entry from the ubiquitous Wolfgang Puck (this restaurant originated in San Francisco, where it's highly acclaimed). **Zeffirino's** chef Paolo Belloni has cooked for some of the most eminent judges of Italian food: the pope and Sinatra. There's much more, including spa food at **Canyon Ranch,** and a food court. There are several comfortable and inviting lounges and bars; the casino is elegant but confusingly laid out.

Amenities: 24-hour room service, concierge, shoe shine, dry cleaning/laundry, beauty salon, car rental, airport transportation, cellular phone rental, baby-sitting, and foreign-currency exchange. The Venetian has five pools and whirlpools, but so far its pool area is disappointing—sterile and bland.

The ✪ **health club/spa** is run by Canyon Ranch, a branch of arguably the finest getaway spa in America. This is an unbelievably lavish facility, certainly the finest hotel spa in town. From the

Bed Head and Bumble & Bumble products on sale in the shop, to the nutritionists, physical therapists, and acupuncturists on staff and ready for consultations, to the vibrating massage chairs you rest in during pedicures—geez, what more could you want? The $25 a day fee is high, but it does include a full day's worth of classes. Did we mention the rock-climbing wall?

The ✪ **Grand Canal Shoppes** are an absolute must-see. It's a mock Italian village with a blue, cloud-studded, painted sky overhead. But down the middle runs a canal, complete with singing gondoliers. (The 10-minute ride costs about $12, which seems steep, but trust us, it's a *lot* more in the real Venice.) The whole thing finishes up at a small re-creation of St. Mark's Square, which features glass blowers, traveling musicians, flower sellers, and the like. Expect to run into famous Venetians such as a flirty Casanova and a travel-weary Marco Polo. It's ambitious and a big step up from Animatronic figures. Oh, and the stores are also probably worth a look—a decent mixture of high-end fashion and more affordable outlets.

EXPENSIVE

The Flamingo Las Vegas. 3555 Las Vegas Blvd. S. (between Sands Ave. and Flamingo Rd.), Las Vegas, NV 89109. ☎ **800/732-2111** or 702/733-3111. Fax 702/733-3353. www.flamingolv.com. 3,999 units. A/C TV TEL. $69–$299 double; $250–$580 suite. Extra person $20. Children 17 and under stay free in parents' room. Inquire about packages and time-share suites. AE, CB, DC, DISC, JCB, MC, V. Free self- and valet parking.

The Flamingo is the Strip's senior citizen, with a colorful history. It's changed a great deal since Bugsy Siegel opened his 105-room oasis "in the middle of nowhere" in 1946. It was so luxurious for its time that even the janitors wore tuxedos. Jimmy Durante was the opening headliner, and the wealthy and famous flocked to the tropical paradise of swaying palms, lagoons, and waterfalls. A fresh, new look, enhanced by a recent $130-million renovation and expansion, has made Siegel's "real class joint" better than ever—including making it somewhat easier to reach the outside world, which in the past was often difficult. The Flamingo is no longer a Hilton property, though we have yet to see if that will affect anything you might care about.

For those planning some leisure time outside the casino, the Flamingo's exceptional pool area, spa, and tennis courts are a big draw. One of the best in Vegas, the pool is smashing, with countless trees and foliage, live birds, two waterslides, waterfalls, and so on. Although the water can be a little chilly, kids should be able to spend hours in there.

Rooms occupy six towers and are variously decorated. All accommodations offer in-room safes; TVs have in-house information and gaming instruction stations, a keno channel, video checkout, message retrieval, and account review.

Dining/Diversions: Dining choices are what you would expect in a Vegas hotel: Italian, Japanese, steakhouse, gourmet dining room, buffet, and so on, plus **Lindy's Deli,** a pleasant and spacious 24-hour coffee shop. There is a similar complement of bars, plus a huge casino and two big production shows (see chapter 8).

Amenities: 24-hour room service, guest services desk, translation services, foreign-currency exchange, car-rental desk, tour and show desks, full-service salon, wedding chapel, four night-lit championship tennis courts with pro shop and practice alley (tennis clinics and lessons are available), and shopping arcade.

Five gorgeous swimming pools, two whirlpools, waterslides, and a kiddie pool are located in a 15-acre Caribbean landscape amid lagoons, meandering streams, fountains, waterfalls, a rose garden, and islands of live flamingos and African penguins. Ponds can have ducks, swans, and koi, and a grove of 2,000 palms graces an expanse of lawn.

A health club ($20 fee per day) offers a variety of Universal weight machines, treadmills, stair machines, free weights, sauna, steam, a TV lounge, and hot and cold whirlpools. Exercise tapes are available, and spa services can be booked.

Harrah's Las Vegas. 3475 Las Vegas Blvd. S. (between Flamingo and Spring Mountain rds.), Las Vegas, NV 89109. ☎ **800/HARRAHS (427-7247)** or 702/369-5000. Fax 702/369-4147. www.harrahs.lv.com. 2,700 units. A/C TV TEL. $65–$195 standard "deluxe" double, $85–$250 standard "superior" double; $195–$1,000 suite. Extra person $15. Children 12 and under stay free in parents' room. AE, CB, DC, DISC, MC, V. Free self- and valet parking.

A recent radical facelift has completely transformed Harrah's. It used to look like a Mississippi River showboat, but now it looks nothing like that. It's less gauche, with a European carnival theme. Everywhere there are large murals celebrating different international festivals, plus lots of accents of marble, bright colors, mirrors, and gold trim. A neat trick involving the confetti-strewn pattern carpeting and the fiber-optic fireworks on the ceiling creates a festive effect.

Overall, Harrah's has done a terrific job with its remodeling, creating a comfortable and fun environment while somehow eschewing both kitsch and the haughtiness that followed in the wake of other hotels' conversion to more upscale images.

Guest rooms, featuring marble fixtures and light wood accents, were slowly being refurbished at press time. All the rooms are larger than average. Spacious minisuites, offering large sofas and comfortable armchairs, are especially desirable. In all rooms, TVs offer hotel information and keno channels, pay movies, Nintendo, and video account review and checkout.

Dining/Diversions: The Range steakhouse is one of the few hotel restaurants that overlooks the Strip. You'll find other choices for basic tastes, as well, including a buffet. Several new bars have also opened, including **La Playa,** an open-air lounge featuring live reggae bands and outdoor seating right on the Strip. The casino has a fun, festive atmosphere, complete with "party pits." Harrah's showroom usually hosts some kind of big show or revue, though the 2001 offering had not been announced at press time.

Amenities: 24-hour room service, complimentary gaming lessons, car-rental desk, tour and show desks, nice-size video-game arcade, coin-op laundry, and unisex hair salon. **Carnavale Court** is a festive, palm-fringed shopping plaza where strolling entertainers perform.

Harrah's has a beautiful Olympic-size swimming pool and sundeck area with waterfall and trellised garden areas, a whirlpool, kids' wading pool, cocktail and snack bars, and a poolside shop selling T-shirts and sundries.

The hotel's health club has doubled in size. One of the better facilities on the Strip, it has a spa offering a full range of services and a health club with Lifecycles, treadmills, stair machines, rowing machines, lots of Universal equipment, free weights, and two TVs and a VCR for which aerobic exercise tapes are available. Its $15-a-day access charge is more reasonable than fees in other hotels.

✪ **The Mirage.** 3400 Las Vegas Blvd. S. (between Flamingo Rd. and Sands Ave.), Las Vegas, NV 89109. ☎ **800/627-6667** or 702/791-7444. Fax 702/791-7446. www.themirage.com. 3,323 units. A/C TV TEL. Sun–Thurs $79–$399 double, Fri–Sat and holidays $159–$399 double; $250–$3,000 suite. Extra person $30. AE, CB, DC, DISC, MC, V. Free self- and valet parking.

We really like this place. Many consider it the most beautiful hotel in Vegas. Occupying 102 acres, the Mirage is fronted by more than a city block of cascading waterfalls and tropical foliage centering on a very active **"volcano,"** which, after dark, erupts every 15 minutes, spewing fire 100 feet above the lagoons below. To be honest, it's not very volcanolike; just expect a really neat light show. The lobby is dominated by a 53-foot, 20,000-gallon simulated coral reef aquarium stocked with more than 1,000 colorful tropical fish, including six sharks.

Next it's through the rain forest, which occupies a 90-foot domed atrium—a path meanders through palms, banana trees, waterfalls, and serene pools. If we must find a complaint with the Mirage, it's with the next bit, as you have to negotiate 8 miles (or so it seems) of casino mayhem to get to your room, the pool, food, or the outside world. It gets old, fast. (On the other hand, the sundries shop is located right next to the guest room elevators, so if you forgot toothpaste you don't have to travel miles to get more.)

The rooms have marble entryways, mirrors, vanity tables, and canopies over the beds headboards that give even the standards a luxurious appearance. The bathrooms are marble and slightly on the small size, depending on the room. Oak armoires house 25-inch TVs, and phones are equipped with fax and computer jacks. Further up the price scale are super-deluxe rooms with whirlpool tubs. The staff is genuinely helpful; any problems that may arise are quickly smoothed out.

Off the casino is a habitat for Siegfried and Roy's white tigers, a plaster enclosure that allows for photo-taking and "aaaahhhs." Behind the pool is the dolphin habitat and Siegfried and Roy's Secret Garden, which has a separate admission.

Dining/Diversions: Choices include **Onda,** for superb Italian food; a good buffet; **Alex Stratta,** for fine French food in a formal setting; **Kokomo's,** situated in the tropical rain forest atrium; and a **California Pizza Kitchen** in the casino.

The main lounge right next to the rain forest is a particularly happening Vegas nightspot. The highly recommended production shows by **Siegfried and Roy** and **Danny Gans** are reviewed in chapter 8, and the Mirage has one of our favorite casinos.

Amenities: 24-hour room service, newspaper delivery, car-rental desk, shops, unisex salon offering all beauty services, video arcade, business services center, foreign-currency exchange. A free tram travels between the Mirage and Treasure Island almost around the clock.

Out back is the pool, one of the nicest in Vegas; it has a quarter-mile shoreline, a tropical paradise of waterfalls, trees, waterslides, and so forth. It looks inviting, but truth be told, it's sometimes on the chilly side and isn't very deep. But it's so pretty you hardly care. Free swimming lessons and water aerobics classes take place daily at the pool. Private poolside cabanas (equipped with phones, TVs, free snacks and soft drinks, refrigerators, misting systems, rafts, and radios) can be rented for $85 a day.

The **Mirage Day Spa** teems with friendly staff anxious to pamper you, bringing you iced towels to cool you during your workout and refreshing juices afterward. After a workout in the gym, soak in the whirlpool, take a steam, a sauna, a shower, and you'll be prepared for an evening of wild abandon (there's a flat $20 fee for access to all of the above facilities). Massages and treatments are also available.

Rio Suites. 3700 W. Flamingo Rd. (at I-15), Las Vegas, NV 89103. ☎ **800/752-9746** or 702/252-7777. Fax 702/252-0080. www.playrio.com. 2,582 units. A/C TV TEL. Sun–Thurs $95 suite, Fri–Sat $149 suite. Extra person $15. Inquire about golf packages. AE, CB, DC, MC, V. Free self- and valet parking.

The Rio Hotel stands somewhat removed from the Strip. The original hotel was joined by a $200-million addition: a 41-story tower and the Masquerade Village. Diverging from the rest of the tropically themed hotel, this new section simulates a European village, complete with shops, restaurants, and a bizarre live-action show in the sky. The addition is actually quite nice—this part of the casino is much more airy, thanks to the very tall ceilings.

Rio pushes itself as a "carnival" atmosphere hotel, which in this case means hectic, crowded, and noisy. The older section's low ceilings only seem to accentuate how crowded the area is. All this party atmosphere, by the way, is strictly for adults; the hotel actively discourages guests from bringing children.

The rooms are touted because of their size. Every one is a "suite," which does not mean two separate rooms but rather one large room with a sectional, corner sofa, and coffee table at one end. The dressing areas are certainly larger than average and feature a number of extra amenities, such as refrigerators, coffeemakers, and small snacks. Windows, running the whole length of the room, are floor to ceiling, with a pretty impressive view. Expect, by the way, a long wait on the phone for reservations and a not-very-helpful staff. As we went to press, the hotel announced some layoffs and the fact that some of its restaurants would no longer stay open 7 days a week. It's not yet clear whether these financial woes will translate into any other changes that might affect guests.

Dining/Diversions: The restaurants include **Napa** (from celebrity chef Jean Louis Palladin), **Fiore,** and a first-rate buffet, plus several other options, including the **Wine Cellar Tasting Room.**

The **Voodoo Lounge** and **Club Rio** are among the nightspots here. **Mambo's Entertainment Lounge** in the casino has dancing from 9pm to 3am (except Sunday). The Rio's big production show, *At the Copa,* starring David Cassidy, is reviewed in chapter 8.

To keep shoving that party, carnival theme down your throat, there is a new, live-action show called *The Masquerade Show in the Sky.* Three differently themed shows alternate, from noon to 10pm Sunday to Tuesday, from 1 to 11pm Thursday to Saturday (it's dark Wednesday). Sets modeled after Mardi Gras floats (sort of) move on grids set in the ceiling, filled with costumed performers who lip sync to songs designed to rev up the crowd. These floats are best viewed from the second floor of the village. Down below, dancers do their thing on a stage, while even stranger costumes (ostriches, dragons, and so on) prance next to them. Guests can also don costumes and ride a float, but you have to pay for the privilege.

Amenities: Guest services desk, 24-hour room service, foreign-currency exchange, complimentary shuttle bus to/from the MGM and the Forum Mall, casino, tour and show desks, unisex hair salon (offering all beauty services, including massage and facials), small video-game arcade, fitness room with cardio machines, and shops.

Out back is a pool with a sandy beach, and two new pools in imaginative fish and shell shapes that seem inviting until you get up close and see how small they are. Three whirlpool spas nestle amid rocks and foliage, there are two sand volleyball courts, and blue-and-white-striped cabanas can be rented for $8 per hour or $25 per day. The 18-hole championship **Rio Secco golf course** was designed by Rees Jones.

○ **Treasure Island at the Mirage.** 3300 Las Vegas Blvd. S. (at Spring Mountain Rd.), Las Vegas, NV 89177-0711. ☎ **800/944-7444** or 702/ 894-7111. Fax 702/894-7446. www.treasureislandlasvegas.com. 2,891 units. A/C TV TEL. From $69 double; from $109 suite. Extra person $30. Inquire about packages. AE, DC, DISC, JCB, MC, V. Free self- and valet parking.

They will deny it now if you ask them, but Treasure Island was originally conceived (more or less) as the family alternative to the more grown-up Mirage. Why else would you build a hotel that is essentially a blown-up version of Disneyland's Pirates of the Caribbean? But that's all behind them. Sure, the pirate theme remains, though the skulls, crossbones, treasure chests, pirate ships' figureheads, Animatronic skeletons, and pirate nautical paraphernalia has been toned down and minimized. A $25-million face-lift has added more marble and gilded the bones, so to speak (actually, literally in some cases). It's still Pirates of the Caribbean, but with lots and lots of money thrown at it. Despite this, it still remains a top family choice, and many kids are often running about, which some vacationers may not find desirable.

This is modern Vegas kitsch; not nearly as out there as, say, Excalibur, but loads of fun to gawk at anyway. The outside is an entire 18th-century pirate village, with the front consisting of a wooden dock from which spectators can view the free live-action pirate stunt show that plays every 90 minutes.

The rooms all have tasteful monochromatic color schemes and good bathrooms with large soaking tubs. For those of us who get disoriented in these giant hotels, the hallways have different wall-paper patterns, so you know instantly which of the several choices is yours. Best of all, Stripside rooms have a view of the pirate battle—views are best from the sixth floor on up.

Dining/Diversions: The hotel's premier restaurant is the **Buccaneer Bay Club.** The **Black Spot Grille** is described in chapter 4, as are its buffet offerings. **Madame Ching's** is a good choice for an intimate Chinese dinner.

Captain Morgan's Lounge is a piano bar that overlooks the highly themed casino. The **Battle Bar** airs sports on TV monitors overhead and offers live music nightly except Monday. More importantly, it provides patio seating overlooking Buccaneer Bay; for the best possible view of the ship battle, arrive at least 45 minutes before the show and snag a table by the railing.

Treasure Island is home to ✪ **Cirque du Soleil's** *Mystère,* one of the best production shows in town. See chapter 8.

Amenities: 24-hour room service, Mutiny Bay (state-of-the-art video-game arcade and carnival midway), limo rental, foreign-currency exchange, tour and sightseeing desks, car-rental desk, travel agency, two wedding chapels, full-service unisex salon (days of beauty are an option), and a shopping arcade.

A free tram travels between Treasure Island and the Mirage almost around the clock.

There's a full-service spa and health club with a complement of machines, sauna, steam, whirlpool and massage, on-site trainers, TVs and stereos with headsets, and anything else you might need (including a full line of Sebastian grooming products in the women's locker rooms). There's an $18-per-day fee to use the facilities.

The pool is not that memorable. It's a large free-form swimming pool with a 230-foot loop slide and a nicely landscaped sundeck area. There's a kiddie pool and whirlpool, and cabanas (equipped with overhead fans, small refrigerators, phones, cable TVs, rafts, tables, and chairs) can be rented for $75 a day.

MODERATE

Imperial Palace. 3535 Las Vegas Blvd. S. (between Sands Ave. and Flamingo Rd.), Las Vegas, NV 89109. ☎ **800/634-6441** or 702/731-3311. Fax 702/735-8578. www.imperialpalace.com. 2,700 units. A/C TV TEL. $49–$99 double; $79–$149 "luv tub" suite, $159–$299 other suites. Extra person $15. Inquire about packages. AE, CB, DC, DISC, MC, V. Free self- and valet parking.

Though appearing even older than its 20 years, the Imperial Palace has much more going for it than a first impression might yield. The Strip location, right in the middle of the action, can't be beat. The standard rooms are just that, but they all have balconies, which is exceedingly rare in Vegas. A perfect Vegas hoot, the "luv tub" rooms are one of the best deals on the Strip, especially if you can get them for the cheapest end of the price range; you get a larger bedroom (with a mirror over the bed!) while the larger-than-usual bathroom features a 300-gallon sunken "luv tub" (with still more mirrors). In fact, serious Vegas budget vacationers adore the Imperial Palace because its regular rooms can often go for as little as $29—again, given the Strip location, one hell of a deal.

The room amenities are all environmentally sensitive, with biodegradable paper containers and cruelty-free products. They are in an "ongoing" process of upgrading the furniture. TVs offer in-house information channels, video message review and check-out, and pay-per-view movies.

Dining/Diversions: Buffet, Asian, Italian—whatever you want, it's here but none of it is worth really highlighting. There's a total of 10 cocktail bars/lounges and a casino. From April to

October, the hotel holds "luaus" at the pool, with a Polynesian revue and buffet. Expect tiki torches. The hotel is also home to the long-running *Legends in Concert* impersonator show, which is reviewed in chapter 8.

A unique feature is the **Imperial Palace Auto Collection** of more than 800 antique, classic, and special-interest vehicles spanning a century of automotive history (details in chapter 5).

Amenities: 24-hour room service, free gaming lessons, health club, show and tour desks, car-rental desk, travel agency, unisex hairdresser, wedding chapel, and shopping arcade. An Olympic-size swimming pool is backed by a rock garden and waterfalls, and its palm-fringed sundeck area also has a whirlpool. The hotel spa is adequate for exercise needs; there's a $10 fee to use it, which, sadly, is a good deal in Vegas. You can also book a massage.

3 North Strip

EXPENSIVE

Riviera Hotel & Casino. 2901 Las Vegas Blvd. S. (at Riviera Blvd.), Las Vegas, NV 89109. ☎ **800/634-6753** or 702/734-5110. Fax 702/794-9451. www. theriviera.com. 2,136 units. A/C TV TEL. $59–$95 double; $125–$500 suite. Extra person $20. Inquire about "Gambler's Spree" packages. AE, CB, DC, MC, V. Free self- and valet parking.

As a reaction to the ultimately futile attempt to restyle Vegas as a "family resort," the Riviera began to promote itself as an "alternative for grown-ups" and an "adult-oriented hotel." In addition to absolutely no attractions for kids, what this means is that they aren't shy about plastering posters of their flesh-intensive, naughty show *Crazy Girls* over most surfaces. Parents should probably take the hint and take their tykes elsewhere.

Opened in 1955 (Liberace cut the ribbon and Joan Crawford was the official hostess of opening ceremonies), the Riviera was the first "high-rise" on the Strip, at nine stories. Today, it tries to evoke the Vegas of the good old days—"come drink, gamble, and see a show"—and while it is appropriately dark and glitzy, it's also very crowded and has a confusing layout. Don't miss your chance to take your photo with the bronze memorial to the Crazy Girls, and their butts, outside on the Strip. Rooms have recently been redone; amenities include in-room safes and cable TV with pay-movie options and in-house information stations.

Dining/Diversions: A predictable assortment of dining choices, including an extremely attractive food court. There are two casino bars: the **Splash Bar** and **Le Bistro Lounge;** the latter offers nightly live entertainment. The Riviera's enormous casino is one of the world's largest; see chapter 8 for reviews of its production shows.

Amenities: 24-hour room service, large arcade with carnival and video games, well-equipped health club ($10 fee for access; treatments can be booked), Olympic-size swimming pool and sundeck, wedding chapel, beauty salon/barbershop, comprehensive business center, America West airlines desk, tour and show desks, car-rental desk, shops, and two Har-Tru tennis courts lit for night play. *Warning:* Buyers, beware the booth by the Strip entrance to the casino that offers free or discounted tickets to many shows; they're hawking time-shares.

MODERATE

Sahara Hotel & Casino. 2535 Las Vegas Blvd. S. (at E. Sahara Ave.), Las Vegas, NV 89109. ☎ **800/634-6666** or 702/737-2111. Fax 702/737-2027. www.saharahotelandcasino.com. 2,035 units. A/C TV TEL. $35–$55 standard double, $55–$85 deluxe double; $200–$600 suite. Extra person $10. Children under 14 stay free in parents' room. AE, CB, DC, DISC, MC, V. Free self- and valet parking.

One of the few venerable old casino hotels remaining in Vegas (it's come a long way since it opened in 1952), the Sahara has completed a major face-lift. A new entrance features an arched neon dome with Moroccan detail, with plenty of marble and chandeliers, plus little tiles and other Arabian Nights details. This entrance is quite a hike from the actual registration area—be sure to bring your camel. And then to top it all off, they added a roller coaster around the outside (quite a good ride, enthusiasts assure us).

Unfortunately, none of this really adds up to a nice hotel experience. Recent guests find the place, renovations notwithstanding, just a bit dreary and maybe even shabby. Again, this may simply be in comparison to the gleaming new kids in town, a fate suffered by most of the older hotels. It should be noted that the Sahara feels they are not as well-equipped as other hotels for children and discourage you from bringing yours—and yet, they added a roller coaster. Go figure.

The room decor suffers from overkill, with stars and stripes assaulting the eyes and not looking terribly Moroccan. The boldly striped bedspreads on the otherwise comfortable beds are a

North Strip Accommodations

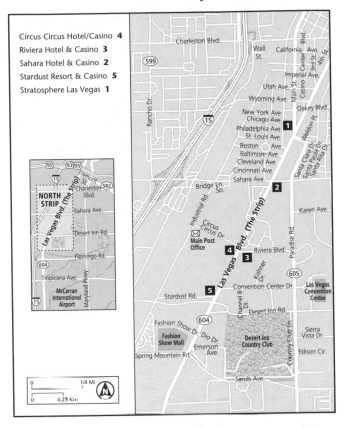

Circus Circus Hotel/Casino **4**

Riviera Hotel & Casino **3**

Sahara Hotel & Casino **2**

Stardust Resort & Casino **5**

Stratosphere Las Vegas **1**

particular mistake. The windows open, which is unusual for Vegas.

Dining/Diversions: You got your coffee shop, steakhouse, and Mexican food. The **Sahara Buffet** is detailed in chapter 4. Bar/lounges include a 24-hour casino bar (the **Safari Bar**), plus the **Casbah Lounge,** offering top-notch live entertainment daily from 2 to 6pm and 7pm to 4am. There's a casino and a headliner showroom.

Amenities: 24-hour room service, beauty salon/barbershop, car-rental desk, tour and show desks, shops, and video-game arcade. There is a handsome Olympic-size pool, done in Moroccan mosaic tiles, with misters on the palm trees and a pool shop and poolside bar in nearby thatch-roofed structures. Unfortunately, it is also right by the parking garage, which means you might be giving some casino-bound tourist an eyeful. A smaller pool shares the same courtyard setting. Note that there's no health club.

Stardust Resort & Casino. 3000 Las Vegas Blvd. S. (at Convention Center Dr.), Las Vegas, NV 89109. ☎ **800/634-6757** or 702/732-6111. Fax 702/ 732-6257. www.stardustlv.com. 2,200 units. A/C TV TEL. From $60 standard double; from $250 suite; $36–$200 Motor Inn rooms (2-person max). Extra person $10. Children 12 and under stay free in parents' room. AE, CB, DC, DISC, JCB, MC, V. Free self- and valet parking.

Opened in 1958, the Stardust is a longtime resident of the Strip, and its 188-foot starry sign is one of America's most recognized landmarks. In 1991, it added a 1,500-room tower and a 35,000-square-foot state-of-the-art meeting and conference center. It's a likable hotel, but has no personality. Rooms in the Towers are perfectly adequate, nice even, but forgettable. You can rent an adjoining parlor room with a sofa bed, whirlpool, refrigerator, and wet bar—a good choice for families. Also quite nice are Villa rooms in two-story buildings surrounding a large swimming pool; they have private shaded patios. The least expensive rooms are in the Stardust's Motor Inn, set far back on the property. Motor Inn guests can park at their doors. All Stardust accommodations offer in-room safes, and TVs have Spectravision movie options and in-house information channels.

Dining/Diversions: The **Tony Roma's** chain has a home at the Stardust. Otherwise, your dining choices are predictable: buffet, steak, seafood, diner, coffee shop, Mexican, and so on. There are eight bars and cocktail lounges in the hotel, including the **Starlight Lounge,** featuring live music nightly. The casino is huge and usually crowded.

Mr. Wayne Newton himself has taken up residency at the Stardust, performing regularly in its showroom.

Amenities: 24-hour room service, video-game arcade, car-rental desk, show desk, free ice on every floor, beauty salon/barbershop, and shops. There are two large swimming pools: one in the Villa section, the other between the East and West Towers. Both have attractively landscaped sundecks and poolside bars; the Towers pool area has three whirlpool spas. For $12, guests can use the **Las Vegas Sporting House** directly behind the hotel, a state-of-the-art, 24-hour health club with extensive facilities.

Stratosphere Las Vegas. 2000 Las Vegas Blvd. S. (between St. Louis St. and Baltimore Ave.), Las Vegas, NV 89104. ☎ **800/99-TOWER (998-6937)** or 702/380-7777. Fax 702/383-5334. www.grandcasinos.com. 1,500 units. A/C TV TEL. Sun–Thurs $39–$99 double, Fri–Sat $59–$139 double; $69–$400 suite. Extra person $15. Children 12 and under stay free in parents' room. Rates may be higher during special events. AE, CB, DC, DISC, JCB, MC, V. Free self- and valet parking.

A really neat idea, in that Vegas way, in a really bad location. At 1,149 feet, it's the tallest building west of the Mississippi. In theory, this should have provided yet another attraction for visitors: Climb (okay, elevator) to the top and gaze at the stunning view. But despite being on the Strip, it's a healthy walk from anywhere—the nearest casino is the Sahara, which is 5 very long blocks away. This and possibly the hefty price charged for the privilege of going up in said Tower may have conspired to keep the crowds away. Stay away they did; the hotel is in severe financial trouble, and construction on additions and upgrades has halted.

But in an effort to lure crowds back, prices have dropped, and some changes have been made. The casino has been toned down, and the shopping arcade has been expanded. You can still ride the incredible thrill rides (provided the wind isn't blowing too hard that day) on top of the tower: the world's highest roller coaster (it careens around the outer rim of the tower 909 feet, 108 stories, aboveground) and the Big Shot, a fabulous free-fall ride that thrusts passengers up and down the tower at speeds of up to 45 miles per hour. Indoor and outdoor observation decks offer the most stunning city views you will ever see, especially at night.

The rooms are furnished in Biedermeier-style cherrywood pieces with black lacquer accents. Enhanced by bright abstract paintings, they offer TVs with in-house information channels and pay-movie options, safes, phones with modem ports, and hair dryers. Ask for a high floor when you reserve to optimize your view.

Dining/Diversions: Two notable restaurants here are the revolving **Top of the World,** featuring panoramic vistas of Las Vegas from 800 feet, and the **Montana's Steakhouse,** offering Cajun food and all-you-can-eat dinners. There's also a buffet and a '50s-themed diner. Bars and lounges include **Oasis,** featuring live Caribbean/reggae music and tropical drinks; a cocktail lounge on the 107th floor; and the **Big Sky Lounge,** which features country music nightly after 8pm. There's a casino, and the production show is reviewed in chapter 8.

Amenities: 24-hour room service, foreign-currency exchange, guest-services desk, tour and show desk, video-game arcade, shopping arcade, three wedding chapels (offering incredible views from the 103rd floor), and car-rental desk.

INEXPENSIVE

✪ **Circus Circus Hotel/Casino.** 2880 Las Vegas Blvd. S. (between Circus Circus Dr. and Convention Center Dr.), Las Vegas, NV 89109. ☎ **800/444-CIRC (444-2472),** 800/634-3450, or 702/734-0410. Fax 702/734-2268. www. circuscircus-lasvegas.com. 3,744 units. A/C TV TEL. Sun–Thurs $39–$79 double, Fri–Sat $59–$99 double. AE, CB, DC, DISC, MC, V. Free self- and valet parking.

Perhaps the strongest evidence that things are changing in Las Vegas is the massive remodeling and renovation of this classic hotel and casino. The circus theme remains, but Jumbo the Clown has been replaced by commedia dell'arte harlequins. Like everyone else, even the venerable Circus Circus, once the epitome of kitsch, is trying to be taken more seriously. Gone are the bright primary colors and garish trims in favor of subtle, muted tones and more high-rent touches that appeal less to big-top buffs and more to the Cirque du Soleil crowd.

Despite the changes, don't come expecting an adult atmosphere; the kid appeal remains. The midway level features dozens of carnival games, a large arcade (more than 300 video and pinball games), trick mirrors, and ongoing circus acts under the big top from 11am to midnight daily. The world's largest permanent circus (according to the *Guinness Book of World Records*), it features renowned trapeze artists, stunt cyclists, jugglers, magicians, acrobats, and high-wire daredevils. Circus clowns wander the midway creating balloon animals and cutting up in various ways.

The thousands of rooms here occupy sufficient acreage to warrant a free Disney World–style aerial shuttle (another kid pleaser) and minibuses connecting its many components. Tower rooms have brand-new, just slightly better-than-average furnishings, and offer safes and TVs with in-house information and gaming instruction stations. The Manor section comprises five white three-story buildings out back, fronted by rows of cypresses. Manor guests can park at their doors, and a gate to the complex that can be opened only with a room key assures security. These rooms are usually among the least expensive in town, but we've said it before and we'll say it again: You get what you pay for. (However, as this was being written, the rooms were undergoing—at last—a needed renovation.) All sections of this vast property have their own swimming pools; additional casinos serve the main tower and Skyrise buildings; and both towers provide covered parking garages.

Adjacent to the hotel is **Circusland RV Park,** with 384 full-utility spaces and up to 50-amp hookups. It has its own 24-hour convenience store, swimming pools, saunas, whirlpools, kiddie playground, fenced pet runs, video-game arcade, and community room. The rate is $12 Sunday to Thursday, $16 Friday and Saturday, $18 holidays.

Dining/Diversions: Highly esteemed by locals (but frankly, we aren't sure why, as the food is pretty mediocre), the **Steak House** is elegant and candlelit. The very reasonably priced **Pink Pony** is Circus Circus's cheerful 24-hour eatery with a wide array of coffee-shop fare. In addition to other basic dining options, there are seven casino bars, including the carousel-themed **Horse-A-Round Bar** on the midway level. **Circus Circus Buffet** is discussed in chapter 4.

In addition to the ongoing circus acts, there's also the upgraded **Adventuredome** indoor theme park out back (see chapter 5 for details). The three full-size casinos are all crowded and noisy (what do you expect when you gamble in the middle of a circus?).

Amenities: Two swimming pools, two video-game arcades, an all-new shopping arcade, 24-hour room service (continental breakfast and drinks only), wedding chapel, tour and show desks, car-rental desk, and unisex hairdresser. There's no health club on the premises, but guests have access to a facility across the street for $12.

4 East of the Strip

In this section, we've covered hotels close by the Convention Center, along with those farther south on Paradise Road, Flamingo Road, and Tropicana Avenue.

VERY EXPENSIVE

✪ **Hard Rock Hotel & Casino.** 4455 Paradise Rd. (at Harmon Ave.), Las Vegas, NV 89109. ☎ **800/473-ROCK (473-7625)** or 702/693-5000. Fax 702/693-5010. www.hardrock.com. 657 units. A/C TV TEL. Sun–Thurs $79–$359 double; Fri–Sat $145–$300 double; from $250 suite. Extra person $25. Children 12 and under stay free in parents' room. AE, DC, MC, V. Free self- and valet parking.

As soon as you check out the Hard Rock clientele, you know you are in a Vegas hotel that's like no other. The hip—from Hollywood and the music industry, among others—flock to the Hard Rock, drawn by the cool 'n' rockin' ambience and the goodies offered by a boutique hotel (657 room is boutique only in Vegas).

It's that Boomer-meets-Gen-X sensibility that finds tacky chic most hip, and that may explain the rooms, which are a big let-down, even though they're large and have fine rock photos on the walls. The spare furnishings in the older section are a little too close to '60s "no-tell motel" for comfort. Suites are actually uglier than standard rooms, with a bath/shower combo crammed into a small chamber, and sinks outside in a dimly lit dressing area. Standard double rooms are quite large and are somewhat more attractive, with less cramped bathrooms. The rooms and suites in the new addition are much nicer by comparison (if still a bit too '60s-futuristic hip to come off as posh), but they're certainly less immediately drab and more comfortable. Bathrooms are a big step forward—bigger, brighter, shinier. On a high note, the beds have feather pillows, and mattresses are surprisingly comfortable. Uncharacteristically large 27-inch TVs offer pay-movie options and special music channels.

Dining/Diversions: There are several fine restaurants, includ-ing **AJ's Steakhouse; Nobu,** a branch of highly famed chef Nobu Matsuhisa's wildly popular Japanese restaurant, less expensive and less acclaimed than his other ventures; the Mexican- and folk-art-filled **Cantina Pink Taco;** and more. The Hard Rock's premier restaurant, **Mortoni's,** is a beautiful spot for Italian fare. The **Hard Rock Cafe** is adjacent to the hotel.

Baby is the new hot nightspot offering from L.A. club impre-sario Sean MacPherson, not that that matters; its velvet-rope pol-icy may keep the likes of us out of there. There are several other bars, all with a buzzing scene. The casino itself has a playful decor but an unbelievable noise level. **The Joint** is a major showroom that often hosts big-name rock musicians.

Amenities: 24-hour room service, concierge, small video-game arcade, gift/sundry shop, immense Hard Rock retail store, show desk (for The Joint only; tickets to other shows can be arranged by the concierge), and foreign-currency exchange.

If you've ever dreamed of being in a beach party movie, or on the set of one of those MTV summer beach houses, the recon-structed pool at the Hard Rock is for you. Multiple pools are all joined by a lazy river, fringed in spots by actual sand beaches. You won't get much swimming done—the water is largely so shallow

Accommodations East of the Strip

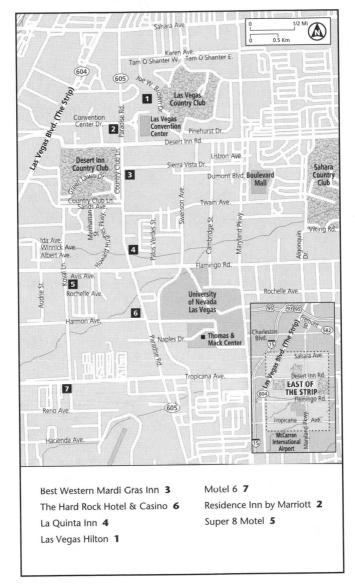

Best Western Mardi Gras Inn **3**

The Hard Rock Hotel & Casino **6**

La Quinta Inn **4**

Las Vegas Hilton **1**

Motel 6 **7**

Residence Inn by Marriott **2**

Super 8 Motel **5**

it won't hit your knees—but there is swim-up blackjack, while a stage features live music in the summer. On warm days and nights, this is *the* hangout scene.

The newly refurbished spa is smaller than its Strip counterparts but is soothing in its posh Space Age Zen way, and the health club is plenty large and well-equipped, offering a full complement of Cybex equipment, stair machines, treadmills, massage, and steam rooms. There's a $15 per day fee to use the health club facilities.

✪ **Las Vegas Hilton.** 3000 Paradise Rd. (at Riviera Blvd.), Las Vegas, NV 89109. ☎ **800/732-7117** or 702/732-5111. Fax 702/794-3611. www.lv-hilton.com. 3,174 units, A/C TV TEL. $49–$349 double. Extra person $30. Children of any age stay free in parents' room. AE, CB, DC, DISC, ER, MC, V. Free self- and valet parking.

This is really quite a classy hotel, which is probably why so many business travelers prefer it. (That, and its location next to the Convention Center.) The lobby, glittering with massive chandeliers and gleaming marble, is lovely, and the casino is actually separate from it. There are quite a few terrific restaurants, plus the largest hotel convention and meeting facilities in the world.

The newly remodeled rooms have partly marble floors and slightly larger marble bathtubs. They're nothing particularly special in terms of decor, but they are very comfortable. All offer TVs (cached in handsome armoires) with HBO, On-Command pay-movie options, an in-house information channel, and video-checkout capability.

Note: Just as we went to press, the Hilton was sold. While the initially announced changes do not sound too radical, be aware that by the time you read this, some of the information contained here may have changed.

Dining/Diversions: The Hilton has a strong showing of restaurants, including a Benihana's and a buffet that's reviewed in chapter 4. *Note:* Children 12 and under dine in any Hilton restaurant for half the listed menu prices. The **Nightclub,** a first-rate casino lounge, has live entertainment nightly. There's also a major headliner showroom, and a well-designed casino with some fun gimmicks.

A serious renovation has added a number of new shops, plus **Star Trek: The Experience,** a themed attraction and accompanying space-themed casino. We've heard totally unconfirmed rumors that this attraction may be moving to another hotel, so if this is something that may lure you to the Hilton, call first to make sure it still exists.

Amenities: 18-hole golf course, 24-hour room service, foreign-currency exchange, car-rental desk, tour desk, travel agency, shops, small video-game arcade, business center, multiservice beauty salon/barbershop, and jogging trail.

The third-floor roof comprises a beautifully landscaped 8-acre recreation deck with a large swimming pool, a 24-seat whirlpool spa, six Har-Tru tennis courts lit for night play, Ping-Pong, and a putting green. Also on this level is a luxurious 17,000-square-foot, state-of-the-art health club offering Nautilus equipment, Lifecycles, treadmills, rowing machines, three whirlpool spas, steam, sauna, massage, and tanning beds. There's a $15-per-day fee to use the facilities, but guests are totally pampered.

EXPENSIVE

La Quinta Inn. 3970 Paradise Rd. (between Twain Ave. and Flamingo Rd.), Las Vegas, NV 89109. ☎ **800/531-5900** or 702/796-9000. Fax 702/796-3537. www.laquinta.com. 251 units. A/C TV TEL. $79–$95 standard double; $89–$99 executive queen; $115–$169 suite. Rates include continental breakfast; inquire about seasonal discounts. AE, CB, DC, DISC, MC, V. Free self-parking.

This is a tranquil alternative to Strip hubbub, featuring court-yards, attractive pools, barbecue grills, and picnic tables. The staff is terrific—friendly and incredibly helpful. The rooms are immaculate and attractive. Executive rooms feature one queen-size bed, a small refrigerator, a wet bar, and a microwave oven. Double queens are larger but have no kitchen facilities. And two-bedroom suites are not just spacious—they are really full apart-ments, with large living rooms (some with sofa beds), dining areas, and full kitchens. Ground-floor accommodations have patios, and all accommodations feature bathrooms with oversize whirlpool tubs. TVs offer satellite channels and HBO.

Dining: A hearty and complimentary continental breakfast is served daily in the **Patio Café.**

Amenities: Car rentals/tours arranged at the front desk, coin-op washers/dryers, medium-size swimming pool, and adjoining whirlpool. A free 24-hour shuttle offers pickup and return to and from the airport and several Strip casino hotels.

✪ **Residence Inn by Marriott.** 3225 Paradise Rd. (between Desert Inn Rd. and Convention Center Dr.), Las Vegas, NV 89109. ☎ **800/331-3131** or 702/796-9300. www.marriott.com. 192 units. A/C TV TEL. $119 and up for studio; $149 and up for penthouse. Rates include continental breakfast. AE, CB, DC, DISC, MC, V. Free self-parking.

Staying here is like having your own apartment in Las Vegas. The property occupies 7 acres of perfectly manicured lawns, tropical foliage, and neat flower beds. It's a great choice for families and business travelers.

Accommodations, most with working fireplaces, are housed in condolike, two-story wood-and-stucco buildings, fronted by little gardens. Studios have adjoining sitting rooms with sofas and armchairs, dressing areas, and fully equipped eat-in kitchens complete with dishwashers. Every guest receives a welcome basket of microwave popcorn and coffee. TVs offer visitor information channels and VCRs (you can rent movies nearby), and all rooms have balconies or patios. Duplex penthouses, some with cathedral ceilings, add an upstairs bedroom (with its own bath, phone, TV, and radio) and a full dining room.

Dining: A big continental buffet breakfast is served each morning. Daily papers are set out each morning; there's a large-screen TV and a stereo for guest use; and a selection of toys, games, and books is available for children. Weekday evenings from 5:30 to 7pm, complimentary buffets with beverages (beer, wine, coffee, and soda), fresh popcorn, and daily varying fare are served in the gatehouse. Local restaurants deliver food, and there's also a complimentary food-shopping service (maids wash your dishes).

Amenities: Good-size swimming pool and whirlpool with a sundeck, car-rental desk, barbecue grills, coin-op washers/dryers, sports court (paddle tennis, volleyball, and basketball). Guests can use the health club next door at the Courtyard by Marriott.

MODERATE

Best Western Mardi Gras Inn. 3500 Paradise Rd. (between Sands Ave. and Desert Inn Rd.), Las Vegas, NV 89109. ☎ **800/634-6501** or 702/731-2020. Fax 702/733-6994. www.mardigrasinn.com. 315 units. A/C TV TEL. $40–$125 double. Extra person $8. Children 18 and under stay free in parents' room. AE, CB, DC, DISC, JCB, MC, V. Free parking at your room door.

This well-run little casino hotel has a lot to offer. A block from the Convention Center and close to major properties, its three-story building sits on nicely landscaped grounds. Accommodations are all spacious, queen-bedded minisuites with sofa-bedded living room areas and eat-in kitchens, the latter equipped with wet bars, refrigerators, and coffeemakers. All are attractively decorated and offer TVs with HBO and pay-movie options. Staying here is like having your own little Las Vegas apartment.

Dining: A pleasant restaurant/bar serves typical coffee-shop fare; a 12-ounce prime rib dinner here is just $9. There's a small casino, with 64 slots/video-poker machines.

Amenities: Large swimming pool with a duplex sundeck and whirlpool, free transportation to/from airport and major Strip hotels, small video-game arcade, car-rental desk, tour and show desks, coin-op washers/dryers, unisex hairdresser, and RV parking.

INEXPENSIVE

Motel 6. 195 E. Tropicana Ave. (at Koval Lane), Las Vegas, NV 89109. ☎ 800/4-MOTEL-6 (466-8356) or 702/798-0728. Fax 702/798-5657. 602 units. A/C TV TEL. Sun–Thurs $35 single, Fri–Sat $58 single. Extra person $6. Children under 17 stay free in parents' room. AE, CB, DC, DISC, MC, V. Free parking at your room door.

Fronted by a big neon sign, Las Vegas's Motel 6 is the largest in the country, and it happens to be a great budget choice. Most Motel 6 properties are a little out of the way, but this one is quite close to major Strip casino hotels (the MGM is nearby). It has a big, pleasant lobby, and the rooms are clean and attractively decorated. Some rooms have showers only; others, tub/shower baths. Local calls are free, and your TV offers HBO.

Note: At press time there were plans to turn a portion or all of this property into a new 1940s gangster-themed hotel called Bugsy's. A portion of Motel 6 may still be operating or may be entirely closed by the end of 2000.

Dining: Three restaurants (including a pleasant 24-hour family restaurant called **Carrows**) adjoin.

Amenities: Two nice-size swimming pools in enclosed courtyards, whirlpool, gift shop, vending machines, tour desk, and coin-op washers/dryers.

Super 8 Motel. 4250 Koval Lane (just south of Flamingo Rd.), Las Vegas, NV 89109. ☎ 800/800-8000 or 702/794-0888. 290 units. A/C TV TEL. Sun–Thurs $41–$43 double, Fri–Sat $56–$58 double. Extra person $8. Children 12 and under stay free in parents' room. AE, CB, DC, DISC, MC, V. Free self-parking. Pets $8 per night (1 pet only).

Billing itself as "the world's largest Super 8 Motel," this friendly property occupies a vaguely Tudor-style stone-and-stucco building. Free coffee is served in a pleasant little lobby furnished with comfortable sofas and wing chairs. Rooms are clean and well-maintained. Some have safes, and TVs offer free movie channels.

Dining/Diversions: The nautically themed **Ellis Island Restaurant,** open 24 hours, offers typical coffee-shop fare at reasonable prices. There's also a sports bar, a karaoke bar, and a casino.

Amenities: Small kidney-shaped pool/sundeck and adjoining whirlpool, limited room service via Ellis Island, free airport transfer, car-rental desk, and coin-op washers/dryers.

5 Downtown

EXPENSIVE

✪ **Golden Nugget.** 129 E. Fremont St. (at Casino Center Blvd.), Las Vegas, NV 89101. ☎ **800/634-3454** or 702/385-7111. Fax 702/386-8362. www. goldennugget.com. 1,907 units. A/C TV TEL. $59–$299 double; $275–$500 suite. Extra person $20. AE, CB, DC, DISC, MC, V. Free self- and valet parking.

The Golden Nugget opened in 1946, as the first building in Las Vegas constructed specifically for casino gambling. Steve Wynn took it over as his first major project in Vegas, in 1973. He gradually transformed the Old West/Victorian interiors (typical for Downtown) into something more high rent; marble and brass gleam, and the whole package seems luxurious, especially for Downtown. The sunny interior spaces are a welcome change from the Vegas tradition of dim lighting.

If the decor of the Mirage sounded appealing to you and you want to stay Downtown, come here, since the same people own them and the rooms look almost identical. They have marble entryways, half-canopy beds, vanity tables with magnifying makeup mirrors, armoires, and marble bathrooms complete with hair dryers. Cable TVs feature pay-movie options. In the North Tower, the rooms are slightly larger than in the South (and also slightly larger than at the Mirage).

Dining/Diversions: The **Carson Street Café** is the Nugget's 24-hour restaurant. There are also superb buffets, 24-hour Sunday brunch, a branch of the **California Pizza Kitchen,** and four casino bars, including the elegant **Claude's** and the **38 Different Kinds of Beer Bar.**

Amenities: Lovely and immense tropical pool with poolside bar, 24-hour room service, concierge, casino, car-rental desk, full-service unisex hair salon, shops, video-game arcade, and foreign-currency exchange.

The Nugget's top-rated health club ($15-per-day fee to use the facilities) offers a full line of cardio and weight equipment and a sauna. Salon treatments include everything from leg waxing to

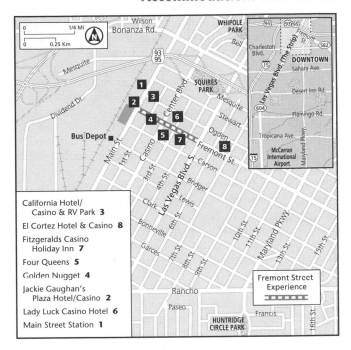

California Hotel/
  Casino & RV Park **3**

El Cortez Hotel & Casino **8**

Fitzgeralds Casino
  Holiday Inn **7**

Four Queens **5**

Golden Nugget **4**

Jackie Gaughan's
  Plaza Hotel/Casino **2**

Lady Luck Casino Hotel **6**

Main Street Station **1**

seaweed-mask facials. Free Sebastian products are available for sprucing up afterward.

MODERATE

✪ **Fitzgeralds Casino Holiday Inn.** 301 Fremont St. (at 3rd St.), Las Vegas, NV 89101. ☎ **800/274-LUCK (274-5825)** or 702/388-2400. Fax 702/388-2181. 652 units. A/C TV TEL. $40–$85 double; $60–$105 suite. Extra person $10. Children under 19 stay free in parents' room. AE, CB, DC, DISC, MC, V. Free self- and valet parking.

Fitzgeralds is a Holiday Inn franchise and has upgraded its rooms to fit said chain's code. The result is attractive and has received an award for best redesign from the Governor's Conference. The restaurants have all been given serious facelifts, and a sort of Irish country village walkway, complete with big giant fake tree, leads to the room elevators. Fitzgeralds has the only balcony in Downtown from which you can watch the Fremont Street Experience. You can also sit in their McDonald's and gawk at the light show through the atrium windows.

The look in the rooms is clean and comfortable, standard hotel room decor. Because this is the tallest building in Downtown (34 stories), you get excellent views: either snowcapped mountains, Downtown lights, or the Strip. Whirlpool tub rooms are $20 more and are slightly larger with wraparound windows. All rooms offer safes and 25-inch TVs with pay-movie options.

Dining/Diversions: **Limerick's,** an upscale Irish pub, is described in chapter 4. There's also an Italian choice, a coffee shop, and more. The balcony of the second-floor **Lookout Lounge** is a good vantage point for viewing the Fremont Street Experience. A **McDonald's** and three bars are on the casino floor.

Amenities: 24-hour room service, complimentary gaming lessons, casino, tour and show desks, car-rental desk.

✪ **Four Queens.** 202 Fremont St. (at Casino Center Blvd.), Las Vegas, NV 89101. ☎ **800/634-6045** or 702/385-4011. Fax 702/387-5122. www. savenet.com/702/4queen.htm. 700 units. A/C TV TEL. $29–$179 double; $119–$350 suite. Extra person $15. AE, CB, DC, DISC, MC, V. Free self- and valet parking.

Opened in 1966 with a mere 120 rooms, the Four Queens (named for the owner's four daughters) has evolved over the decades into a major Downtown property occupying an entire city block. The lobby is small but elegant—in a slightly faded, slightly dated way (with mirrors and huge chandeliers). In the Four Queens, you just know you're in old Las Vegas. And are glad. As the staff says, this is the place to stay if you just want to gamble. Their clientele is on the older side (50-plus), and doesn't usually include those coming to Las Vegas for the first time.

Notably nice rooms, decorated in basic hotel-room style, are located in 19-story twin towers. Especially lovely are the North Tower rooms, decorated in a Southwestern motif and, in most cases, offering views of the Fremont Street Experience. Mini-suites, decorated in traditional styles, have living rooms (separated from the bedrooms by a trellised wall) and dining areas, double-sink baths, and dressing areas. All accommodations offer TVs with in-house information and pay-movie channels. Some rooms are equipped with small refrigerators and coffeemakers.

Dining/Diversions: **Hugo's Cellar** is the main restaurant; it also has a cozy lounge with a working fireplace, and two bars serve the casino. There are a couple of other restaurants for your Italian or coffee-shop cravings, and a casino.

Amenities: 24-hour room service, gift shop, car-rental desk, tour and show desks, small video-game arcade, plus a basic workout room that is free.

INEXPENSIVE

California Hotel/Casino & RV Park. 12 Ogden Ave. (at 1st St.), Las Vegas, NV 89101. ☎ **800/634-6255** or 702/385-1222. Fax 702/388-2660. 855 units. A/C TV TEL. Sun–Thurs $50 double, Fri–Sat $60 double, holidays $70 double. Extra person $5. Children 12 and under stay free in parents' room. AE, CB, DC, DISC, MC, V. Free self- and valet parking.

This is a hotel with a unique personality. California-themed, it markets mostly in Hawaii, and since 85% of the guests are from the Aloha State, it offers Hawaiian entrees in several of its restaurants and even has an on-premises store specializing in Hawaiian foodstuff. You'll also notice that dealers are wearing colorful aloha shirts. The rooms have mahogany furnishings and attractive marble baths. In-room safes are a plus, and TVs offer pay-per-view movies and keno channels.

Dining/Diversions: The **Redwood Bar and Grill,** featuring steak and seafood, looks like a ski lodge. There's piano bar entertainment in the adjoining lounge. There are a couple of other dining choices, plus two 24-hour casino bars.

Amenities: Small rooftop pool, room service (breakfast only), car-rental desk, car wash, small video-game arcade, shops, food store.

El Cortez Hotel & Casino. 600 Fremont St. (between 6th and 7th sts.), Las Vegas, NV 89101. ☎ **800/634-6703** or 702/385-5200. Fax 702/474-3626. www.elcortez.net. 428 units. A/C TV TEL. $32 double; $40 minisuite. Extra person $3. AE, DISC, MC, V. Free self- and valet parking.

This small hotel is popular with locals for its casual, "just-folks" Downtown atmosphere and its frequent big-prize lotteries (up to $50,000) based on Social Security numbers. The nicest accommodations are the enormous minisuites in the newer 14-story tower. Some are exceptionally large king-bedded rooms with sofas; others have separate sitting areas with sofas, armchairs, and tables, plus small dressing areas. The rooms in the original building are furnished more traditionally and with less flair, and they cost less. Local calls are just 25¢. Under the same ownership is **Ogden House,** just across the street, with rooms that go for just $18 a night.

Dining/Diversions: One fancy restaurant, plus a large 24-hour coffee shop called the **Emerald Room,** where you can enjoy a bacon-and-eggs breakfast with hash browns, toast, and coffee for $1. A "soup-to-nuts" 18-ounce porterhouse steak dinner is $6.45 here. Four bars serve the casino.

Amenities: Small video-game arcade, beauty salon, gift shop, and barbershop.

Jackie Gaughan's Plaza Hotel/Casino. 1 Main St. (at Fremont St.), Las Vegas, NV 89101. ☎ **800/634-6575** or 702/386-2110. Fax 702/386-2378. www.jackiegaughan.com. 1,037 units. A/C TV TEL. $40–$120 double; $80–$150 suite. Extra person $8. Children under 12 stay free in parents' room. AE, DC, DISC, MC, V. Free self- and valet parking.

Built in 1971 on the site of the old Union Pacific Railroad Depot, the Plaza, a double-towered, 3-block-long property, permanently altered the Downtown skyline. Las Vegas's Amtrak station (currently unused) is right in the hotel, and the main Greyhound terminal adjoins it. Fremont Street literally ends right at the Plaza's front door, so you can't fault the location.

Accommodations are spacious and adequately decorated. The suites, in particular, are huge, and the two-bedroom suite would be a terrific option for a large party of friends to share. Rooms in the North Tower look down on the Fremont Street Experience.

Dining/Diversions: The **Center Stage** restaurant offers fabulous views of Glitter Gulch and the Fremont Street Experience. There's a 24-hour diner, a coffee bar, several casino cocktail bars, and the **Omaha Lounge,** offering live entertainment in the casino almost around the clock.

Amenities: Sports deck with a nice-size swimming pool, a ¼-mile outdoor jogging track, and four Har-Tru tennis courts; guest-services desk (also handles in-house shows); tour desk; car-rental desk; shops; wedding chapel; and beauty salon/barbershop.

Lady Luck Casino Hotel. 206 N. 3rd St. (at Ogden Ave.), Las Vegas, NV 89101. ☎ **800/523-9582** or 702/477-3000. Fax 702/382-2346. www.ladyluck.com. 792 units. A/C TV TEL. $40–$155 double; Sun–Thurs $55–$75 junior suite, Fri–Sat $70–$105 junior suite. Extra person $8. AE, CB, DC, DISC, JCB, MC, V. Free self- and valet parking.

The Lady Luck, which includes sleek 17- and 25-story towers, is a major Downtown player taking up an entire city block. What it retains from earlier times is a friendly atmosphere, one that has kept customers coming back for decades. Eighty percent of Lady Luck's clientele is repeat business.

Neon tubing overhead in the casino and hotel is color-coded to your room key, so you know which way to go to the particular tower where you are staying. This is good, as one of those towers is actually across the street (an over-the-street enclosed walkway takes you there). Tower rooms are decorated in a variety of attractive color schemes, mostly using muted Southwestern hues and handsome oak furnishings. It's all larger, brighter, and lighter than you might expect (though again, just your basic hotel-room decor). Rooms also have full-length mirrors, small refrigerators, and TVs with pay-per-view movies. Junior suites in the West Tower have parlor areas with sofas and armchairs, separate dressing areas, and baths with whirlpool tubs. The original Garden Rooms, by the pool, are a little smaller and less spiffy-looking.

Dining/Diversions: The usual stuff: fancy dining room, Italian place, and coffee shop. In addition, there is a daily buffet, and ESPN is aired on three TV monitors in the **Casino Bar.**

Amenities: Unheated swimming pool; sundeck; 24-hour room service; multilingual front desk; complimentary airport shuttle; casino, tour, show, and car-rental desks; gift shop.

✪ **Main Street Station.** 200 N. Main St. (between Fremont St. and I-95), Las Vegas, NV 89101. ☎ **800/465-0711** or 702/387-1896. Fax 702/386-4466. 452 units. A/C TV TEL. $45–$175 standard double. AE, CB, DC, DISC, MC, V. Free self- and valet parking.

Though not actually on Fremont Street, the Main Street Station is just 2 short blocks away, barely a 3-minute walk. Considering how terrific it is, this is hardly an inconvenience. We think it's one of the nicest hotels in Downtown and one of the best bargains in the city.

The overall look here, typical of Downtown, is turn-of-the-century San Francisco. The details here are outstanding, producing a beautiful hotel by any measure. Outside, gas lamps flicker on wrought-iron railings and stained-glass windows. Inside are hammered tin ceilings, ornate antique-style chandeliers, and lazy ceiling fans. The small lobby is filled with wood panels, long wooden benches, and a front desk straight out of the Old West. Even the cashier cages look like antique brass bank tellers' cages. It's all very appealing and just plain pretty. An enclosed bridge connects the hotel with the California across the street, where you will find shopping and a kids' arcade.

The long and narrow rooms are possibly the largest in Downtown. The ornate decorating downstairs does not extend up here, but everything is simple, clean, and in good taste. The bathrooms are small but well-appointed. (Rooms on the north side overlook the freeway, and the railroad track is nearby. The soundproofing seems quite strong, but if you're concerned, request a room on the south side.) Each room has Nintendo for a charge and movies for free.

Dining/Diversions: The stylish **Triple 7 Brew Pub** is described in detail in chapter 8. The **Pullman Grille** is a reasonably priced steak-and-seafood place, and there's an excellent buffet. The casino, thanks to some high ceilings, is one of the most smoke-free around.

Amenities: Dry cleaning and laundry service, in-room massage, safe-deposit boxes, show desk, and shopping and game-room arcade at California Hotel accessible via connecting walkway.

4

Dining

*A*mong the many images that people have of Las Vegas are cheap food deals, bargains so good the food is practically free. They think of the buffets—all a small country can eat—for only $3.99!

All that is true, but frankly, eating in Las Vegas is no longer something you don't have to worry about budgeting for. The buffets are certainly there—no good hotel would be without one— as are the cheap meal deals, but you get what you pay for. Some of the cheaper buffets, and even the more moderately priced ones, are mediocre at best, ghastly and inedible at worst. And we don't even want to *think* about those 69¢ beef stew specials.

However, there is some good, indeed, almost unheard-of news on the Vegas food scene. Virtually overnight, there has been an explosion of new restaurants that are actually of high quality. All of a sudden, Vegas is able to hold its head up alongside other big cities as a legitimate foodie destination.

Look at this partial list: Celebrity chefs Wolfgang Puck and Emeril Lagasse between them have half a dozen restaurants in town; deservedly famed chefs Julian Serrano and Jean Louis Palladin have set up shop in Bellagio's **Picasso** and the Rio's **Napa**, respectively; and branches of L.A., New York, San Francisco, and Boston high-profile names such as **Pinot, Le Cirque, Aqua, Aureole, Olives, Star Canyon, Lutèce, Border Grill, Matsuhisa,** and still others have all rolled into town.

There are tricks to surviving dining in Vegas. If you can, make reservations in advance, particularly for the better restaurants (you might well get to town, planning to check out some of the better spots, only to find they are totally booked throughout your stay). Eat as much as you can during off-hours, which admittedly are hard to find. But you know that noon to, say, 1:30 or 2pm is going to be prime for lunch, and 5:30 to 8:30pm (and just after the early shows get out) for dinner. Speaking of time, give yourself plenty of it, particularly if you have to catch a show.

1 South Strip

VERY EXPENSIVE

Aureole. In Mandalay Bay, 3950 Las Vegas Blvd. S. ☎ **702/632-7401.** Reservations required. Fixed-price dinner $65. AE, DISC, MC, V. Daily 5–10:15pm. NOUVELLE AMERICAN.

This branch of a New York City fave (it's pronounced are-ree-*all*) run by Charlie Palmer is most noted locally for its glass wine tower. Four stories of carefully chosen bottles (including the largest collection of Austrian wines outside of that country—well worth trying for a new wine experience) are plucked from their perches by comely, cat-suited lasses who fly up and down via pulleys. It's quite the show, and folks come in just to watch.

Should you come for the food? Perhaps. Certainly the Asian-influenced fusion is solid, but it's more underwhelming than outstanding, and since it's currently a fixed-price three-course meal, it may simply not be worth the price.

Coyote Cafe. In the MGM Grand, 3799 Las Vegas Blvd. S. ☎ **702/891-7349.** Reservations recommended for the Grill Room, not accepted for the Cafe. Grill Room main courses $15–$32. Cafe main courses $7.50–$17.50 (many are under $10). AE, CB, DC, DISC, JCB, MC, V. Grill Room daily 5:30–10pm. Cafe daily 7:30am–11pm. SOUTHWESTERN.

Mark Miller was one of the first celebrity chefs to hit Vegas, way back before the current trendy boom. His robust regional cuisine combines elements of traditional Mexican, Native American, Creole, and Cajun cookery. The Grill Room menu changes monthly, but on a recent visit, we enjoyed a bibb lettuce salad with a lovely light lemon dressing, and some fine spicy pork chops. Desserts include chocolate banana torte served on banana crème anglaise and topped with a scoop of vanilla ice cream. The wine list includes many by-the-glass selections, including champagnes and sparkling wines, which nicely complement spicy Southwestern fare; Brazilian daiquiris are a house specialty.

The Cafe menu offers similar but somewhat lighter fare. Southwestern breakfasts ($6 to $9.50) range from huevos rancheros to blue-corn pancakes with toasted pine nuts, honey butter, and real maple syrup.

✪ Emeril's New Orleans Fish House. In the MGM Grand, 3799 Las Vegas Blvd. S. ☎ **702/891-7374.** Reservations required. Main courses $12–$18 at lunch, $18–$38 at dinner (more for lobster). AE, CB, DC, DISC, MC, V. Daily 11am–2:30pm and 5:30–10:30pm. CONTEMPORARY CREOLE.

South Strip Dining

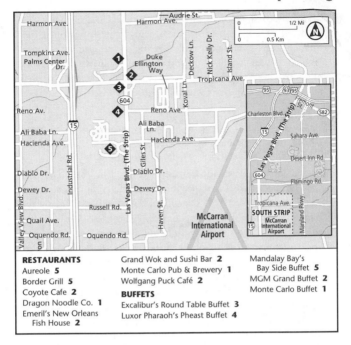

RESTAURANTS
Aureole **5**
Border Grill **5**
Coyote Cafe **2**
Dragon Noodle Co. **1**
Emeril's New Orleans
  Fish House **2**

Grand Wok and Sushi Bar **2**
Monte Carlo Pub & Brewery **1**
Wolfgang Puck Café **2**

BUFFETS
Excalibur's Round Table Buffet **3**
Luxor Pharaoh's Pheast Buffet **4**

Mandalay Bay's
  Bay Side Buffet **5**
MGM Grand Buffet **2**
Monte Carlo Buffet **1**

Chef Emeril Lagasse, a ubiquitous presence on cable's Food Network, has brought his popular New Orleans restaurant to the MGM Grand, where it is tucked into an almost unseen corner of the hotel. The restaurant's quiet and comforting decor provides the stage for creative, exciting, "BAM!" food.

Although Lagasse caters to the tastes of everyone from poultry lovers to vegetarians, seafood is the specialty here, flown in from Louisiana or from anywhere that he finds the quality of the ingredients to be the very finest. We started off with the most recent edition of Lagasse's legendary savory "cheesecakes": a lobster cheesecake with tomato-tarragon coulis, topped with a dollop of succulent Louisiana choupique caviar. It's a heady, rich appetizer that may be completely unlike anything you've ever had.

Our entrees did not fail to elicit a "Wow!" from everyone at the table. A Creole-seasoned seared ahi steak was stuffed with Hudson Valley foie gras and served in a bed of Lagasse's famous "smashed" potatoes, creamy and rich, with roasted shallots and a part-shallot reduction—absolutely luxurious. And in a dish that bordered on the sinful, there was a marvelously seasoned filet mignon stuffed with a crawfish dressing and topped with bordelaise sauce with crawfish tails and sliced andouille sausage. A slice of the banana cream pie with banana crust and caramel drizzle is one of the finest desserts you will ever have.

EXPENSIVE

✪ **Border Grill.** In Mandalay Bay, 3950 Las Vegas Blvd. S. ☎ **702/632-7403.** Reservations recommended. Main courses $15–$20. AE, DC, DISC, MC, V. Sun–Thurs 11:30am–10pm, Fri–Sat 11:30am–11pm. MEXICAN.

For our money, here's the best Mexican food in town. This big, cheerful space (like a Romper Room for adults) houses a branch of the much-lauded L.A. restaurant, conceived and run by the Food Network's "Two Hot Tamales," Mary Sue Milliken and Susan Feniger. This is truly authentic Mexican home cooking, but with a nuevo twist. So don't expect precisely the same dishes you'd encounter in your favorite corner joint, but do expect fresh and fabulous food, arranged as brightly on the plates as the decor on the walls. Stay away from the occasionally bland fish and head right towards rich and cheesy dishes like chili rellenos (with perfect black beans) and chicken *chilaquiles,* or try things like mushroom empanadas. Don't miss the dense but fluffy Mexican chocolate cream pie (with a meringue crust).

MODERATE

See also the listing for the **Coyote Café,** above; it's fronted by a more moderately priced cafe.

✪ **Dragon Noodle Co.** In the Monte Carlo Resort & Casino, 3770 Las Vegas Blvd. S. (between Flamingo Rd. and Tropicana Ave.). ☎ **702/730-7965.** Reservations not accepted. Main courses $5.50–$17 (many under $10). AE, CB, DC, DISC, MC, V. Sun–Thurs 11am–10pm, Fri–Sat 11am–11pm. ASIAN FUSION.

Dragon Noodle is one of the better Chinese restaurants in town. We were glad to see that in addition to the usual suspects, there are some other interesting (if not radically less safe) choices on the menu. Food is served family-style, and prepared in an open kitchen, so you know it's fresh. Be sure to try the very smooth house green tea. You might let your waiter choose your meal for you, but try the crispy Peking pork, the sweet pungent shrimp, the potstickers, and perhaps the generous seafood soup. We were a little disappointed by the popular sizzling black-pepper chicken.

✪ **Grand Wok and Sushi Bar.** In the MGM Grand, 3799 Las Vegas Blvd. S.
☎ **702/891-7777.** Reservations not accepted. Main courses $8.95–$13.95;
sushi $4.50–$9.50. AE, DC, DISC, MC, V. Daily 11am–11:30pm. PAN-ASIAN.

A pan-Asian restaurant runs the risk of attempting to be a jack of
all trades and master of none, but somehow, this new MGM
eatery pulls it off. We didn't try every cuisine offered (Japanese,
Chinese, Korean, Vietnamese and maybe more!), but a random
sampling (including lovely fresh sushi, fat dumplings, and a huge
Vietnamese combo soup that was full of noodles and different
kinds of meat) produced really superb food, delicately prepared.
Hotel Asian restaurants are often a bit dubious, this one really is
marvelous—and the primarily Asian clientele clearly agrees. Note
that soup portions are most generous; four people could easily
split one order and have a nice and very cheap lunch, one of the
best bargain meals in town.

✪ **Wolfgang Puck Café.** In the MGM Grand, 3799 Las Vegas Blvd. S.
☎ **702/895-9653.** Reservations not accepted. Main courses $9–$15.
AE, DC, MC, V. Daily 11am–11pm. CALIFORNIA.

A brightly colored riot of mosaic tiles and other experiments in
geometric design, the Wolfgang Puck Café stands out in the
MGM Grand. It's more or less Spago Lite: downscaled salads,
pizzas, and pastas, all showing the Puck hand. While perhaps a
little pricier than what you'd find at your average cafe, the food is
comparably better, if sometimes not that special. However, it's all
very fresh nouvelle cuisine, which makes a nice change of pace.
There does tend to be a line to get in, particularly after *EFX* lets
out just across the casino.

INEXPENSIVE

✪ **Monte Carlo Pub & Brewery.** In the Monte Carlo Resort & Casino, 3770
Las Vegas Blvd. S. (between Flamingo Rd. and Tropicana Ave.). ☎ **702/
730-7777.** Reservations not accepted. Main courses $6–$8. AE, CB, DC, DISC,
MC, V. Sun–Thurs 11am–1am, Fri–Sat 11am–3am. PUB FARE.

Lest you think we are big, fat foodie snobs who can't appreciate a
meal unless it comes drenched in truffles and caviar, we hasten to
direct you to this lively, working microbrewery (with a sort of rus-
tic factory appearance) and its hearty, not-so-high-falutin' food.
No fancy French frills, and best of all, no inflated prices. Combine the general high quality with generous portions—a nachos
appetizer could probably feed eight (though it was not the best
nachos appetizer ever)—and this may be a better deal than most

buffets. It's not, however, the place for a quiet rendezvous, with about 40 TVs spread throughout (a sports fan's dream) and music blaring. Earning recent raves were the short ribs, in a fine barbecue sauce, cooked just right; the excellent chicken fingers and shrimp fried in beer appetizers; and the garlic pizza with mounds of our favorite aromatic herb. We also highly enjoyed the double-chocolate-fudge suicide brownie, though really, what's not to love about something like that? After 9pm, only pizza is served, and dueling pianos provide dance music and entertainment.

2 Mid-Strip

VERY EXPENSIVE

✪ **Aqua.** In Bellagio, 3600 Las Vegas Blvd. S. ☎ **702/693-7223**. Reservations recommended. Main courses $29–$34 (lobster and whole foie gras higher). AE, DISC, MC, V. Daily 5:30–10pm. SEAFOOD.

Fish fans should certainly head quickly over to Aqua, a branch of a highly respected San Francisco restaurant. You can start your meal with a non-seafood choice like Hudson Valley foie gras, which comes with a warm apple Charlotte. The mixed seasonal greens salad looks like a flower, and is a light, amiable mix of flavors. For a main course, fish fans should go straight to the vaguely Japanese miso-glazed Chilean sea bass in a rich, but not heavy, shellfish consommé. More timid fish eaters might try the robust Hawaiian swordfish au poivre, though its side of pancetta-wrapped shrimp dumplings (think fancy bacon-wrapped shrimp) is not as successful. The lobster pot pie is cooked in a pot, then brought to the table and disassembled with great ceremony, as 1½ pounds of lobster is laid out, a creamy sauce with veggies is poured over it, and it's all topped with the crust. Do try some of their dainty and clever desserts, particularly their signature root beer float—no, really. It's got root beer sorbet, sasaparilla ice cream, a chocolate straw, and warm cookies right out of the oven.

Chinois. In Caesars Palace, 3570 Las Vegas Blvd. S. ☎ **702/737-9700**. Reservations recommended. Main courses $11–$16.50 in the cafe; $19.75–$28 in the restaurant. AE, JCB, MC, V. Restaurant daily 5pm–10pm; cafe daily 11:30am–10pm. EURASIAN.

From Wolfgang Puck, the man who brought you Spago and gourmet frozen pizzas, comes another entry in the world of fine dining and innovative cuisine. It's not the groundbreaker that Spago was, and it's probably more about presentation than truly

Mid-Strip Dining

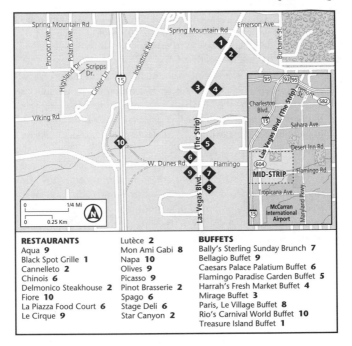

RESTAURANTS
Aqua **9**
Black Spot Grille **1**
Cannelleto **2**
Chinois **6**
Delmonico Steakhouse **2**
Fiore **10**
La Piazza Food Court **6**
Le Cirque **9**

Lutèce **2**
Mon Ami Gabi **8**
Napa **10**
Olives **9**
Picasso **9**
Pinot Brasserie **2**
Spago **6**
Stage Deli **6**
Star Canyon **2**

BUFFETS
Bally's Sterling Sunday Brunch **7**
Bellagio Buffet **9**
Caesars Palace Palatium Buffet **6**
Flamingo Paradise Garden Buffet **5**
Harrah's Fresh Market Buffet **4**
Mirage Buffet **3**
Paris, Le Village Buffet **8**
Rio's Carnival World Buffet **10**
Treasure Island Buffet **1**

remarkable meals, but it's still good to have it on the Vegas foodie scene.

Food is served family-style, which helps spread around the rather high prices. There are specials every night, but you can count on Chinois "classics" every evening. Appetizers include Szechuan pancakes with stir-fried Peking duck, spring veggies, and wild mushrooms—everything combines into one new savory taste. Always free to spend your money, we also recommend the lovely sautéed foie gras with rhubarb compote (it has a citrus zing to it) and a sauce made from port wine, figs, and spices. For entrees, the Shanghai lobster with a rich coconut curry sauce is marvelous, though also pricey. More budget-minded is the whole sizzling catfish, which along with a couple of appetizers will easily feed two people. The Cantonese duck with divine sesame crêpes is also superb, a light, nearly perfect rendering of that difficult fowl. Skip the ordinary Mongolian lamb chops, but save room for the scrumptious chocolate mint gâteau dessert.

Delmonico Steakhouse. In The Venetian, 3355 Las Vegas Blvd. S. ☎ **702/ 414-3737.** Reservations strongly recommended for dinner. Main courses $21– $36. AE, DC, DISC, MC, V. Daily 11:30am–2pm; Sun–Thurs 5:30–10:30pm, Fri–Sat 5:30–11pm. CONTEMPORARY CREOLE/STEAK.

Watching the Food Network, you might well feel Emeril Lagasse is omnipresent. Slowly but surely, he's becoming as ubiquitous here in Vegas as he is in New Orleans (though he has a long way to go to match Puck), as he brings variations on his Big Easy brand-name eateries to town. This latest is a steakhouse version of his hard-core classic Creole restaurant.

You can try both Emeril concoctions and fabulous cuts of red meat. You can't go wrong with most appetizers, especially the superbly rich smoked mushrooms with homemade tasso over pasta—it's enough for a meal in and of itself—any of the specials, or the gumbo, particularly if it's the hearty, near-homemade country selection. If you want to experiment, definitely do it with the appetizers. You're better off steering clear of complex entrees, no matter how intriguing they sound. We've found them to be generally disappointing, while the more deceptively simple choices are more successful. The bone-in rib steak is rightly recommended (skip the gummy béarnaise sauce in favor of the fabulous homemade Worcester or the A.O.K. sauce). Sides are hit or miss—the creamed spinach was too salty, but a sweet potato purée (a special, but maybe they'll serve you a side if you ask sweetly) is most definitely a winner. Too full for dessert? No, you aren't. Have a chocolate soufflé, a bananas Foster cream pie, or the lemon ice-box pie.

Fiore. In the Rio Suites, 3700 W. Flamingo Rd. (at I-15). ☎ **702/252-7702.** Reservations recommended. Main courses $26–$48. AE, CB, DC, DISC, MC, V. Daily 6–11pm. ITALIAN/PROVENÇAL.

Once the Rio's standout restaurant, Fiore has lost ground to the more high-profile, and, truthfully, far superior Napa, but it's still a worthwhile second choice, with a very attentive staff. Try to get a seat on the patio; outdoor dining is rare in Vegas, so it's worth taking advantage of. Comparisons are odious, but when you see what's going on upstairs at Napa, you wish the menu here were a little less pedestrian. Still, you can't go wrong with the perfectly done rack of lamb with roasted garlic sauce, or the appetizer of panchetta-wrapped shrimp with port-wine glaze (sure, it's just a more tony version of bacon-wrapped shrimp, but it's good!). Skip the disappointingly overdone Chilean sea bass. Save room for a cheese plate and especially, the gooey chocolate desserts—they have a very talented pastry chef.

✪ **Le Cirque.** In Bellagio, 3600 Las Vegas Blvd. S. ☎ **702/693-8150.** Reservations required. Jacket and tie for gentlemen required. Main courses $29–$39. AE, DC, DISC, MC, V. Daily 5:30–10pm. FRENCH.

The influx of haute-cuisine, high-profile restaurants in Vegas means there are ever so many places now where you may feel like you have to take out a bank loan in order to eat there—and you may wonder why you ought to. Always feeling free to spend your money, we suggest you just blow it all at Le Cirque. A branch of the much beloved New York City classic, this is the one gourmet restaurant where it all comes together.

The subtlety of flavors demonstrates that this is truly sophisticated cuisine, rather than a place with just pretensions toward the same. The menu changes seasonally, but here's what had us in raptures on a recent visit: appetizers of sea scallops layered with black truffle, wrapped in puff pastry, and a creamy foie gras du Tochon, marinated in sauterne and topped with more black truffle; and main courses like properly aged filet topped with exquisite foie gras, and a vaguely Moroccan roasted honey-spiced glazed duck with figs (the caramelized onion on the side didn't quite work, but the figs most assuredly did). Desserts tickle your fancy as they cavort on the plate.

✪ **Lutèce.** In The Venetian, 3355 Las Vegas Blvd. S. ☎ **702/414-2220.** Reservations strongly recommended for dinner. Main courses $26–$38. AE, DC, DISC, MC, V. Daily 11:30am–3:30pm and 5:30–10:30pm. FRENCH.

A branch of the highly esteemed New York City French restaurant, Lutèce is yet another example of how, if you want to dine well in Vegas, you've got to pay for it. This place is full of style, style, style. It's genuinely chic, which is unusual for Vegas, but it's not threatening nor cavernous. A self-aware, self-confident place, this may prove to be one of our favorite dining spots in Vegas. Try to get a table in the little nook area that looks out at the Strip— it's more romantic than it sounds.

The presentation of the food is just lovely. The menu will probably change periodically, but on our recent visit, we enjoyed the appetizer of smoked codfish and white truffle oil and arugula, a combo that works surprisingly well. For a main course, we loved the crisp black bass with lobster sauce and herb noodles, and the turbot poached in tarragon broth with baby veggies.

✪ **Napa.** In the Rio Suites, 3700 W. Flamingo Rd. ☎ **702/247-7962.** Reservations strongly recommended. Main courses $28–$42; degustation menu $110. AE, CB, DC, DISC, MC, V. Tues–Sat. 6–11pm. FRENCH.

Aside from the price issue, one major drawback to the whole celebrity chef boom in Vegas is that most of the chefs have restaurants elsewhere, and are rarely actually in residence. The lone exceptions are Picasso and Napa—and the difference is obvious. Here, highly praised chef Jean Louis Palladin can be found in the kitchen at least 2 weeks out of every 4, so odds are that you can personally enjoy his rep for really brilliant cooking. Voted the best restaurant in Vegas by *Wine Spectator* and *Los Angeles* magazines, among others, this is another place where we feel perfectly justified urging you to spend your money. It won't be cheap, but you'll get what you pay for.

The menu changes seasonally, but here's what we ate one recent delightful summer evening. Cold soup fans will be thrilled by the slightly spicy, distinct flavors of the outstanding cold red and yellow tomato soup with rock shrimp; it's cleverly presented, as it's poured from two pitchers. It's not on the menu, but always available is a perfectly done oven-seared Hudson Valley foie gras (with seasonal glazes like rhubarb, huckleberry, or white peach). We loved the melt-in-your-mouth roasted rack of lamb, and another evening, we swooned over roast suckling pig wrapped around herbed forcemeat and drizzled with a rosemary-infused broth. Desserts were a riot of delicate bits of summer: peach soup (a clear consommé) with almond milk sherbet, roasted banana with fresh banana ice cream (like a deconstructed bananas Foster), and mission figs gratin with toasted pine nut ice cream. Oh, my. It's all set in a pretty, subdued space from which you can look down into the rather garish pool area, or out to the passing Mardi Gras parade. As if you will tear your eyes away from the delicate presentation.

✪ **Picasso.** In Bellagio, 3600 Las Vegas Blvd. S. ☎ **702/693-7111.** Reservations recommended. Fixed-price 4-course dinner $70, 5-course degustation $80. AE, CB, DC, DISC, MC, V. Sun–Tues and Thurs 6–10pm, Fri–Sat 6–11pm. FRENCH.

A Spanish chef who cooks French cuisine in an Italian-themed hotel in Vegas? Trust us, it works. This may well be the best restaurant in Vegas, and given the sudden serious competition for such a title, that says a lot. Madrid-born chef Julian Serrano (whose Masa was considered the finest French restaurant in San

Francisco) offers an extraordinary dining experience (plus, $30 million worth of Picassos gaze down over your shoulders while you eat).

Needless to say, Serrano's cooking is a work of art that can proudly stand next to the masterpieces. The menu changes nightly and is always a choice between a four- or five-course fixed-price dinner or tasting menu. The night we ate there, we were bowled over by roasted Maine lobster with a "trio" of corn—kernels, sauce, and a corn flan that was like eating slightly solid sunshine. Hudson Valley foie gras was crusted in truffles and went down most smoothly. A fillet of roasted sea bass came with a light saffron sauce and dots of cauliflower purée. And finally, pray that they're serving the lamb rôti—it was an outstanding piece of lamb, perfectly done, tender, and crusted with truffles. Portions are dainty, but so rich that you'll have plenty to eat without groaning and feeling heavy when you leave. Desserts are powerful, yet prettily constructed. A molten chocolate cake leaves any other you may have tried in the dust, and comes with ice cream made with imported European chocolate. Everything is delivered by an attentive staff who make you feel quite pampered.

Spago. In Caesars Palace, 3570 Las Vegas Blvd. S. ☎ **702/369-6300.** Reservations recommended for the dining room; not accepted at the cafe. Dining room main courses $14–$31; cafe main courses $9.50–$23. AE, CB, DC, DISC, JCB, MC, V. Dining room Sun–Thurs 6–10pm, Fri–Sat 5:30–11pm. Cafe Sun–Thurs 11am–11pm, Fri–Sat 11am–midnight. AMERICAN/ASIAN/CALIFORNIA.

With Wolfgang Puck showing up in a different incarnation at every hotel in town these days (or so it seems), his original creation might get lost in the shuffle. Certainly, it's no longer what it used to be—the only foodie game in town—and you get the feeling they were so far ahead of the pack for so long that they've gotten a bit complacent. Which is not to say Spago is not worth the expense—it just means that others have caught up with, and in some cases surpassed, them.

But it's still an experience. Call it California casual elegance. The post-industrial interior is the very model of a modern major restaurant, while the exterior cafe on the Forum Shops is more relaxed and provides an opportunity for people watching as fine as at any European sidewalk cafe. The interior dining room menu changes seasonally; your choices might include scallops with a divine basil risotto, an appetizer of tuna sashimi in hot olive oil and sesame, or porcini mushrooms with a truffle sauce. The pumpkin-squash soup reminds you that soup is good food indeed. The signature dish is a Chinese-style duck, moist but with a perfectly crispy skin. It's about as good as duck gets, served with a doughy steamed bun and Chinese vegetables. The wine list is impressive, but the house wine was a disappointment and possibly not worth the cost.

EXPENSIVE

Cannelleto. In The Venetian, 3355 Las Vegas Blvd. S. ☎ **702/733-0070.** Reservations recommended for dinner. Main courses $9.95–$21.95. AE, DC, MC, V. Sun–Thurs 11:30am–10:30pm, Fri–Sat 11:30am–11:30pm. ITALIAN.

Come here for solid, true Italian fare—and that means less sauce-intensive than the red-checked-tablecloth establishments of our American youths. Here, the emphasis is on the pasta, not the accompaniments. This place is all the more enjoyable for being perched on the faux St. Mark's Square; in theory, you can pretend you are sitting on the edge of the real thing, a fantasy we don't mind admitting we briefly indulged in. A risotto of porcini, sausage, and white truffle oil was full of strong flavors, while the wood-fired roast chicken was perfectly moist. You know, a properly roasted chicken should be a much-celebrated thing and that alone may be a reason to come here.

✪ **Pinot Brasserie.** In The Venetian, 3355 Las Vegas Blvd. S. ☎ **702/735-8888.** Reservations recommended for dinner. Main courses $11.50–$16.95 at lunch, $18.50–$22.50 at dinner. AE, DISC, JCB, MC, V. Daily 11am–11pm. BISTRO.

This is the latest incarnation of a series of well-regarded Los Angeles restaurants whose mother ship, Patina, regularly tops "Best of" lists among City of Angels foodies. While the more innovative cooking is going on back in L.A., Pinot reliably delivers French and American favorites that are thoughtfully conceived and generally delicious. It's an excellent choice if you want a special meal that is neither stratospherically expensive nor too complex.

Salads are possibly fresher and more generous than other similar starters in town (thank that California influence), and they can come paired with various toppings for *crostini* (toasted slices of French bread) such as herbed goat cheese. The signature dish, beloved by many, is a roasted chicken accompanied by heaping mounds of garlic fries, but if you wish to get a little more elaborate (and yet rather light), thin slices of smoked salmon with

🛈 Family-Friendly Restaurants

Buffets   Cheap meals for the whole family. The kids can choose what they like, and there are sometimes make-your-own sundae machines. Section 7 of this chapter reviews all the buffets, and notes which ones have reduced prices for the kids.

Dive!   Housed in a submarine and featuring a zany high-tech show every hour projected on a video wall, this is the most fun family-oriented spot of all.

Rain Forest Cafe   This is like eating in the Jungle Book Ride at Disneyland. Animals howl, thunder wails, everywhere there is something to marvel at. There is a decent kids' menu, and they might even learn a little bit about ecology and the environment.

Hard Rock Cafe   Kids adore this restaurant, which throbs with excitement and is filled with rock memorabilia.

Pink Pony   This bubble-gum pink circus-motif 24-hour coffee shop at Circus Circus will appeal to kids. Mom and Dad can linger while the kids race upstairs to watch circus acts and play carnival games.

Sherwood Forest Cafe   Kids love to climb on the lavender dragons fronting this 24-hour coffee shop at Excalibur, and they also enjoy numerous child-oriented activities while you're on the premises.

Monte Carlo Pub & Brewery   Despite the "pub" part of the name, this is a noisy place in the Monte Carlo hotel with many TV's to distract short-attention kids and broody teenagers, all of whom will like the BBQ, pizza, and chicken fingers, while parents will be pleased with the low prices.

celery rémoulade could be a way to go. Desserts are lovely, and ice cream is homemade—the chocolate alone should make you wish you'd never eaten at 31 Flavors, because it was wasted calories compared to this. *Note:* It's easy to graze through this menu and have a less costly meal here than at most other high-end places, and the constant operating hours mean you can also pop in for a nosh at times when other fine-dining options are closed.

✪ **Star Canyon.** In The Venetian, 3355 Las Vegas Blvd. S. ☎ **702/ 414-3772.** Reservations recommended for dinner. Main courses $10–$17 at lunch, $21–$30 at dinner. AE, MC, V. Daily 11:30am–2:30pm; Sun–Thurs 6–10pm, Fri–Sat 6–11pm. SOUTHWESTERN.

Texas-based chef Stephen Pyles is more or less credited with inventing Southwestern cuisine, and this new branch of his highly touted Dallas restaurant not only gives Coyote Cafe a serious run for the title of Best Southwestern Restaurant in Vegas, but it might just be the Best American Restaurant.

For this reason, we urge you to take some chances (or what you may view as chances) with appetizers—we'd go a bit more plain, though with equal satisfaction, with the main courses. All use classic Southwestern flavors, and more importantly, spices, and combine them with just the right nouvelle cuisine influences. A tamale pie's spicy crust is cooled by its filling of roast-garlic custard, topped with crabmeat, while that gourmand's delight, seared foie gras, is most happily paired with a more humble corn cake, itself dressed up with pineapple salsa. Molasses-coated quail is dainty and sweet tasting atop arugula, poached pear, and a bit of cambazola cheese. Be sure to try the hearty, serious, chewy breads, which can come in flavors like pesto and chipolte. While you may justly feel tempted to make a meal of appetizers, don't. For then you would miss their signature dish, a bone-in ribeye, cowboy-style (think Western spices), an utterly tender, flavorful dish (topped with a mile-high tower of crispy onions) that makes it hard to imagine a better piece of meat. Desserts are perhaps not quite as joy-producing.

MODERATE

See also the listing for **Spago** and **Chinois** (both above), expensive restaurants fronted by more moderately priced cafes.

Black Spot Grille. In Treasure Island, 3300 Las Vegas Blvd. S. (at Spring Mountain Rd.) ☎ **702/894-7352.** Reservations not accepted. Main courses $7.95–$13.95. AE, DC, DISC, MC, V. Sun–Thurs 11am–11pm, Fri–Sat 11am–12:30pm. ITALIAN/AMERICAN.

This is a very reliable, reasonably priced place to grab a bite, particularly if you are heading to or from a showing of *Mystère*. Unfortunately, everyone else heading to or from the show will have the same idea (it's on the way to the theater). Otherwise, you might want to time your meal during performances to avoid what can be a lengthy line. Try one of the hearty pastas—including a very good Cajun chicken penne (with a parmesan cream sauce), and a nearly-as-good spaghetti primavera (loaded with veggies). The pizzas will give no cause for complaint (we liked the five-cheese entry), and there's a fine dessert called the Cannonball (white-chocolate ice cream dipped in white-chocolate nuggets with blackberry sauce).

✪ **Mon Ami Gabi.** In Paris–Las Vegas, 3655 Las Vegas Blvd. S. ☎ **702/ 944-GABI (944-4224).** Reservations recommended. Main courses $8.95– $26.95. AE, CB, DC, DISC, MC, V. Daily 11:30am–3:30pm; Sun–Thurs 5–11pm, 5pm–midnight. BISTRO.

This charming bistro is our new favorite local restaurant. It has it all: a delightful setting, better than average food, affordable prices. Sure, it goes overboard in trying to replicate a classic Parisian bistro, but the results are less cheesy than most Vegas attempts at atmosphere, and there's patio seating on the Strip (no reservations taken there—first-come, first-served). You can be budget-conscious and order just the very fine onion soup, or you can eat like a real French person and order classic steak and pomme frites (the filet mignon is probably the best cut, if not the cheapest). Especially at lunch, there are plenty of cheaper options (which is why we listed this place in the "moderate" category, by the way). Yes, they have snails, and we loved 'em. Desserts, by the way, are massive and should be shared (another way to save). The baseball-size profiteroles (three or four to an order) filled with fine vanilla ice cream and the football-size bananas Foster crêpe are particularly recommended. Oo, la la!

✪ **Olives.** In Bellagio, 3600 Las Vegas Blvd. S. ☎ **702/693-8181.** Reservations recommended. Main courses $15–$19 at lunch, $20–$33.50 at dinner; flatbreads $10–$14.50. AE, DC, DISC, MC, V. Daily 11am–3pm and 5– 11:30pm. ITALIAN/MEDITERRANEAN.

If there were an Olives cafe in our neighborhood, we would eat there regularly. The less expensive relative of the Mirage's Onda (as well as a branch of Todd English's original Boston-based restaurant), Olives is a strong choice for a light lunch that need not be as expensive as you might think. Here's how to enjoy a moderately priced meal here: Don't fill up too much on the focac-cia bread and olives they give you at the start (on the other hand, budget-obsessives, go ahead), and skip the small-size and thus costly salads and instead go right to the flatbreads. Think pizza with an ultra-thin crust (like a slightly limp cracker), topped with delicious combinations like the highly recommended Moroccan spiced lamb, eggplant purée, and feta cheese, or fig, prosciutto, and gorgonzola. They are rich and wonderful—split one between two people, along with that salad we just maligned, and you have an affordable and terrific lunch. Or try a pasta; we were steered toward the simple but marvelous spaggatini with roasted tomatoes, garlic, and Parmesan, and were glad. The constructed, but not too fussy, food gets more complicated and costly at night, adding an array of meats and chickens, plus pastas like butternut squash with brown butter and sage.

✪ **Stage Deli.** In Caesars Palace, 3570 Las Vegas Blvd. S. ☎ **702/ 893-4045.** Reservations accepted for large parties only. Main courses $10– $14; sandwiches $6–$14. AE, DC, DISC, JCB, MC, V. Sun–Thurs 7:30am– 10:30pm, Fri–Sat 7:30am–midnight. DELI.

New York City's legendary Stage Deli has been slapping pastrami on rye for more than half a century. Its Las Vegas branch retains the Stage's brightly lit, Big Apple essence. Walls are embellished with subway graffiti and hung with Broadway theater posters, bowls of pickles grace the white Formica tables, and, in the New York tradition, comics and celebrities like Buddy Hackett and Arnold Schwarzenegger drop by whenever they're in town.

Most of the fare—including fresh-baked pumpernickel and rye, meats, chewy bagels, lox, spicy deli mustard, and pickles— comes in daily from New York. The Stage dishes up authentic 5-inch-high sandwiches stuffed with pastrami, corned beef, brisket, or chopped liver. Unless you have a hearty appetite, are feeding two, or have a fridge in your room for leftovers, you might want to try the half sandwich and soup or salad combos. Other specialties here include matzo ball soup, knishes, kasha varnishkes, cheese blintzes, kreplach, pirogen, and smoked fish platters accompanied by bagels and cream cheese. Or you might prefer a full meal consisting of pot roast and gravy, salad, homemade dinner rolls, potato pancakes, and fresh vegetables. Desserts run the gamut from rugelach cheesecake to Hungarian-style apple strudel.

INEXPENSIVE

La Piazza Food Court. In Caesars Palace, 3570 Las Vegas Blvd. S. (just north of Flamingo Rd.). ☎ **702/731-7110.** Complete meals $7–$15. AE, DC, DISC, MC, V. Sun–Thurs 11am–11pm, Fri–Sat 11am–midnight. FOOD COURT.

Essentially an upscale cafeteria, this is a great choice for families. Food stations are located along an attractive arched walkway lit by pink neon, and the brass-railed dining area, under massive domes, is rather elegant, with gold-topped columns and comfortable upholstered seating. The food is top quality—terrific deep-dish pizzas, an excellent salad bar, fresh-baked pies and cakes, sushi, smoked fish, immense burritos, Chinese stir-fry, rotisserie chicken, and a New York–style deli, Häagen-Dazs bars, and a selection of beverages that includes herbal teas, wine, beer, espresso, and cappuccino. Just about any single beverage you can think of, from virtually all over the world, you can find here. There's something for every dining mood. Waffle cones are baked on the premises, creating a delicious aroma.

3 North Strip

EXPENSIVE

Chin's. In the Fashion Show Mall, 3200 Las Vegas Blvd. S. (turn at the Frontier sign). ☎ **702/733-8899.** Reservations recommended. Main courses $10–$12 at lunch, $10–$29.50 at dinner. AE, DC, MC, V. Mon–Sat 11:30am–9:30pm, Sun noon–9:30pm. CHINESE.

Chin's has been a Vegas fixture for 20 years and is consistently voted by locals in the *Las Vegas Review* as their favorite Chinese restaurant. The simple, stark decor produces an ambience of low-key elegance. This is upscale Chinese food, but it's carefully prepared and presented in a traditionally stylish way. However, anyone with broad experience with Chinese food won't find anything terribly surprising here. Experiments with more radical dishes failed (too-timid tourists?), and so the menu is on the safe side. Standouts include the sweetly cloying strawberry chicken (think lemon chicken but with a different fruit; Chin's created this twist on a familiar dish, and other local restaurants have copied it); an appetizer of sinful deep-fried shrimp puffs (stuffed with minced shrimp and mildly curried cream cheese); splendid spring rolls; and barbecued pork-fried rice that strikes that tricky, careful balance between dry and greasy.

INEXPENSIVE

Capriotti's. 324 W. Sahara Ave (at Las Vegas Blvd. S.). ☎ **702/474-0229.** All sandwiches under $10. No credit cards. Mon–Sat 10am–7pm. SANDWICHES.

Don't be fooled by the sizes listed at the no-frills, mom-and-pop Capriotti's sandwich shop. The so-called "small" should actually be called "too big." Plan to share. They roast their own beef and turkeys on the premises, and providing the help gets the stuff out of the ovens in time, it's mighty tasty and special (but otherwise, the meat can be too dry). Interesting combinations and tastes are the standard here, and the result is a very good sandwich indeed. The standout sandwich is the "Bobby," which combines a virtual Thanksgiving dinner—turkey, dressing, and cranberry sauce—on a French roll, for a taste sensation so marvelous you wonder why no one thought of it before. We also liked the "Slaw-by Joe"—roast beef, coleslaw, and provolone. The shop is convenient to Downtown and is right off the Strip, but those farther away should note they will deliver with a $10 minimum.

Chang's of Las Vegas. In Gold Key Shopping Center, 3055 Las Vegas Blvd. S. ☎ **702/731-3388.** Dim sum $1.80–$5; main courses $9.95–$16.95. AE, MC, V. Daily 10am–2am (dim sum 10am–3pm). CHINESE.

Dim sum are little Chinese nibbles, most often spiced and diced bits of meat and shellfish stuffed into buns or wrapped with dough, then steamed or deep-fried. A menu will list the options, but not explain what the heck anything is (here's one, just to help you out—*hai gow* are steamed balls of dough-wrapped shrimp). Don't bother ordering from it, but instead wait as steam carts are pushed around the room and toward you, and the cart pusher pulls lids off many little pots, exposing various tasties within. (Dim sum service stops at 3pm except by special order.) Be brave and just point at something that looks good. Find out what you ate later. Or never. Sometimes it's just better that way.

Dona Maria Tamales. 910 Las Vegas Blvd. S. (corner of Charleston Blvd.). ☎ **702/382-6538.** Main courses $5.45–$8 at breakfast, $6–$13 at lunch or dinner. AE, CB, MC, V. Sun–Thurs 8am–10pm, Fri–Sat 8am–11pm. MEXICAN.

Decorated with Tijuana-style quiltwork and calendars, this is your quintessential Mexican diner, convenient to both the north end of the Strip and Downtown. They use lots of lard, lots of cheese, and lots of sauce. As a result, the food is really good—and really fattening. Yep, the folks who did those health reports showing how bad Mexican food can be for your heart probably did some research here. That just makes it all the better, in our opinion. Locals apparently agree; even at lunchtime the place is crowded.

✪ **Liberty Cafe at the Blue Castle Pharmacy.** 1700 Las Vegas Blvd. S. ☎ **702/383-0101.** Reservations not accepted. Nothing over $6.50. No credit cards. Daily 24 hours. DINER.

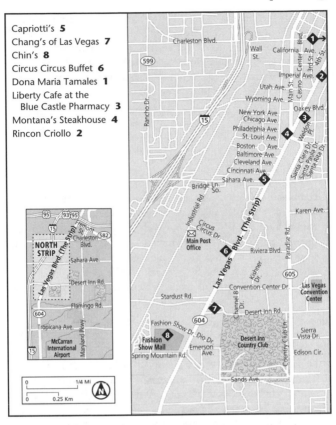

Capriotti's **5**
Chang's of Las Vegas **7**
Chin's **8**
Circus Circus Buffet **6**
Dona Maria Tamales **1**
Liberty Cafe at the
  Blue Castle Pharmacy **3**
Montana's Steakhouse **4**
Rincon Criollo **2**

You can go to any number of retro soda-fountain replicas (such as Johnny Rockets) and theme restaurants that pretend to be cheap diners, but why bother when the real thing is just past the end of the Strip? The decidedly unflashy soda fountain/lunch counter at the Blue Castle Pharmacy was Las Vegas's first 24-hour restaurant, and it has been going strong for 60 years. Plunk down at the counter, and watch the cooks go nuts trying to keep up with the orders. The menu is basic comfort food: standard grill items (meat loaf, ground round steak, chops, and so on), fluffy cream pies, and classic breakfasts served "anytime"—try the biscuits and cream gravy at 3am. They also serve gyros and the like.

But the best bet is a ⅓-pound burger and "thick creamy shake," both the way they were meant to be and about as good as they get. At around $5, this is half what you would pay for a comparable meal at the Hard Rock Cafe. And as waitress Beverly says, "This is really real." Places like this are a vanishing species—it's worth the short walk from the Stratosphere.

Montana's Steakhouse. In the Stratosphere Las Vegas, 2000 Las Vegas Blvd. S. (between St. Louis St. and Baltimore Ave.). ☎ **702/780-7777.** Complete steak dinners from $10, all-you-can-eat barbecue dinner $13, free for children under 6. AE, CB, DC, DISC, JCB, MC, V. Daily 24 hours. AMERICAN.

A place to consider for a solid food bargain. Entree choices include prime rib with creamed horseradish sauce, a barbecue combination (beef brisket, St. Louis ribs, Carolina-pulled pork, and fried chicken), and steaks. Whatever you select, it will come with a huge salad, scrumptious corn muffins (don't fill up on them; there's lots more food coming), corn on the cob, seasoned steak fries, coleslaw, Texas toast, and baked beans with pork. And when you've eaten your fill, you can waddle over to the dessert table and help yourself to apple cobbler, fresh berries and cream, and bread pudding with rum sauce. There's a full bar.

Rincon Criollo. 1145 Las Vegas Blvd. S. ☎ **702/388-1906.** Reservations not accepted. Main courses $6.50–$10; paella (for 3) $20. AE, DISC, MC, V. Tues–Sun 11am–10pm. CUBAN.

Located beyond the wedding chapels on Las Vegas Boulevard, Rincon Criollo has all the right details for a good, cheap ethnic joint: It's full of locals and empty of frills. It's not the best Cuban food ever, but it gets the job done. The main courses (featuring Cuban pork and chicken specialties) are hit or miss; try the marinated pork leg or, better still, ask your server for a recommendation. Paella is offered, but only for parties of three or more (and starts at $20). The side-course *chorizo* (a spicy sausage) is excellent, and the Cuban sandwich (roast pork, ham, and cheese on bread, which is then pressed and flattened out) is huge and tasty. For only $3.50, the latter makes a fine change-of-pace meal.

4 East of the Strip

In this section, we cover restaurants close by the Convention Center, along with those farther south on Paradise Road, Flamingo Road, and Tropicana Avenue.

VERY EXPENSIVE

✪ **Lawry's The Prime Rib.** 4043 Howard Hughes Pkwy. (at Flamingo Rd., between Paradise Rd. and Koval Lane). ☎ **702/893-2223.** Reservations recommended. Main courses $20–$30. AE, DC, DISC, JCB, MC, V. Sun–Thurs 5–10pm, Fri–Sat 5–11pm. STEAK/SEAFOOD.

If you love prime rib, come here. If you could take or leave prime rib, Lawry's will turn you into a believer. Because Lawry's does one thing, and it does it better than anyone else.

Eating at Lawry's is a ceremony, with all the parts played the same way for the last 60 years. You tell the waitress what side dishes you might want (sublime creamed spinach, baked potato, and so on) for an extra price. Later, she returns with a spinning salad bowl (think of salad preparation as a Busby Berkeley musical number). The bowl, resting on crushed ice, spins as she pours Lawry's special dressing in a stream from high over her head. Tomatoes garnish. Applause follows. Eventually, giant metal carving carts come to your table, bearing the meat. You name your cut (the regular Lawry's, the extra-large Diamond Jim Brady for serious carnivores, and the wimpy thin English cut), and specify how you'd like it cooked. It comes with terrific Yorkshire pudding, nicely browned and not soggy, and some creamed horseradish that is combined with fluffy whipped cream, simultaneously sweet and tart.

Flavorful, tender, perfectly cooked, lightly seasoned, this will be the best prime rib you will ever have. Okay, maybe that's going too far, but the rest is accurate, honest. It just has to be tasted to be believed. Incidentally, other Lawry's are decorated English-manor style, but the Vegas branch has instead tried to re-create a 1930s restaurant, with art-deco touches all around and big band music on the sound system.

Morton's of Chicago. 400 E. Flamingo (at Paradise Rd.). ☎ **702/893-0703.** Reservations recommended. Main courses $18–$30. AE, CB, DC, JCB, MC, V. Mon–Thurs 5:30–11pm, Fri–Sat 5–11pm, Sun 5–10pm. STEAK/SEAFOOD.

Note: Just before press time, this branch of the Morton's steakhouse chain moved from its old North Strip location to the address listed above. Although we didn't get a chance to visit the new location, we are confident that the review below holds true.

Frequent power diners here include most hotel/casino owners as well as Strip entertainers Siegfried and Roy. Robert de Niro and Joe Pesci came in frequently during the filming of *Casino,* and, one night, Tony Curtis joined the waitstaff in singing "Happy Birthday" to a guest.

Start off with an appetizer, perhaps a lump crabmeat cocktail with mustard-mayonnaise sauce. Entree choices include succulent prime Midwestern steaks prepared to your exact specifications, plus lemon oregano chicken, lamb chops, Sicilian veal, grilled swordfish, and whole baked Maine lobster. Side orders such as flavorfully fresh al dente asparagus served with hollandaise or hash browns are highly recommended. Portions are bountiful; plan to share. A loaf of warm onion bread on every table is complimentary. Leave room for dessert, perhaps a Grand Marnier soufflé. There's an extensive wine list.

○ **Pamplemousse.** 400 E. Sahara Ave. (between Santa Paula and Santa Rita drs., just east of Paradise Rd.). ☎ **702/733-2066.** Reservations required. Main courses $17.50–$26. AE, CB, DC, DISC, MC, V. Seatings daily at 6–10pm. FRENCH.

A little bit off the beaten path, Pamplemousse is a long-established Vegas restaurant that shouldn't be overlooked in the crush of new high-profile eateries. The menu, which changes nightly, is recited by your waiter. The meal always begins with a large complimentary basket of crudités (about 10 different crisp, fresh vegetables), a big bowl of olives, and, in a nice country touch, a basket of hard-boiled eggs. Recent menu offerings have included out-of-this-world soups (like French onion and cream of asparagus), and appetizers like shrimp in cognac cream sauce or Maryland crab cakes with a macadamia nut crust. Recommended entrees include a sterling veal with mushrooms and a dijon sauce, and an even-better rack of lamb with a pistaccio nut crust and a rosemary cream sauce (all sauces, by the way, are made with whatever the chef has on hand that evening in the kitchen). That's not to mention fabulous desserts like homemade ice cream in a hard chocolate shell.

Gordon-Biersch Brewing Company. 3987 Paradise Rd. (just north of Flamingo Rd.). ☎ **702/312-5247.** Main courses $11–$16. AE, DISC, MC, V. Sun–Thurs 11:30am–10pm, Fri–Sat 11:30am–11pm; bar open until 2am. CALIFORNIA.

This is a traditional brewpub (exposed piping and ducts, but the place is still comfortable and casual), but it's worth going to for a nosh as well. The menu is pub fare meets California cuisine (kids

Dining & Nightlife East of the Strip

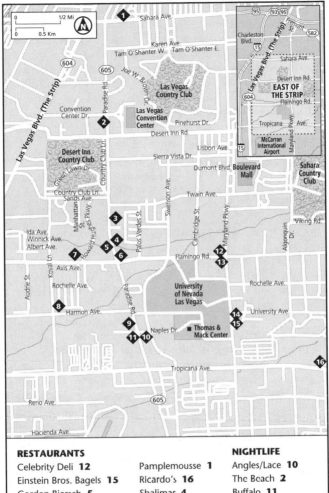

RESTAURANTS

Celebrity Deli **12**
Einstein Bros. Bagels **15**
Gordon Biersch **5**
Lawry's The Prime Rib **7**
Mediterranean Café & Market **13**
Morton's of Chicago **6**
Pamplemousse **1**
Ricardo's **16**
Shalimar **4**
Z Tejas Grill **3**

NIGHTLIFE

Angles/Lace **10**
The Beach **2**
Buffalo **11**
Drink **8**
Gipsy **9**
Tom & Jerry's **14**

will probably find the food too complicated), and naturally, there are a lot of beers (German-style lagers) to choose from. Appetizers include satays, potstickers, calamari, baby-back ribs, delicious beer-battered onion rings, and amazing garlic-encrusted fries. A wood-burning pizza oven turns out pies with California-type toppings: eggplant, shrimp, and so forth. The dinner menu offers rosemary chicken, steaks, fish items, and, just in case you forgot it was a brew-pub-type joint, beer everything: beer-glazed ham, beer meat loaf, and beer-barbecued glazed ribs. Doesn't that make you want to order a glass of milk?

Ricardo's. 2380 Tropicana Ave. (at Eastern Ave., on the northwest corner). ☎ **702/798-4515.** Reservations recommended. Main courses $7.50–$13; lunch buffet $7.25; children's plates $3–$4, including milk or soft drink with complimentary refills. AE, CB, DC, DISC, MC, V. Sun–Thurs 11am–10pm, Fri–Sat 11am–11pm. MEXICAN.

This hacienda-style restaurant is a great favorite with locals. Start off with an appetizer of deep-fried battered chicken wings served with melted cheddar (ask for jalapeños if you like your cheese sauce hotter). Nachos smothered with cheese and guacamole are also very good here. For an entree, you can't go wrong with chicken, beef, or pork fajitas, served sizzling on a hot skillet atop sautéed onions, mushrooms, and peppers; they come with rice and beans, tortillas, a selection of salsas, guacamole, and tomato wedges with cilantro. All the usual taco/enchilada/tamale combinations are also listed. A delicious dessert is *helado* Las Vegas: ice cream rolled in corn flakes and cinnamon, deep-fried, and served with honey and whipped cream. Be sure to order a pitcher of Ricardo's great margaritas. The same menu is available all day, but a buffet is offered at lunch. The kids' menu, on a placemat with games and puzzles, features both Mexican and American fare.

✪ **Shalimar.** In the Citibank Plaza, 3900 S. Paradise Rd. ☎ **702/796-0302.** Reservations recommended. Lunch buffet $7.50; main courses $10.50–$16 at dinner. AE, DISC, MC, V. Mon–Fri 11:30am–2:30pm; daily 5:30–10:30pm. INDIAN.

In a town full of buffet deals, it's hard to get excited about another one, but on the other hand, all those other buffet deals offer pretty much the identical food: carving stations, various cafeteria hot dishes, and so forth. Here at Shalimar, a lunch buffet means about two dozen different North Indian–style dishes, all for about $7.50. It's not as colorful or huge (in fact, it's just a table covered with steam trays) as those buffets up the street, but it is far more interesting. It's also a great deal and one of the first places to run to if you're sick of Strip food. Just ask the locals, who voted it their favorite ethnic restaurant in the *Las Vegas Review Journal* annual poll.

Z Tejas Grill. 3824 Paradise Rd. (between Twain Ave. and Corporate Dr.). ☎ **702/732-1660.** Reservations recommended. Main courses $7.25–$12 at lunch, $8.75–$17 at dinner. AE, CB, DC, DISC, JCB, MC, V. Daily 11am–11pm. TEX-MEX.

This Austin, Texas–based restaurant's rather odd name came about because its original chef, a Frenchman, kept referring to it as "zee" Tejas Grill. Featuring self-proclaimed "South by Southwestern" cuisine, it recently got a handsome makeover, lining the interior with streamlined warm woods and black accents. In particular, we like the generously portioned grilled-fish tacos, which come wrapped in fresh tortillas, stuffed with all kinds of veggies and served with a spicy Japanese sauce. Not your usual drippy, fattening tacos. Less of a bargain, but mighty tasty, is the tender and piquant black sesame tuna, with a black-peppercorn vinaigrette and a soy mustard sauce. (There's a larger version of this found under the entrees; it's called "Voodoo Tuna," and it's not quite as good.) A better main course choice would be the spicy-grilled Jamaican-jerk chicken, nuanced with lime and served with peanut sauce and rum-spiked coconut-banana ketchup; it comes with two side dishes—when we were there, garlic mashed potatoes and a corn casserole soufflé.

INEXPENSIVE

Celebrity Deli. 4055 S. Maryland Pkwy. (at Flamingo Rd.). ☎ **702/733-7827.** Reservations not accepted. Main courses $7–$12. AE, MC, V. Mon–Sat 9am–8pm, Sun 9am–4pm. DELI.

A basic, solid New York deli, the Celebrity lacks the mammoth portions of the Stage Deli (though perhaps that's a good thing) but lacks also the occasionally mammoth prices of same. It also does not require navigating the Strip and the Caesars Forum Shops (which means it's more convenient for those staying at accommodations east of the Strip), and in many ways, it's more authentic, from its revolving pastry case to the middle-aged waitresses with thick foundation and thick ankles who shout your order back to the kitchen. The clientele are classic Vegas characters, of an age to have been fans of the youthful Paul Anka. If you are lucky, you might sit next to a table full of dealers swapping war stories about their pit bosses.

Einstein Bros. Bagels. In the University Gardens Shopping Center, 4626 S. Maryland Pkwy. (between Harmon and Tropicana aves.). ☎ **702/795-8110.** All items under $6. MC, V. Mon–Sat 6am–8pm (until 5pm in summer), Sun 7am–5pm. BAGELS.

You may not like digging into an enormous buffet first thing in the morning, and the continental breakfast in most hotels is a rip-off. A welcome alternative is a fresh-baked bagel, of which there are 15 varieties here—everything from onion to wild blueberry. Cream cheeses also come in many flavors, anything from sun-dried tomato to vegetable and jalapeño. Einstein's is a pleasant place for the morning meal, with both indoor seating and out-door tables cooled by misters. Service is friendly, and four special-blend coffees are available each day.

✪ **Mediterranean Café & Market.** 4147 S. Maryland Pkwy. (at Flamingo Rd., in the Tiffany Square strip mall). ☎ **702/731-6030.** Reservations not accepted. Main courses $8–$16 (all sandwiches under $5). AE, DISC, MC, V. Mon–Sat 11am–9pm. MEDITERRANEAN.

It's a thrill to find this totally authentic, mom-and-pop Middle Eastern restaurant in Las Vegas, where high-quality ethnic eater-ies are scarce. Everything here is homemade and delicious. You might order up a gyro (slivers of rotisseried beef and lamb enfolded into a pita with lettuce and tomato). Other good choices are a filo pie layered with spinach and feta cheese, served with hummus; skewers of grilled chicken and vegetable kabobs with lavash bread and hummus; and a combination platter of hummus, tabbouleh, stuffed grape leaves, and falafel. All entrees come with pita bread and salad. Try a side order of *bourrani* (creamy yogurt dip mixed with steamed spinach, sautéed garlic, and slivered almonds). Wine and beer are available. A Mediterranean market adjoins.

5 West Las Vegas

INEXPENSIVE

✪ **Enigma Cafe.** 918½ S. Fourth St. (at Charleston Blvd.). ☎ **702/386-0999.** Reservations not accepted. No items over $6. No credit cards. Mon 7am–3pm, Tues–Fri 7am–midnight, Sat–Sun 9am–midnight. CALIFORNIA/MEDITERRANEAN.

Finding the Enigma Cafe is almost as good as finding a breeze on a really hot Vegas day. Or maybe it's more like suddenly finding yourself transported out of Vegas and into California. Owners Julie and Len have taken two 1930s-era cottages and turned them into a cafe/coffeehouse/art space that, during the day, is a restful garden patio setting with folk and classical music playing. Orders are taken inside one house; inside the other is the art gallery, with more seating. At night, the space blooms with candles, live music, and poetry readings.

The menu is a huge relief: healthful, interesting sandwiches ("Mossy Melt" is tuna salad revved up with horseradish and havarti, and toasted open-face) and familiar ones (ham and Swiss, but well-garnished), salads (again with a range from the ordinary green variety to "Dr. Bombay's" curried chicken breast with veggies), hummus burritos, and the "Tippy Elvis Supreme" (named after a local polka band/art project), which is peanut butter and bananas (what else?). You can get a side platter of hummus, feta cheese, veggies, and pita, or have a thick fruit smoothie. And that doesn't even begin to cover their wide range of coffee drinks. Best of all, it's cheap. This is actually very close to both the Strip and Downtown, particularly the latter, where good (and healthful) food is hard to find.

6 Downtown

VERY EXPENSIVE

✪ **Andre's.** 401 S. 6th St. (at Lewis St., 2 blocks south of Fremont St.). ☎ **702/385-5016.** Reservations required. Main courses $20–$33. AE, CB, DC, MC, V. Daily from 6pm; closing hours vary. FRENCH.

Andre's has long been the bastion of gourmet dining in Vegas, but with all those new big boys crowding the Strip, it runs the risk of getting overlooked. It shouldn't. Besides, it still dominates Downtown. (This is also a celebrity haunt where you're likely to see Strip headliners. One night, Tom Hanks, Steven Spielberg, and James Spader were all spotted joining some pals for a bachelor party. The staff played it cool, though.) In a small, converted 1930s house, you find an elegant French provincial atmosphere, overseen by owner-chef Andre, who brings over 40 years of experience to the table. Much of the waitstaff is also French but not the sort who give the French a bad name. They will happily lavish attention on you and guide you through the menu.

The food presentation is exquisite, and choices change seasonally. On a recent visit, an appetizer of Northwest smoked salmon *mille feulle* with cucumber salad and sevruga caviar was especially enjoyed, as was a main course of grilled provini veal tornados with chive sauce accompanied by a mushroom and foie gras crêpe. You get the idea. Desserts are similarly lovely, an exotic array of rich delights. An extensive wine list (more than 900 labels) is international in scope and includes many rare vintages; consult the sommelier.

Note: An additional branch of Andre's has opened in the **Monte Carlo Hotel & Casino,** 3775 Las Vegas Blvd. S. (☎ **702/798-7151**).

EXPENSIVE

Limerick's. In Fitzgeralds Casino Holiday Inn, 301 Fremont St. (at 3rd St.). ☎ **702/388-2400.** Reservations recommended. Main courses $18–$40. AE, DISC, MC, V. Thurs–Mon 5–11pm, closed Tues–Wed. STEAK/SEAFOOD.

Decorated in the classic Olde English gentlemen's club style, Limerick's is meant to be an oasis of gracious dining away from hectic casino life, and the overall effect is comforting and moderately womblike, particularly in the cozy booths at the back. Unfortunately, casino "ca-chings" still creep in, but it's not overly bothersome. The menu is classic, upscale steakhouse: beef, chops, some lobster, and chicken. The portions are Vegas-size (the small prime rib was 14 ounces), so bring an appetite (and a love of red meat), or take your leftovers back to the room to feed the kids for a couple days. The filet mignon was tender enough to cut with a fork, while the lamb chops came with a pecan mustard glaze. Patrons who don't eat red meat might want to try the apricot chicken. The wine list is good and extensive.

☉ **Second Street Grill.** In the Fremont Hotel & Casino, 200 E. Fremont St. ☎ **702/ 385-3232.** Main courses $17–$23. Reservations recommended. AE, DC, DISC, MC, V. Sun–Mon and Thurs 5–10pm, Fri–Sat 5–11pm. INTERNATIONAL/ PACIFIC RIM.

One of the better-kept secrets of Las Vegas, this is a Downtown jewel, a lovely bit of romantic, cozy class tucked away inside the Fremont Hotel, with excellent food to boot. There is hardly a misstep on the menu, from taste to beautiful presentation. To call this Hawaiian-influenced would be accurate, but don't think of the "Polynesian" craze of the '60s and '70s—this is more like what you would find in a top-flight restaurant on the Big Island. You begin with warm sourdough bread accompanied by a garlic, eggplant, and olive oil dipping sauce. For starters, try the unusual lemon-chicken potstickers and the duck confit. Entrees include lobster, ahi tuna, and filet mignon, but the whole fish (opaka paka on a recent visit), served in a bowl with a giant tea-leaf lid, is the best bet. It comes with sautéed mushrooms that will melt

Andre's **7**
Binion's Horseshoe
  Coffee Shop **2**
Carson Street Café **3**
El Sombrero Cafe **6**
Limerick's **5**
Second Street Grill **4**
BUFFETS
Fremont Paradise
  Buffet **4**
Golden Nugget
  Buffet **3**
Main Street Station
  Garden Court **1**

in your mouth. Other notable side dishes include some fabulous pesto mashed potatoes. Don't skip the Chocolate Explosion: a piece of chocolate cake topped with chocolate mousse, covered with a rich chocolate shell.

INEXPENSIVE

✪ **Binion's Horseshoe Coffee Shop.** In Binion's Horseshoe, 128 E. Fremont St. (at Casino Center Blvd.). ☎ **702/382-1600.** Reservations not accepted. Main courses $4.25–$15 (most under $8). AE, CB, DC, DISC, MC, V. Daily 24 hours. AMERICAN.

The menu lists all the traditional Las Vegas coffee-shop items: sandwiches, burgers, Southern-fried chicken, steak, seafood, and breakfast fare. And you can't beat Binion's specials: two eggs with an immense slab of grilled ham, home fries, toast, and tea or coffee ($3 from 6am to 2pm); a 7-ounce New York steak with eggs, home fries, and toast ($3 from 10pm to 5:45am); a 10-ounce prime-rib dinner, including soup or salad, potato, and vegetables ($5.25 from 5 to 9:45pm, and $6.25 if you make it a 16-ounce

T-bone steak instead of prime rib). Although these particular specials may not be available when you visit, you get the basic idea. All bar drinks are available, and there's peanut-butter cream pie for dessert.

Carson Street Café. In the Golden Nugget, 129 E. Fremont St. (between 1st St. and Casino Center Blvd.). ☎ **702/385-7111.** Reservations not accepted. Main courses $6–$15. AE, CB, DC, DISC, MC, V. Daily 24 hours. AMERICAN.

Here's a slightly better than adequate hotel coffee shop, though it's a mixed bag in terms of quality of food. Sandwiches are better than ribs, burgers, and fries, all of which are merely just filling. On the other hand, linguine with shrimp is surprisingly good, while desserts, especially pecan pie à la mode and the famous bread pudding (former Golden Nugget owner Steve Wynn's mom's own recipe and a heavily guarded secret) more than earns its rep.

✪ **El Sombrero Cafe.** 807 S. Main St. ☎ **702/382-9234.** Everything under $10. AE, MC, V. Mon–Sat 11am–10pm. MEXICAN.

This kind of hole-in-the-wall Mexican joint can be found all over California but not always so readily elsewhere. It's also the kind of family-run (since 1950) place increasingly forced out of Vegas by giant hotel conglomerates, making it even more worth your time (it's becoming harder and harder, particularly in Downtown, to find budget options that present you with food that is more than just mere fuel). Mexican food fans in particular should seek this friendly place out, though it's not in an attractive part of town. Portions are generous, better than average, and unexpectedly spicy. They also cater to special requests—changing the beef burrito to a chicken one (an option that comes highly recommended), for example, without batting an eyelash. The enchilada and taco combo also won raves.

7   Buffets & Sunday Brunches

Lavish, low-priced buffets are a Las Vegas tradition, designed to lure you to the gaming tables, and to make you feel that you got such a bargain for your meal you can afford to drop more money. They're a gimmick, and we love them. Something about filling up on too much prime rib and shrimp just says "Vegas" to us. Of course, there is quite a range. Some are just perfunctory steam-table displays and salad bars that are heavy on the iceberg lettuce, while others are unbelievably opulent spreads with caviar and free-flowing champagne. Some are quite beautifully presented, as well. Some of the food is awful, some of it merely works as fuel, and some of it is memorable.

Note: Buffet meals are extremely popular, and reservations are usually not taken (we've indicated when they are accepted, and in all those cases, they are highly recommended). Arrive early (before opening) or late to avoid a long line, especially on weekends.

SOUTH STRIP
MODERATE

Mandalay Bay's Bay Side Buffet. 3950 Las Vegas Blvd. S. ☎ **702/ 632-7402.** Breakfast $8.50, lunch $9.50, dinner $13.50; Sun brunch $14.50. AE, CB, DC, DISC, MC, V. Daily 7am–10pm.

This is a particularly pretty, not overly large buffet. Actual windows, floor to ceiling, no less, overlooking the beach part of the elaborate pool area, make it less stuffy and eliminate that closed-in feeling that so many of the other buffets in town have. The buffet itself is adequately arranged but features nothing particularly special, though there are some nice cold salads, hearty meats, and a larger and better-than-average dessert bar (they make their own desserts and it shows).

INEXPENSIVE

✪ **Excalibur's Round Table Buffet.** 3850 Las Vegas Blvd. S. ☎ **702/ 597-7777.** Breakfast $7, lunch $8, dinner $10. AE, CB, DC, DISC, MC, V. Sun–Thurs 6:30am–10pm, Fri–Sat 6:30am–11pm.

This one strikes the perfect balance of cheap prices, mandatory tacky decor, and adequate food. It's what you want in a cheap Vegas buffet. But on a recent trip they didn't have mashed potatoes or macaroni salad, which are essential for an archetypal buffet. The plates are large, so you don't have to make as many trips to the buffet tables.

✪ **Luxor's Pharaoh's Pheast Buffet.** 3900 Las Vegas Blvd. S. ☎ **702/ 262-4000.** Breakfast $7.50, lunch $8, dinner $11.50. AE, DC, DISC, MC, V. Daily 6:30am–11pm.

Located on the lower level, where the Luxor showroom used to be, this huge new buffet looks like it was set in the middle of an archaeological dig, complete with wood braces holding up the ceiling, pot shards, papyrus, and servers dressed in khaki-dig outfits. It's a unique and fun decor—be sure to avoid tripping on the mummies and their sarcophagi sticking half up out of the ground. The food is better than that at most cheap buffets. There's a Mexican station with some genuinely spicy food, a Chinese stir-fry station, and different Italian pastas. Desserts were disappointing, though. A beer and wine cart makes the rounds. Word has probably gotten out, unfortunately, because the lines are always enormous.

MGM Grand Buffet. 3799 Las Vegas Blvd. S. ☎ **702/891-7777.** Brunch $8.95, dinner $12.95; reduced prices for children under 10, free for children under 4. AE, DC, DISC, MC, V. Daily 7am–2:30pm and 4–10pm.

This rather average buffet does feature a fresh Belgian waffle station at breakfast. Dinner also has all-you-can-eat shrimp and an all-you-can-eat shrimp and prime-rib option. Also available: low-fat, sugar-free desserts! And at all meals, you get a full pot of coffee on your table.

Monte Carlo Buffet. 3770 Las Vegas Blvd. S. ☎ **702/730-7777.** Breakfast $7, lunch $7.25, dinner $10; Sun brunch $10.95. AE, CB, DC, DISC, MC, V. Daily 7am–10pm.

A "courtyard" under a painted sky, the Monte Carlo's buffet room has a Moroccan market theme, with murals of Arab scenes, Moorish archways, oriental carpets, and walls hung with photographs of, and artifacts from, Morocco. Dinner includes a rotisserie (for chicken and pork loin, or London broil), a Chinese food station, a taco/fajita bar, a baked potato bar, numerous salads, and more than a dozen desserts, plus frozen yogurt and ice-cream machines. Lunches are similar. At breakfast, the expected fare is supplemented by an omelet station, and choices include crêpes, blintzes, and corned beef hash. Fresh-baked New York–style bagels are a plus.

MID-STRIP
VERY EXPENSIVE

✪ **Bally's Sterling Sunday Brunch.** 3645 Las Vegas Blvd. S. ☎ **702/739-4111.** Reservations recommended. Brunch $49.95. AE, CB, DC, JCB, MC, V. Sun 9:30am–2:30pm.

Now, the admittedly high cost of this brunch seems antithetical to the original purpose of a buffet, which was a lot of food for minimal money. However, if you're a dedicated buffet fan, this is probably a better spree than one of the many new high-priced restaurants. It works out to less money in the long run, and you will get, for your purposes, more bang for your buck. It's a fancy deal—linen and silver bedecked tables, waiters to assist you if you choose—and while the variety of food isn't as massive as at regular buffets, the quality is much higher in terms of both content and execution. We're talking unlimited champagne, broiled lobster, caviar, sushi and rotating dishes of the day (items such as monkfish with pomegranate essence, tenderloin wrapped in porcini mushroom mousse, and even ostrich). No French toast that's been sitting out for days here! Perfect for a wedding breakfast or business brunch or just a big treat; stay a long time and eat as much as you can.

EXPENSIVE

✪ **Bellagio Buffet.** 3600 Las Vegas Blvd. S. ☎ **888/987-6667.** Breakfast $8.95, lunch $12.95, dinner $19.95, brunch $18.95. AE, CB, DC, DISC, MC, V. Breakfast Mon–Fri 7–10:30am; lunch Mon–Fri 11am–3:30pm; dinner Sun–Thurs 4–10pm, Fri–Sat 4–11pm; brunch Sat–Sun 8am–4pm.

Though even pricier than its counterpart over at the Mirage, the new Bellagio buffet gets nearly as high marks. The array of foods is fabulous, with one ethnic cuisine after another (Japanese, Chinese that includes unexpected buffet fare like dim sum, build-it-yourself Mexican items, and so on). There are elaborate pastas and semitraditional Italian-style pizza from a wood-fired oven. The cold fish appetizers at each end of the line are not to be missed—scallops, smoked salmon, crab claws, shrimp, oysters, and assorted condiments. Specialties include breast of duck and game hens. There is no carving station, but you can get the meat pre-carved. The salad bar is more ordinary, though prepared salads have some fine surprises like eggplant tofu and an exceptional Chinese chicken salad. Desserts, unfortunately, look better than they actually are.

✪ **Paris, Le Village Buffet.** 3665 Las Vegas Blvd. S. ☎ **888/266-5687.** Breakfast $10.95, lunch $14.95, dinner $22, brunch $21. AE, CB, DC, DISC, MC, V. Breakfast daily 7:30–10:30am, lunch Mon–Thurs 10:30am–5:30pm; dinner Mon–Thurs 5:30–10:30pm, Fri–Sat 11am–11pm, Sun 3–10pm; brunch Sun 11:30am–3pm.

We don't like this trend of increasingly less-bargain-priced buffets, but we have to admit the food at these places can be considerably better than at their cheaper brethren. The Paris buffet is a fine example of same. Serving stations are offered up according to various regions in France (Provence, Alsace, Burgundy, and so forth) featuring dishes you don't find at your run-of-the-mill buffet, such as chicken mushroom vol au vent and bay scallops with apple cider vinaigrette. There are special sauces (chateaubriand, cherry escoffier, and so on) for the roast meats. And it's all pretty darn good. Yes, there is quiche, plus fresh bread and cheese. The room is particularly nice-looking as well.

MODERATE

Caesars Palace Palatium Buffet. 3570 Las Vegas Blvd. S. ☎ **702/ 731-7110.** Breakfast $7.35, lunch $9.25, dinner $14.95; Fri seafood dinner $23.35 (includes 1 lobster); Sat–Sun brunch $14.95 adults (includes unlimited champagne), $7 children ages 4–12, free for children under 4. AE, CB, DC, DISC, MC, V. Daily 7:30am–10pm.

Named for the 2nd-century meeting place of Rome's academy of chefs, this is a rather busy, stuffy room with slightly better than run-of-the-mill buffet quality. Selections at lunch and dinner include elaborate salad bars and fresh-baked breads, while the evening meal includes a cold seafood station. Weekend brunches are quite lavish, with omelet stations (in addition to egg dishes), breakfast meats, fresh-squeezed juices, potatoes prepared in various ways, pastas, rice casseroles, carved meats, cold shrimp, smoked salmon, and a waffle and ice-cream sundae bar, in addition to two dessert islands spotlighting cakes and pastries. Now *that's* a buffet!

Harrah's Fresh Market Buffet. 3475 Las Vegas Blvd. S. ☎ **702/ 369-5000.** Breakfast $9, lunch $10, dinner $15; Sat–Sun champagne brunch $15. AE, CB, DC, DISC, MC, V. Mon–Fri 7am–10pm, Sat–Sun 10am–10pm.

The theme here is farmer's market, which means lots of big sculptures of fresh fruits and vegetables, if not actual fresh fruits and vegetables. It follows the new trend of various food stations, as opposed to one long buffet. You'll find seafood, pasta, Mexican, Asian, and American specialties ranging from meat loaf to Cajun entrees. Above-average food combined with an extremely friendly staff makes this one of the better buffet choices.

✪ **Mirage Buffet.** 3400 Las Vegas Blvd. S. ☎ **702/791-7111.** Breakfast $8.95, lunch $9.95, dinner $14.95; Sun brunch $14.95; reduced prices for children ages 4–10, free for children under 4. AE, CB, DC, DISC, MC, V. Mon–Sat 7am–10pm; Sun 8am–10pm.

The Mirage offers lavish spreads in a lovely garden-themed setting with palm trees, a plant-filled stone fountain, and seating under verdigris eaves and domes embellished with flowers. You pay somewhat more here than at other buffets, but you certainly get what you pay for. The salad bars alone are enormous, filled with at least 25 different choices such as Thai beef, seafood, salad Niçoise, tabbouleh, Chinese chicken, Creole rice, and tortellini. At brunch, champagne flows freely, and a scrumptious array of smoked fish is added to the board, along with such items as fruit-filled crêpes and blintzes. And every meal features a spectacular dessert table (the bread pudding in bourbon sauce is notewor-thy). For healthful eating, there are many light items to choose from, including sugar- and fat-free puddings. And on Sunday, a non-alcoholic sparkling cider is a possible champagne alternative.

INEXPENSIVE

Flamingo Paradise Garden Buffet. 3555 Las Vegas Blvd. S. ☎ **702/ 733-3111.** Champagne brunch $8.75, lunch/dinner $14. AE, CB, DC, DISC, JCB, MC, V. Daily 6–11:30am (brunch) and 11:30am–11pm (lunch/dinner).

The buffet here occupies a vast room, with floor-to-ceiling win-dows overlooking a verdant tropical landscape of cascading water-falls and a pond filled with ducks, swans, and flamingos. The interior, one of the most pleasant in Las Vegas, is equally lush, though its palm trees and tropical foliage are faux. At dinner, there is an extensive international food station (which changes monthly) presenting French, Chinese, Mexican, German, or Ital-ian specialties. A large salad bar, fresh fruits, pastas, vegetables, potato dishes, and a vast dessert display round out the offerings. Lunch is similar, featuring a mix of international cuisines as well as a stir-fry station and a soup/salad/pasta bar. At breakfast, you'll find all the expected fare, including a made-to-order omelet sta-tion and fresh-baked breads.

✪ **Rio's Carnival World Buffet.** 3700 W. Flamingo Rd. ☎ **702/ 252-7777.** Breakfast $7.95, lunch $9.95, dinner $12.95. AE, CB, DC, MC, V. Daily 8am–10:30am and 11am–11pm.

The buffet here is located in a festively decorated room with var-iegated wide, sequined ribbons looped overhead and seating amid planters of lush, faux tropical blooms. Chairs and booths are upholstered in bright hues. This is an excellent buffet with cheer-fully decorative food booths set up like stations in an upscale food court. A barbecued chicken and ribs station offers side dishes of baked beans and mashed potatoes. Other stations offer stir-fries, Mexican taco fixings and accompaniments, Chinese fare, a Japanese sushi and teppanyaki grill, a Brazilian mixed grill, Ital-ian pasta and antipasto, and fish-and-chips. There's even a diner setup for hot dogs, burgers, fries, and milk shakes. All this is in addition to the usual offerings of most Las Vegas buffets. A stunning array of oven-fresh cakes, pies, and pastries (including sugar-free and low-fat desserts) is arranged in a palm-fringed circular display area, and there's also a make-your-own sundae bar. A full cash bar is another Rio plus. Everything is fresh and beautifully prepared and presented.

Treasure Island Buffet. 3300 Las Vegas Blvd. S. ☎ **702/894-7111.** Breakfast $7, lunch $7.50, dinner $11.50; Sun brunch $11.50. AE, DC, DISC, JCB, MC, V. Mon–Sat 7–10:45am and 11am–3:45pm; daily 4–10:30pm; Sun 7am–3:30pm.

The buffet is served in two internationally themed rooms. The American room, under a central rough-hewn beamed canopy hung with the flags of the 13 colonies, re-creates New Orleans during the era of Jean Lafitte. And the Italian room, modeled after a Tuscan villa overlooking a bustling piazza, has strings of festival lights overhead and food displays under a striped awning. Both rooms are filled with antiques and artifacts typical of their locales and time periods. And both also serve identical fare, including extensive American breakfasts. Dinners offer a Chinese food station, peel-and-eat shrimp, a salad bar, potato and rice side dishes, cheeses and cold cuts, fresh fruits and vegetables, breads, and a large choice of desserts. Lunch is similar, and Sunday brunch includes unlimited champagne.

NORTH STRIP
INEXPENSIVE

Circus Circus Buffet. 2880 Las Vegas Blvd. S. ☎ **702/734-0410.** Breakfast $5.50, lunch $6.50, dinner $8; Sat–Sun brunch $6.50. AE, CB, DC, DISC, MC, V. Mon–Fri 7–11:30am, noon–4pm, and 4:30–10pm; Sat–Sun 7am–4pm and 4:30–11pm.

Here's a tradeoff: It's just about the cheapest buffet on the Strip but also the worst buffet food in town. Here you'll find 50 items of typical cafeteria fare, and none of them all that good. Kids love it; some adults find it inedible. If food is strictly fuel for you, you can't go wrong here. Otherwise, trundle off to another buffet.

EAST OF THE STRIP
MODERATE

Las Vegas Hilton Buffet of Champions. 3000 Paradise Rd. ☎ **702/732-5111.** Breakfast $8, lunch $9, dinner $13; weekend brunch $12 (includes unlimited champagne); half price for children age 12 and under. CB, DC, DISC, ER, MC, V. Daily 8am–2:30pm and 5–10pm.

As the name implies, the room, located near the casino entrance to the race and sports SuperBook, is sports-themed, with attractive murals and photographs of hockey, football, boxing, and horse racing, plus bookshelves stocked with sporting literature. All in all, it's one of the better-looking buffet rooms in town. And the fare is fresh and delicious, with special mention going to the prime rib and the outstanding cream puffs and superior rice pudding (it's hard to find good desserts at Vegas buffets). Dinner additionally features all-you-can-eat crab and shrimp. The Friday-night seafood selection is particularly large and palatable.

DOWNTOWN
MODERATE

✪ **Golden Nugget Buffet.** 129 E. Fremont St. ☎ **702/385-7111.** Breakfast $5.75, lunch $7.50, dinner $10.25; Sun brunch $11. AE, CB, DC, DISC, MC, V. Mon–Sat 7am–3pm and 4–10pm; Sun 8am–10pm.

This buffet has often been voted number one in Las Vegas. Not only is the food fresh and delicious, but it's served in an opulent dining room with marble-topped serving tables amid planters of greenery and potted palms. Mirrored columns, beveled mirrors, etched glass, and brass add sparkle to the room, and swagged draperies provide a note of elegance. Most of the seating is in plush booths. The buffet tables are also laden with an extensive salad bar (about 50 items), fresh fruit, and marvelous desserts including the famous bread pudding made from the secret recipe of Zelma Wynn (Steve's mom). Every night, fresh seafood is featured. Most lavish is the all-day Sunday champagne brunch, which adds such dishes as eggs Benedict, blintzes, pancakes, creamed herring, and smoked fish with bagels and cream cheese. *Note:* This stunning buffet room is also the setting for a $3 late-night meal of steak and eggs with home fries and biscuits with gravy; it's served 11pm to 4am.

INEXPENSIVE

✪ **Fremont Paradise Buffet.** 200 E. Fremont St. ☎ **702/385-3232.** Breakfast $5, lunch $6.50, dinner $10; $15 for Seafood Fantasy; Sun brunch $9. AE, CB, DC, DISC, JCB, MC, V. Mon–Sat 7–10:30am and 11am–3pm; Mon and Wed–Thurs 4–10pm, Sat 4–11pm; Seafood Fantasy Sun and Tues 4–10pm, Fri 4–11pm; Sun 7am–3pm.

This buffet is served in an attractive, tropically themed room. Diners sit in spacious booths amid lush jungle foliage—birds of paradise, palms, and bright tropical blooms—and the buffet area is surrounded by a "waterfall" of Tivoli lighting under a reflective ceiling. Island music, enhanced by bird calls and the sound of splashing waterfalls, helps set the tone. Meals here are on the lavish side.

✪ Main Street Station Garden Court. 200 N. Main St. ☎ **702/ 387-1896.** Breakfast $5, lunch $7, dinner $10; Fri seafood buffet $14; Sat and Sun champagne brunch $9; free for children 3 and under. AE, CB, DC, DISC, MC, V. Daily 7am–10:30am, 11am–3pm, and 4–10pm.

Set in what is truly one of the prettiest buffet spaces in town (and certainly in Downtown), with very high ceilings and tall windows bringing in much-needed natural light, the Main Street Station Garden Court buffet is one of the best in town, let alone Downtown. Featuring nine live-action stations (meaning you can watch your food being prepared), including a wood-fired, brick-oven pizza (delicious), many fresh salsas at the Mexican station, a barbecue rotisserie, fresh sausage at the carving station, Chinese, Hawaiian, and Southern specialties (soul food and the like), and so many more we lost count. On Friday night, they have all this plus nearly infinite varieties of seafood all the way up to lobster. We ate ourselves into a stupor and didn't regret it.

5

What to See & Do in Las Vegas

You aren't going to lack for things to do in Las Vegas. More than likely, you've come here for the gambling, which should keep you pretty busy (we say that with some understatement). But you can't sit at a slot machine forever. (Or maybe you can.) In any event, it shouldn't be too hard to find ways to fill your time between poker hands.

Just walking on the Strip and gazing at the gaudy, garish, absurd wonder of it all can occupy quite a lot of time. This is the number-one activity we recommend in Vegas; at night, it is a mind-boggling sight. And, of course, there are shows and plenty of other nighttime entertainment. But if you need something else to do beyond resting up at your hotel's pool, or if you are trying to amuse yourself while the rest of your party gambles away, this chapter will guide you.

Don't forget to check out the **free hotel attractions,** such as Bellagio's water fountain ballet, Mirage's volcano and white tiger exhibit, Treasure Island's pirate battle, and the masquerade show at the Rio.

1 The Top Attractions

See also the listings for theme parks and other fun stuff in section 3, "Especially for Kids."

There's also the **Bellagio Gallery of Fine Art.** After the MGM Grand bought the Mirage Corp., which owns the Bellagio and other properties, it was announced that Steve Wynn's fine art collection would no longer be displayed here. Though few details were available at press time, expect to see this space used to host traveling art exhibits.

Eiffel Tower Tour. In Paris–Las Vegas, 3655 Las Vegas Blvd. S. ☎ **702/946-7000.** Admission $8. "Tours" leave every half hour. Daily 10am–1am.

Whether this is worth the dough depends on how much you like views. An elevator operator (we refuse to call them guides) delivers a few facts about this Eiffel Tower (this is a half-size exact replica, down to the paint color, of the original) during the minute or so ride to an uppermost platform, where you are welcome to stand around and look out for as long as you want, which probably isn't 2 hours, the length of the average movie, which also costs $8. Nice view, though.

Elvis O' Rama. 3401 Industrial Rd. ☎ **702/309-7200.** Daily 10am–6pm. Admission $9.95 adults, $7.95 seniors, kids under 12 free. (Admission includes a 20-min. Elvis impersonator show, held 4 times daily.)

Three million dollars' worth of Elvis memorabilia—we thought surely this place would give our beloved Liberace museum a run for its spot in our camp-lovin' hearts, but alas, while this is a must for the Elvis faithful (and admittedly, they are legion) looking to view holy relics, it's not the place for a novice to start.

The amount of cool stuff is amazing: Elvis ephemera ranging from his Social Security card (a $14,000 auction purchase) to his "little black book" (entries not divulged, damn it!), his Army uniform, a love letter to his hometown girlfriend, fan club souvenirs (Elvis lipstick!), and on and on it goes. But alas, these precious (and discarded) possessions are exhibited in cases that, as of this writing, are lacking much needed labels and identification. The displays also don't precisely give you a good view of the King's life; it assumes you already know the highlights, and it's hardly complete. Despite our morbid hopes for prescription pill bottles, there was nary a mention of Dr. Nick nor even The Death. There is, however, a whole case displaying what amounts to the contents of Vernon Presley's wallet. It's also all a little too straightfaced and reverent, though the gift shop makes up for it a bit. Best for fans thinking "you know, I really *should* brush up on my Elvis-iania."

⭐ **Fremont Street Experience.** Fremont St. (between Main St. and Las Vegas Blvd.), Downtown. www.vegasexperience.com. Free admission. Shows nightly.

For some years, Downtown Vegas has been losing ground to the Strip. But thanks to a $70-million revitalization project, that's starting to change. Fremont Street, the heart of "Glitter Gulch," has been closed off and turned into a pedestrian mall. The Fremont Street Experience is a 5-block open-air pedestrian mall, a landscaped strip of outdoor cafes, vendor carts, and colorful kiosks purveying food and merchandise. Overhead is a 90-foot-high steel-mesh "celestial vault"; at night, it is the **Sky Parade,** a

Las Vegas Attractions

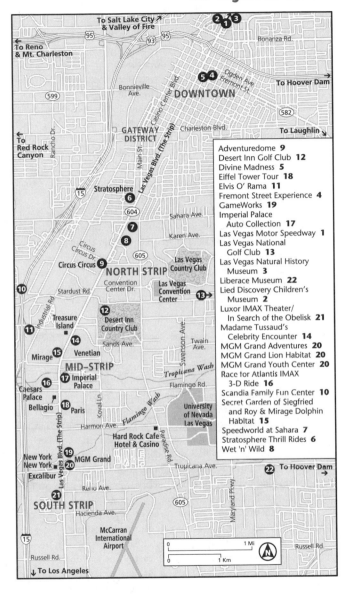

To Salt Lake City
& Valley of Fire

To Reno
& Mt. Charleston

Bonanza Rd.

95

93

95

599

Bonnieville
Ave.

Ogden Ave.
Fremont St.

DOWNTOWN

To Hoover Dam

582

GATEWAY
DISTRICT

Charleston Blvd

To Laughlin

To
Red Rock
Canyon

Rancho Dr.

Main St.

Las Vegas Blvd. (The Strip)

Casino Center Blvd.

Stratosphere

15

604

Sahara Ave.

Karen Ave.

Circus
Circus Dr.

605

Circus Circus

NORTH STRIP

Convention
Center Dr.

Stardust Rd.

Las Vegas
Country Club

Las Vegas
Convention
Center

Industrial Rd.

Treasure
Island

Desert Inn
Country Club

Sands Ave.

Swenson Ave.

Twain
Ave.

Mirage

Venetian

MID-STRIP

Tropicana Wash

Caesars
Palace

Imperial
Palace

Flamingo Rd.

Bellagio

Paris

Koval Ln.

Flamingo Wash

University
of Nevada
Las Vegas

Harmon Ave.

Paradise Rd.

Hard Rock Cafe
Hotel & Casino

New York
New York

MGM Grand

Las Vegas Blvd. (The Strip)

Excalibur

Tropicana Ave.

To Hoover Dam

SOUTH STRIP

Reno Ave.

605

Maryland Pkwy.

Hacienda Ave.

15

McCarran
International
Airport

0   1 Mi

0   1 Km

Russell Rd.

Russell Rd.

To Los Angeles

Adventuredome **9**
Desert Inn Golf Club **12**
Divine Madness **5**
Eiffel Tower Tour **18**
Elvis O' Rama **11**
Fremont Street Experience **4**
GameWorks **19**
Imperial Palace
  Auto Collection **17**
Las Vegas Motor Speedway **1**
Las Vegas National
  Golf Club **13**
Las Vegas Natural History
  Museum **3**
Liberace Museum **22**
Lied Discovery Children's
  Museum **2**
Luxor IMAX Theater/
  In Search of the Obelisk **21**
Madame Tussaud's
  Celebrity Encounter **14**
MGM Grand Adventures **20**
MGM Grand Lion Habitat **20**
MGM Grand Youth Center **20**
Race for Atlantis IMAX
  3-D Ride **16**
Scandia Family Fun Center **10**
Secret Garden of Siegfried
  and Roy & Mirage Dolphin
  Habitat **15**
Speedworld at Sahara **7**
Stratosphere Thrill Rides **6**
Wet 'n' Wild **8**

high-tech light-and-laser show (the canopy is equipped with more than 2.1 million lights) enhanced by a concert-hall-quality sound system, which takes place four times nightly. But there's music between shows as well. Not only does the canopy provide shade, it cools the area through a misting system in summer and warms you with radiant heaters in winter. The difference this makes cannot be overemphasized; what was once a ghost town of tacky, rapidly aging buildings, in an area with more undesirables than not, is now a bustling (at least at night), friendly, safe place (they have private security guards who hustle said undesirables away). It's a place where you can stroll, eat, or even dance to the music under the lights. The crowd it attracts is more upscale than in years past, and of course, it's a lot less crowded than the hectic Strip.

In a further effort to retain as much of classic Las Vegas as possible, the **Neon Museum** is installing vintage hotel and casino signs along the promenade. The first installation is the horse and rider from the old Hacienda, which presently rides the sky over the intersection of Fremont and Las Vegas Boulevard. (Eventually, the Neon Museum hopes to have an indoor installation on the Fremont Street Experience, to showcase some of the smaller signs they have collected.)

✪ **GameWorks.** In the Showcase Mall, 3785 Las Vegas Blvd. S. ☎ **702/ 432-GAME.** Sun–Thurs 10am–midnight, Fri–Sat 10am–2am. Hours may vary.

What do you get when Steven Spielberg and his Dreamworks team get in on the video-game arcade action? Grown-up state-of-the-art fun. High-tech movie magic has taken over all sorts of traditional arcade games and turned them interactive, from a virtual-reality batting cage to a Jurassic Park game that lets you hunt dinosaurs. There are motion simulator rides galore and even actual motion activities like rock climbing. But classic games, from Pacman to pool tables, are here, too, though sometimes with surprising twists such as air hockey, where sometimes multiple pucks will shoot out at once.

All this doesn't exactly come cheap. You purchase a block of time ($20 for an hour, though if you get there at opening you get 2 hours for $20), which goes on a debit card that you then insert into the various machines to activate them. But you do get value for your money, which makes this a viable alternative to casinos, particularly if you have children (though it's clearly geared toward a college age and older demographic). Children probably should be 10 years old and up—any younger and parents will need to stand over them, rather than go off and have considerable fun on their own.

Imperial Palace Auto Collection. In the Imperial Palace Hotel, 3535 Las Vegas Blvd. S. ☎ **702/ 794-3174.** www.autocollections.com. Admission $7 adults, $3 seniors and children under 12, free for children under 5 and AAA members. Daily 9:30am–11:30pm.

Even if you're not a car person, don't assume you won't be interested in this premier collection of antique, classic, and special-interest vehicles. There's more here than just cars and trucks. Check out the graceful lines and handsome sculpture of one of the 43 Model J Dusenbergs (the largest collection in the world, valued at over $50 million). The craftsmanship and attention to detail make these cars, and others here, true works of art.

There's also a great deal of history. Take a walk down President's Row, where you can see JFK's 1962 "bubbletop" Lincoln Continental, Lyndon Johnson's 1964 Cadillac, Eisenhower's 1952 Chrysler Imperial 20-foot-long parade car, Truman's 1950 Lincoln Cosmopolitan with gold-plated interior, FDR's unrestored 1936 V-16 Cadillac, and Herbert Hoover's 1929 Cadillac. Directly opposite this tribute to democracy, in both location and political theory, is the dictator section. Here you will see Adolf Hitler's armored, bulletproof, and mineproof 1936 Mercedes-Benz 770K; Emperor Hirohito's 1935 Packard; Czar Nicholas II's 1914 Rolls-Royce; former Mexican president Lazaro Cardena's black 1939 V-12 Packard (armor-plated to resist 50-caliber machine-gun bullets); and Argentinean strongman Juan Perón's 1939 straight-8 Packard (no pictures of Evita anywhere).

Other highlights are Al Capone's 1930 V-16 Cadillac, Elvis Presley's powder-blue 1976 Cadillac Eldorado, Liberace's pale-cream 1981 Zimmer (complete with candelabra), W. C. Fields's black 1938 Cadillac V-16 touring sedan with built-in bar, Howard Hughes's 1954 Chrysler (because of his phobia about germs, Hughes installed a special air-purification system that cost more than the car itself!), and a 1947 Tucker (one of only 51 manufactured before the company went out of business).

Las Vegas Motor Speedway. 7000 Las Vegas Blvd. N., directly across from Nellis Air Force base (take I-15 north to Speedway exit 54). ☎ **702/ 644-4443** for ticket information. Tickets $10–$75 (higher prices for major events).

This 107,000-seat facility was the first new super-speedway to be built in the Southwest in over 2 decades. A $100-million state-of-the-art motor-sports entertainment complex, it includes a 1½-mile super-speedway, a 2½-mile FIA-approved road course, paved and dirt short-track ovals, and a 4,000-foot drag strip. Also on the property are facilities for Go-Kart, Legends Car, Sand Drag, and Motorcross competition. The new speedway is accessible via shuttle buses to and from the Imperial Palace hotel, though some of the other major hotels have their own shuttles to the Speedway.

✪ **Liberace Museum.** 1775 E. Tropicana Ave. (at Spencer St., 2½ miles east of the Strip on your right). ☎ **702/798-5595.** Admission $6.95 adults, $4.95 seniors over 60 and students, free for children under 12. Mon–Sat 10am–5pm, Sun 1–5pm.

You can keep your Louvres and Vaticans and Smithsonians; *this* is a museum. Housed, like everything else in Vegas, in a strip mall, this is a shrine to the glory and excess that was the art project known as Liberace. You've got your costumes (bejeweled), your many cars (bejeweled), your many pianos (bejeweled), and many jewels (also bejeweled). It just shows what can be bought with lots of money and no taste.

The thing is, Liberace was in on the joke (we think). The people who come here largely aren't. Many of these guests would not have liked him living next door to them if his name was, say, Bruce Smith, but they idolize the-man-the-myth. Not found here is any reference to AIDS or chauffeurs who had plastic surgery to look more like him. But you will find a Czar Nicholas uniform with 22-karat-gold braiding and a blue velvet cape styled after the coronation robes of King George V and covered with $60,000 worth of rare chinchilla. Not to mention a 50.6-pound rhinestone costing $50,000, the world's largest, presented to him by the grateful (I'll bet they were) Austrian firm that supplied all his costume stones. The gift shop has plenty of rhinestone-covered objects plus countless Liberace knickknacks of increasing tackiness. This is a one-of-a-kind place. Unless you have a severely under-developed appreciation for camp or take your museum-going very seriously, you shouldn't miss it.

Luxor IMAX Theater/In Search of the Obelisk. In the Luxor Las Vegas, 3900 Las Vegas Blvd. S. ☎ **702/262-4000.** Admission $7.95 for IMAX 2-D, $8.95 for 3-D, prices may vary depending on the movie; $7 for In Search of the Obelisk. Sun–Thurs 9am–11pm, Fri–Sat 9am–1am. Show times vary depending on the length of the film.

This is a state-of-the-art theater that projects films on a seven-story screen. There are two different films running: one in standard two dimensions, the other 3-D. The glasses for the latter are really cool headsets that include built-in speakers, bringing certain sounds right into your head. The movies change periodically but always include some extraordinary special effects. If you have a fear of heights, make sure to ask for a seat on one of the lower levels.

In Search of the Obelisk is a motion-simulator ride in which technology is used to create an action adventure involving a chase sequence inside a pyramid. In a rapidly plummeting elevator (the cable has broken!), you'll descend to an ancient temple 2 miles beneath the Luxor pyramid. In a thrill ride through the temple's maze, you'll experience an explosive battle with evil forces, rescue Carina from the clutches of Dr. Osiris, and narrowly escape death before returning to the surface. You have an option to take a different route if you have motion sickness, which means you won't get the best special effects. Otherwise, it's a standard thrill ride with interesting touches.

Madame Tussaud's Celebrity Encounter. 3355 Las Vegas Blvd. S. ☎ **702/ 990-3530.** Admission $12.50 adults, $10 children 4–12, $10.75 seniors and Nevada residents. Daily 10am–10pm.

Madame Tussaud's waxworks exhibition has been the top London attraction for nearly 2 centuries, so even if you aren't a fan of wax museums, this is probably worth a stop. Figures here are state-of-the-art, painstakingly constructed to perfectly match the original person. (Truth be told, though some are nearly identical to their living counterparts—Brad Pitt gave us a start—others look about as much like the celebrity in question as a department store mannequin.) There's no Chamber of Horrors, but the exhibit makes up for it, since all the waxworks are free-standing, allowing, and indeed encouraging, guests to get up close and personal. (Go ahead, lay your cheek next to Elvis's or Sinatra's and have your photo taken. You know you want to.) The emphasis here is on film, television, music, and sports celebrities, plus some Vegas icons. There's also a behind-the-scenes look at the lengthy process involved in creating just one of these figures. *Note:* Currently, you can exit only after viewing an 8-minute movie on Vegas, or by reclimbing the many stairs and waiting for a slow elevator.

MGM Grand Lion Habitat. In the MGM Grand, 3799 Las Vegas Blvd. S. ☎ **702/891-7777.** Free admission. Daily; hours vary, so call ahead.

Hit this attraction at the right time and it's one of the best freebies in town. See, it's a large, multilevel glass enclosure, in which various lions frolic during various times of day. In addition to regular angles of viewing, you can walk through a glass tunnel, and get a worm's eye view of the underside of a lion (provided one is in position); note how very big Kitty's paws are. Multiple lions share show duties (about 6 hours on and then 2 days off, heading to a ranch for some free-range activity, so they're never cooped up here for long). So you could see any combo from one giant male to a pack of five females who have grown from cub to near adult-size during their MGM time. Each comes with a trainer or three, who are there to keep the lions busy with play, so they don't act like the big cats they are and sleep the whole time.

Race for Atlantis IMAX 3-D Ride. In Caesars Palace, 3570 Las Vegas Blvd. S. Admission $9.50 adults, $6.75 children under 12. Sun–Thurs 10am–11pm, Fri–Sat 10am–midnight.

Following the trend of virtual-reality theme-park rides, Caesars Palace joined forces with IMAX to create the Race for Atlantis. If you've never been on a virtual-reality ride, you will enjoy it, but the production values pale compared to some others. This experience begins as you walk past a giant statue of Neptune and his chariot drawn by wild-looking sea serpents. The stone hallway appears to lead into an underwater palace. As the line twists around, a sci-fi fantasy world unfolds with mists clouding the multicolored lights of the legendary city of Atlantis. Once in the ride you are treated to a 3-D visor and a silly safety rap sung by Neptune's cowardly secretary. The ride itself is a 3-D motion simulator, which uses computer animation to create the lost city and the racecourse. If you like a bumpy ride, be sure to sit in the very front or very back. During the 4-minute race, your chariot is impeded by flying shrapnel, the evil god, and even by Neptune's own inept secretary. With the 3-D glasses, all of these sharp objects flying at you can get pretty intense. Not for the weak of stomach.

Secret Garden of Siegfried and Roy & ✪ Mirage Dolphin Habitat. In the Mirage, 3400 Las Vegas Blvd. S. ☎ **702/791-7111.** Admission $10, free for children under 10 if accompanied by an adult. On Wed, when only Dolphin Habitat is open, admission $5. Secret Garden open Mon–Tues and Thurs–Fri 11am–5pm, Sat–Sun 10am–5pm. Dolphin Habitat open Mon–Fri 11am–7pm, Sat–Sun 10am–7pm. Hours subject to change and vary by season.

Siegfried and Roy's famous white tigers have long had a free exhibit in the Mirage. They still do, but now they have an additional space, the **Secret Garden,** a gorgeous area behind the dolphin exhibit. Here, the white tigers are joined by white lions, Bengal tigers, an Asian elephant, a panther, and a snow leopard. (Many of these are bred by Siegfried and Roy and are also in their nightly show.) It's really just a glorified zoo, featuring only the big-ticket animals; however, it is a very pretty place, with plenty of foliage and some bits of Indian- and Asian-themed architecture. Zoo purists will be horrified at the smallish spaces the animals occupy, but all the animals are rotated between here and their more lavish digs at the illusionist team's home. What this does allow you to do is get very close up with a tiger, which is quite a thrill—those paws are massive indeed. Visitors are given little portable phonelike objects on which they can play a series of programs, listening to Roy and Mirage owner Steve Wynn discuss conservation or the attributes of each animal and deliver anecdotes.

The **Dolphin Habitat** is more satisfying. It was designed to provide a healthy and nurturing environment and to educate the public about marine mammals and their role in the ecosystem. Specialists worldwide were consulted in creating the habitat, which was designed to serve as a model of a quality, secured environment. The pool is more than eight times larger than government regulations require, and its 2.5 million gallons of man-made seawater are cycled and cleaned once every 2 hours. It must be working, as the adult dolphins here are breeding regularly. The Mirage displays only dolphins already in captivity—no dolphins will be taken from the wild. You can watch the dolphins frolic both above and below ground through viewing windows, in three different pools. (There is nothing quite like the kick you get from seeing a baby dolphin play.) The knowledgeable staff, who surely have the best jobs in Vegas, will answer questions. If they aren't doing it already, ask them to play ball with the dolphins; they toss large beach balls into the pools, and the dolphins hit them out with their noses, leaping out of the water cackling with dolphin glee. You catch the ball, getting nicely wet, and toss it back to them. If you have never played ball with a dolphin, shove that happy child next to you out of the way and go for it. There is also a video of a resident dolphin (Duchess) giving birth (to Squirt) underwater. You can stay as long as you like, which might just be hours.

Speedworld at Sahara. In the Sahara Hotel & Casino, 2535 Las Vegas Blvd. S. ☎ **702/737-2111.** Stock car simulator $8 (you must be at least 48 in. tall to ride); 3-D simulator $3; Speed-The Ride (rollercoaster) $7. Open daily at 10am; closing hour varies seasonally, but usually it's 10pm.

Since auto racing is the fastest-growing spectator sport in America, Speedworld is a popular stop. The first part is an 8-minute **virtual-reality ride** featuring a three-quarter-size replica of an NASCAR race car. Hop aboard for an animated, simulated ride—either the Las Vegas Motor Speedway or a race around the streets of Las Vegas. Press the gas and you lean back and feel the rush of speed; hit a bump and you go flying. Should your car get in a crash, off you go to a pit stop. At the end, a computer-generated report tells you your average speed, how many laps you made, how you did racing against the others next to you, and so forth. It's a pretty remarkable experience.

In a separate **3-D motion theater,** you'll don goggles to view a film that puts you right inside another race car for yet another stomach-churning ride (even more dizzying than the virtual-reality portion). Speed junkies and race-car buffs will be in heaven here, though those with tender stomachs should consider shopping at the well-stocked theme gift shop instead.

Speed: The Ride, is a new roller coaster that blasts riders out through a hole in the wall by the new NASCAR cafe, then through a loop, under the sidewalk, through the hotel's marquee, and finally straight up a 250 foot tower. At the peak, you feel a moment of weightlessness and then you do the whole thing backwards! Not for the faint of heart.

Stratosphere Thrill Rides. Atop the Stratosphere Las Vegas, 2000 Las Vegas Blvd. S. ☎ **702/380-7777.** Admission for Big Shot $6; for Roller Coaster $5; $3 per re-ride, plus $6 to ascend the tower (if you dine in the buffet room or Top of the World, there's no charge to go up to the tower). Multiride packages also available for varying costs. Sun–Thurs 10am–midnight, Fri–Sat 10am–1am. Minimum height requirement for both rides is 48 in.

Atop the 1,149-foot Stratosphere Tower are two marvelous thrill rides. The **Let It Ride High Roller** (the world's highest roller coaster) was recently revamped to go at even faster speeds as it zooms around a hilly track that is seemingly suspended in midair. Even more fun is the **Big Shot,** a breathtaking free-fall ride that thrusts you 160 feet in the air along a 228-foot spire at the top of the tower, then plummets back down again. Sitting in an open car, you seem to be dangling in space over Las Vegas. We have one relative, a thrill-ride enthusiast, who said he never felt more scared than when he rode the Big Shot. After surviving, he promptly put his kids on it; they loved it. *Note:* The rides are shut down in inclement weather and high winds.

2 Getting Married

This is one of the most popular things to do in Las Vegas. Why? It's very easy to get married here. Too easy. See that total stranger standing next to you? Grab him or her, and head down to the **Clark Country Marriage License Bureau,** 200 S. 3rd St., at Briger Avenue (☎ **702/455-3156;** open Monday to Sunday 8am to midnight, 24 hours legal holidays), to get your license. Find a wedding chapel (not hard since there are about 50 of them in town; they line the north end of the Strip, and most hotels have one), and tie the knot. Just like that. No blood test, no waiting period—heck, not even an awkward dating period.

We've listed four of our favorite chapels, though there are many more. The wedding chapels take care of everything; usually they'll even provide a limo to take you to the license bureau and back. Most offer all the accessories, from rings to flowers to a videotaped memory of the event. You can also call **Las Vegas Weddings and Rooms** (☎ **800/488-MATE**), which offers one-stop shopping for wedding services. They'll find a chapel or outdoor garden that suits your taste (not to mention such only-in-Vegas venues as the former mansions of Elvis Presley and Liberace), book you into a hotel for the honeymoon, arrange the ceremony, and provide flowers, a photographer (or videographer), wedding cake, limo, car rental, music, champagne, balloons, and a garter for the bride. Theme weddings are a specialty.

Weddings can be very cheap in Vegas: A license is about $35, and a basic service not much more. Even a full-blown shebang package photos, music, some flowers, video, cake, and other doodads—will run only about $500 total. We haven't quoted any prices here, since the ultimate cost depends entirely on how much you want to spend. Be sure to remember that there are often hidden charges, such as expected gratuities for the minister (about $25 would do; no real need to tip anyone else).

Cupid's Wedding Chapel. 827 Las Vegas Blvd. S. ☎ **800/543-2933** or 702/598-4444. www.cupidswedding.com. Sun–Thurs 10am–10pm, Fri–Sat 10am–1am.

"The little chapel with the big heart." Well, they just might be. The manager explains that, unlike other chapels on the Strip, they schedule weddings an hour apart; this gives them time for the full production number. The folks at Cupid's pride themselves on offering "a traditional church wedding at a chapel price." This includes a bridal processional, dimmed lights as the minister introduces the happy couple, and then a tape of the couple's favorite song, so they can have their first dance right there at the pulpit after their "first" kiss. They also offer family weddings for those couples blending pre-existing ones; the children become a part of the service, and as their parents exchange rings with each other, the kids are given their own small token, to let them know the parents are marrying them as well. "I am a die-hard romantic," said the manager, "I want huggin', kissin', and I don't care if they faint—a wedding is a place for romance." You just know she cries at each and every service they perform. The chapel is pleasantly low-frills and down to earth, with white walls and pews, and modern stained glass with doves and roses. (Kitsch-phobes will be pleased to know the cupids are only in the lobby.) It seats 60 to 70. And, yes, if they don't have something already scheduled, they will take walk-ups.

✪ **Divine Madness.** 111 Las Vegas Blvd. S. (½ block south of Fremont). ☎ **800/717-4734** or 702/384-5660.

Oh, yeah, now *this* is how to do a Vegas wedding. "From innocent lace to erotic leather," this place offers the chance to create your own fantasy wedding. You want to dress up like spacemen? They can do that. Kings and queens? No problem. Scarlett O'Hara? Kid stuff. They've got all the costumes on hand, including well-chosen accessories, and while said outfits may not look that spiffy in person, they will look fabulous in the photographs—and the photographs, after all, are why you have a wedding like this in the first place. The staff is as fun as they ought to be, comfortable, casual, and busy, and the whole thing is infectious, so watch out—you might well find yourself getting married as a cartoon character.

San Francisco Sally's Victorian Chapel. 1304 Las Vegas Blvd. S. ☎ **800/658-8677** or 702/385-7777. www.zip2.com/klas-tv/sfsally. Mon–Thurs 10am–6pm, Fri–Sat 10am–8pm, Sun 10am–4pm.

This is an extremely tiny wedding chapel bursting at the seams with Victorian frills (fringed lamps, swags of lace curtains). They basically offer "an Olde Tyme Parlor Wedding." This is perfect if you want a very intimate wedding—like you, your intended, and someone to officiate. It literally can't hold more than six people. (And the space at the back of the room opens for an even tinier reception area—it can barely fit the cake!) But if you love Victoriana, or you want to play dress-up at your wedding, this is the place. The shop rents out dresses and costumes, so you can wear a Scarlett O'Hara antebellum outfit or some other period number for your big day. (It's all fantasy anyway, so why not go whole hog?) They specialize in extras without extra charges, like altering and whatnot. The women who run it refer to themselves as "a bunch of mother hens"; they're delightful and will pamper you to within an inch of your life. (One couple drops in every year just to say hi.) Some may find it a bit cutesy, but it really is quite charming and has its own distinct personality, unlike most of the other chapels in the area. This is a decidedly special place that might be just right depending on your wedding desires and fantasies.

⊙ **A Special Memory Wedding Chapel.** 800 S. Fourth St. (at Gass Ave.). ☎ **800/962-7798** or 702/384-2211. www.aspecialmemory.com. Sun–Thurs 8am–10pm, Fri–Sat 8am–midnight.

This is a very nice, new-ish wedding chapel, particularly when compared to the rather tired facades of the classics on the Strip. This is absolutely the place to go if you want a traditional, big-production wedding; you won't feel in the least bit tacky. It's a New England church–style building, complete with steeple. The interior looks like a proper church (well, a plain one—don't think ornate Gothic cathedral) with a peaked roof, pews with padded red seats, modern stained-glass windows of doves and flowers, and lots of dark wood. It is all very clean and new and seats about 87 comfortably. There is a short staircase leading to an actual bride's room; she can make an entrance coming down it or through the double doors at the back. The area outside the chapel is like a minimall of bridal paraphernalia stores. Should all this just be too darn nice and proper for you, they also offer a drive-up window (where they do about 300 weddings a month!). It'll cost you $25—just ring the buzzer for service. They have a photo studio on-site and will do a small cake, cold cuts, and champagne receptions. There is a gazebo for outside weddings, and they sell T-shirts!

3 Especially for Kids

Like much of the rest of the world, you may be under the impression that Las Vegas has evolved from an adults-only fantasyland into a vacation destination suitable for the entire family. The only explanation for this myth is that Las Vegas was referred to as "Disneyland for adults" by so many and for so long that the town became momentarily confused and decided it actually *was* Disneyland. Some of the gargantuan hotels then spent small fortunes on redecorating in an attempt to lure families with vast quantities of junk food and a lot of hype. They now vehemently deny that any such notion ever crossed their collective minds, and, no, they don't know how that roller coaster got into the parking lot.

To put things simply, Las Vegas makes money—lots and lots of money—by promoting gambling, drinking, and sex. These are all fine pursuits if you happen to be an adult, but if you haven't reached the magical age of 21, you really don't count in this town. In any case, the casinos and even the Strip itself are simply too stimulating, noisy, and smoky for young kids.

Older progeny may have a tolerance for crowds and the incessant pinging of the slot machines, but they will be thoroughly annoyed with you when casino security chastises them if they so much as stop to tie their shoe laces anywhere near the gaming tables. Since you can't get from your hotel room to the parking lot without ambling through a casino, you can't reasonably expect a teenager to be in a good mood once you stagger outside. And those amusement parks and video halls that haven't yet been purged are expensive places to park your kids for an afternoon or evening, assuming they are old enough to be left unsupervised.

Nevertheless, you may have a perfectly legitimate reason for bringing your children to Las Vegas (like Grandma was busy, or you were just stopping off on your way from somewhere else), so here are some places to take the children both on and off the Strip.

Circus Circus (see p. 52) has ongoing circus acts throughout the day, a vast video-game and pinball arcade, and dozens of carnival games on its mezzanine level. Behind the hotel is the **Adventuredome,** detailed below.

Excalibur (see p. 27) also offers video and carnival games, plus thrill cinemas and free shows (jugglers, puppets, and so on).

At **Caesars Palace** (see p. 34), the Race for Atlantis IMAX ride is a thrill for everyone in the family; a video-game arcade adjoins the OMNIMAX Theatre. Animated talking statues in the **Forum Shops** are also a kick, while kids should also be wowed by clamoring around inside the giant moving Trojan horse outside FAO Schwarz, in the shops, and marveling at the Atlantis fountain show.

The ship battle in front of **Treasure Island** (see p. 44) is sure to please, as will the erupting volcano and the Secret Garden of Siegfried and Roy and Dolphin Habitat at the **Mirage** (see p. 112) and the new aquarium at **Mandalay Bay** (see p. 18). Ditto the various attractions at **Luxor Las Vegas** (the IMAX Theater, p. 110; King Tut's Tomb, p. 29; and simulator ride, p. 110) and Speedworld (p. 114) at the **Sahara.**

Children 10 and up will love the many options for play (from high tech to low tech, from video wonders to actual physical activity) offered at **GameWorks** (see p. 108), as will their parents.

Specifically kid-pleasing attractions are described below.

Adventuredome. 2880 Las Vegas Blvd. S. (behind Circus Circus). ☎ **702/ 794-3939.** Free admission; pay per ride. AE, DC, DISC, MC, V. Park hours vary; call ahead.

This isn't a half-bad place to spend a hot afternoon, especially now that Circus Circus, the casino/hotel that built this indoor amusement park, has undergone a face-lift. The glass dome that towers overhead lets in natural light, a solace to those of us who look peaked under the glow of the artificial kind. A double-loop roller coaster careens around the simulated Grand Canyon, and there's the requisite water flume, a laser tag area, and a modest number of other rides for kids of all ages. A dinosaur-bone excavation area will provide a good time for pre-schoolers, and a place to rest for the supervising adults. Video games and an arcade are separate from the attractions, cutting down just a tad on the noise level. Jugglers and magicians provide impromptu entertainment. Our only caveat is not to leave kids here alone; they could easily get lost.

Las Vegas Natural History Museum. 900 Las Vegas Blvd. N. (at Washington). ☎ **702/384-3466.** Admission $5.50 adults; $4.50 seniors, students, and military; $3 children 4–12; free for children under 4. Daily 9am–4pm.

Conveniently located across the street from the Lied Discovery Children's Museum (described below), this humble temple of taxidermy harkens back to elementary school field trips circa 1965, when stuffed elk and brown bears forever protecting their kill were as close as most of us got to exotic animals. Worn around the edges but very sweet and relaxed, the museum is enlivened by a hands-on activity room and two life-size dinosaurs that roar at one another intermittently. A small boy was observed leaping toward his dad upon watching this display, so you might want to warn any sensitive little ones that the big tyrannosaurs aren't going anywhere. Surprisingly, the gift shop here is particularly well stocked with neat items you won't mind too terribly buying for the kids.

Lied Discovery Children's Museum. 833 Las Vegas Blvd. N. (½ block south of Washington, across the street from Cashman Field). ☎ **702/382-5437.** Admission $5 adults, $4 seniors and children 2–17. Tues–Sun 10am–5pm.

A hands-on science museum designed for curious kids, the bright, airy, two-story Lied makes an ideal outing for toddlers and young children. With lots of interactive exhibits to examine, including a miniature grocery store, a tube for encasing oneself inside a soap bubble, a radio station, and music and drawing areas, you'll soon forget your video poker losses. Clever, thought-inducing exhibits are everywhere. Learn how it feels to be handicapped by playing basketball from a wheelchair. Feed a wooden "sandwich" to a cutout of a snake and to a human cutout, and see how much nutrition each receives. See how much sunscreen their giant stuffed mascot needs to keep from burning. On weekend afternoons from 1 to 3pm, free drop-in art classes are offered, giving you a bit of time to ramble around the gift store or read the fine print on the exhibit placards. The Lied also shares space with a city library branch, so after the kids run around, you can calm them back down with a story or two.

MGM Grand Adventures. Behind the MGM Grand Hotel, 3799 Las Vegas Blvd. S. ☎ **800/929-1111.** Admission $12.95 adults, free for children 42 in. and under. Sky Screamer: 1 person $35, 2 people $30 each, 3 people $25 each (includes general park admission). Open daily generally from Apr until Sept, closed the rest of the year.

This theme park, slapped together without a great deal of thought on a former parking lot, looks as if some Hollywood set designers dropped off a variety of hokey movie facades and then, unburdened, cheerfully rode off into the sunset. The attractions, such as a clothes-soaking log flume and kiddie bumper cars, are sparsely scattered among a great many food and T-shirt emporiums. It leaves you with the impression that fun has a lot to do with the contents of one's pocketbook and/or stomach. For some peculiar reason, the park sports three tiny boxing arenas where you and a friend can suit up like samurai and duke it out. This is also home of the **Sky Screamer,** a combination bungee jump/swing that will thrill kids old enough (and daring enough) to give it a try. (They must be at least 10 years old and 42 inches to ride the Screamer.) There is a separate charge for this ride on top of park admission. It's also fun just to sit on a bench and watch people on this contraption.

MGM Grand Youth Center. In MGM Grand Hotel, 3799 Las Vegas Blvd. S. ☎ **702/891-3200.** For children 3–12 (no diaper wearers). Daily 11am–11pm. Costs vary, depending upon season and whether you are a guest of the hotel (call ahead to get more information).

This is the sole child-care center on the Strip, and according to the genial manager, it's booked solid during summers and on holidays. MGM Grand hotel guests get first priority to leave their youngsters in a warren of brightly decorated and well-supervised, albeit windowless, rooms. Arts and crafts compete with Nintendo and videos for kids' attention, and there are no organized activities (although they do serve meals). You can pay through the nose to have a counselor accompany your child to the theme park (4 hours/$50), but it might be cheaper to bring along a babysitter. If we were children and our parents left us here on a family vacation, we'd never let them forget it.

Scandia Family Fun Center. 2900 Sirius Ave. (at Rancho Dr. just south of Sahara Ave.). ☎ **702/364 0070.** Free admission, but there's a fee for each game or activity. Super Saver Pass $11 (includes 1 round of miniature golf, 2 rides, and 5 game tokens); Unlimited Wristband Package $16 (includes unlimited bumper boat and car rides, unlimited miniature golf, and 10 tokens for batting cages or arcade games). Mar–Oct daily 24 hours; Nov–Feb Sun–Thurs 10am–11pm, Fri–Sat 24 hours.

This family-amusement center, located just a few blocks off the Strip, is still the most viable alternative for those who need to amuse children not quite old enough for GameWorks, or for those on a tighter budget. Certainly it's where local families come for outings, and they keep the batting cages hopping ($1.25 for 25 pitches). The arcade is a bit warm and stinky, and other parts (including miniature car racing and bumper boats, $4 per ride, small children ride free with an adult) are a bit worn, but the miniature golf course (three 18-hole courses, $5.50 per game, free for children under 6) is quite cute. Still, we do have to wonder about those round-the-clock weekend hours; we certainly hope those playing miniature golf at 4am are not parents accompanied by children.

Wet 'n' Wild. 2601 Las Vegas Blvd. S. (just south of Sahara Ave.). ☎ **702/ 871-7811.** www.wetnwild.com. Admission $24 adults, $12 seniors over 55, $18 children 3–10, free for children under 3. Early May–Sept 30 daily 10am–6 or 8pm (sometimes later). Season and hours vary somewhat from year to year, so call ahead.

When temperatures soar, head for this 26-acre water park right in the heart of the Strip and cool off while jumping waves, careening down steep flumes, and running rapids. There is a variety of slides and rides, plus a lazy river and a beach for those looking for more sedentary activities. The noise level can be extraordinarily high (people have to shout to be heard over the rushing water) so don't think of this as relaxing—but when it's 108° in the shade, who cares? Also, be on the lookout for discount coupons. Many Las Vegas packages include a free admission (sometimes partial day).

4 Fore! Great Desert Golf

In addition to the listings below, there are dozens of local courses, including some very challenging ones that have hosted PGA tournaments. *Note:* Greens fees vary radically depending on time of day and year.

If you're a serious golfer, you may want to contact **American Golf** (☎ 800/468-7918), a nationwide reservations service that's based in Arizona. They can help you arrange golf packages, and book hard-to-get tee times.

Angel Park Golf Club. 100 S. Rampart Blvd. (between Summerlin Pkwy. and Alta St.; 20 min. NW of the Strip). ☎ **888/446-5358** or 702/254-4653. www.angelpark.com. Greens fees $60–$145. Discounted twilight rates available.

This 36-hole par-70/71 public course is a local favorite. Arnold Palmer originally designed the Mountain and Palm courses (the Palm Course was redesigned several years later by Bob Cupp). Players call this a great escape from the casinos, claiming that no matter how many times they play it, they never get tired of it. The Palm Course has gently rolling fairways that offer golfers of all abilities a challenging yet forgiving layout. The Mountain Course has rolling natural terrain and gorgeous panoramic views. In addition to these two challenging 18-hole courses,

Angel Park offers a night-lit Cloud 9 Course (12 holes for daylight play, 9 at night), where each hole is patterned after a famous par-3. You can reserve tee times up to 60 days in advance with a credit card guarantee.

Yardage: Palm Course 5,857 championship, 5,438 resort; Mountain Course 6,235 championship, and 5,751 resort.

Facilities: Pro shop, night-lit driving range, 18-hole putting course, restaurant, snack bar, cocktail bar, and beverage cart.

Black Mountain Golf & Country Club. In nearby Henderson, 500 Greenway Rd. ☎ **702/565-7933.** Greens fees $55–$75.

Two new greens have recently been added to this 18-hole, par-72 semiprivate course, which requires reservations 4 days in advance. It's considered a great old course, with lots of wildlife, including roadrunners. However, unpredictable winds may blow during your game.

Yardage: 6,541 championship, 6,223 regular, and 5,478 ladies.

Facilities: Pro shop, putting green, driving range, restaurant, snack bar, and cocktail lounge.

Craig Ranch Golf Club. 628 W. Craig Rd. (between Losee Rd. and Martin Luther King Blvd.). ☎ **702/642-9700.** Greens fees $19 walking, $25 in golf cart.

This is a flat 18-hole, par-70 public course with many trees and bunkers; both narrow and open fairways feature Bermuda turf. The greens fees are a bargain, and you can reserve tee times 7 days in advance.

Yardage: 6,001 regular and 5,221 ladies.

Facilities: Driving range, pro shop, PGA teaching pro, putting green, and snack bar.

✪ **Desert Inn Golf Club.** 3145 Las Vegas Blvd. S. ☎ **702/733-4290.** Greens fees $160 for guests, $250 for non-guests (includes cart rental).

The Desert Inn course gets the nod from champions. It's an 18-hole, par-72 resort course, the most famous and demanding in Las Vegas, with many trees, doglegs, and bunkers. Narrow fairways feature Rye turf, and putting greens feature Bentgrass. *Golf Digest* calls it one of America's top resort courses and what Las Vegas golf is all about, although the high fees may keep it out of many golfers' reach. You can reserve 90 days in advance for Sunday to Thursday, 2 days in advance for Friday and Saturday.

Note: Just as we went to press, it was announced that the Desert Inn was closing, so the future of the golf course is uncertain, but we suspect that the golf course might remain. Call ahead to check on its current status.

Yardage: 7,150 championship, 6,715 regular, and 5,800 ladies.

Facilities: Driving range, putting green, pro shop, and restaurant.

Desert Rose Golf Club. 5483 Clubhouse Dr. (3 blocks west of Nellis Blvd., off Sahara Ave.). ☎ **702/431-4653.** Greens fees $53–$75. Cart rental $12 (walking is allowed).

This is an 18-hole, par-71 public course built in 1963 and designed by Dick Wilson/Joe Lee. Narrow fairways feature Bermuda turf. You can reserve tee times up to 7 days in advance.

Yardage: 6,511 championship, 6,135 regular, and 5,458 ladies.

Facilities: Driving range, putting and chipping greens, PGA teaching pro, pro shop, restaurant, and cocktail lounge.

Las Vegas National Golf Club. 1911 Desert Inn Rd. (between Maryland Pkwy. and Eastern Ave.). ☎ **702/796-0016.** Greens fees $180, including cart rental.

This is an 18-hole (about eight with water on them), par-72 public course, and a classic layout (not the desert layout you'd expect). If you play from the back tees, it can really be a challenge. The 1996 Las Vegas Invitational, won by Tiger Woods, was held here. Discounted tee times are often available. Reservations are taken up to 60 days in advance; a $5 to $7 fee applies.

Yardage: 6,815 championship, 6,418 regular, and 5,741 ladies.

Facilities: Pro shop, golf school, driving range, restaurant, and cocktail lounge.

5 Staying Active

You need not be a slot-hypnotized slug when you come to Vegas. The city and surrounding areas offer plenty of opportunities for active sports. In addition to many highly rated golf courses (described above), just about every hotel has a large swimming pool and health club, and tennis courts abound.

BOWLING The **Showboat Hotel & Casino,** 2800 E. Fremont St. (☎ **702/385-9153**), is famous for housing the largest bowling center in North America (106 lanes) and for being the oldest stop on the Professional Bowlers Tour. A major renovation a few years back made its premises bright and spiffy. Open 24 hours.

TENNIS   Tennis buffs should choose one of the many hotels in town that have tennis courts.

Bally's (☎ 702/739-4111) has eight night-lit hard courts. Fees per hour range from $10 to $15 for guests, $15 to $20 for non-guests. Facilities include a pro shop. Hours vary seasonally. Reservations are advised.

The **Flamingo Las Vegas** (☎ 702/733-3444) has four outdoor hard courts (all lit for night play) and a pro shop. It's open to the public daily from 7am to 7pm. Rates are $20 per hour for non-guests, $12 for guests. Lessons are available. Reservations are required.

In addition to hotels, the **University of Nevada–Las Vegas (UNLV),** Harmon Avenue just east of Swenson Street (☎ 702/895-0844), has a dozen courts (all lit for night play) that are open weekdays from 6am to 9:45pm, weekends 8am to 9pm. Rates are $5 per person per day. You should call before going to find out if a court is available.

6 A Side Trip to Hoover Dam

30 miles SE of Las Vegas

This is one of the most popular excursions from Las Vegas, visited by 2,000 to 3,000 people daily. Why should you join them? Because it's an engineering and architectural marvel and it changed the Southwest forever. Without it, you wouldn't even be going to Vegas. Kids may be bored, unless they like machinery or just plain big things, but expose them to it anyway, for their own good. (Buy them an ice cream and a Hoover Dam snow globe as a bribe.)

The tour itself is a bit cursory, but you do get up close and personal with the dam. Wear comfortable shoes; the tour involves quite a bit of walking. Try to take the tour in the morning to beat the desert heat and the really big crowds. You can have lunch out in Boulder City, and then perhaps drive back through the **Valley of Fire State Park,** which is about 60 magnificently scenic miles from Lake Mead (purchase gas before you start!).

GETTING THERE

Drive east on Flamingo or Tropicana to U.S. 515 south, which automatically turns into I-93 south and takes you right to the dam. This will involve a rather dramatic drive, as you go through Boulder City, come over a rise, and Lake Mead suddenly appears spread out before you. It's a beautiful sight. At about this point, the road narrows down to two lanes and traffic can slow considerably. On busy tourist days, this means the drive can take an hour or more.

Go past the turnoff to Lake Mead. As you near the dam, you'll see a five-story parking structure tucked into the canyon wall on your left. Park here ($2 charge) and take the elevators or stairs to the walkway leading to the new Visitor Center.

If you would rather go on an **organized tour, Gray Line** (☎ **702/384-1234**) offers several Hoover Dam packages, all of them including admission and a tour of the dam. When you're in Las Vegas, look for discount coupons in numerous free publications available at hotels. The 4½-hour **Hoover Dam Shuttle Tour** departs daily at 7:45, 9:45, and 11am and includes pickup, drop-off, and a stop at the Ethel M Chocolate Factory; the price is $29.50 for adults, $22.50 for children 2 to 9. Most elaborate is the **Grand Hoover Dam and Lake Mead Cruise Tour,** departing daily at 9:45am, which includes a 90-minute paddle wheeler cruise on Lake Mead with a light lunch available for an extra cost, plus admission to Hoover Dam; $45 for adults, $39 for children 2 to 9. You can inquire at your hotel sightseeing desk about other bus tours.

A LITTLE BACKGROUND

There would be no Las Vegas as we know it without the Hoover Dam. Certainly not the neon and glitz. In fact, the growth of the entire Southwest can be tied directly to the electricity that came from the dam.

Until the Hoover Dam was built, much of the southwestern United States was plagued by two natural problems: parched, sandy terrain that lacked irrigation for most of the year, and extensive flooding in spring and early summer when the mighty Colorado River, fed by melting snow from its source in the Rocky Mountains, overflowed its banks and destroyed crops, lives, and property. On the positive side, raging unchecked over eons, the river's turbulent, rushing waters carved the Grand Canyon.

In 1928, prodded by the seven states through which the river runs during the course of its 1,400-mile journey to the Gulf of

California, Congress authorized construction of a dam at Boulder Canyon (later moved to Black Canyon). The Senate's declaration of intention was that, "A mighty river, now a source of destruction, is to be curbed and put to work in the interests of society." Construction began in 1931. Because of its vast scope, and the unprecedented problems posed in its realization, the project generated significant advances in many areas of machinery production, engineering, and construction. An army of more than 5,200 laborers was assembled, and work proceeded 24 hours a day. Completed in 1936, 2 years ahead of schedule and $15 million under budget (let's see James Cameron top that!), the dam stopped the annual floods and conserved water for irrigation, industrial, and domestic use. Equally important, it became one of the world's major electrical generating plants, providing low-cost, pollution-free hydroelectric power to a score of surrounding communities. Hoover Dam's $165-million cost has been repaid with interest by the sale of inexpensive power to a number of California cities and the states of Arizona and Nevada. The dam is a government project that paid for itself—a feat almost as awe-inspiring as its engineering.

The dam itself is a massive curved wall, 660 feet thick at the bottom and tapering to 45 feet where the road crosses it at the top. It towers 726.4 feet above bedrock (about the height of a 60-story skyscraper) and acts as a plug between the canyon walls to hold back up to 9.2 trillion gallons of water in Lake Mead, the reservoir created by its construction. Four concrete intake towers on the lake side drop the water down about 600 feet to drive turbines and create power, after which the water spills out into the river and continues south.

All the architecture is on a grand scale, and the design has beautiful art deco elements, unusual in an engineering project. Note, for instance, the monumental 30-foot bronze sculpture, *Winged Figures of the Republic,* flanking a 142-foot flagpole at the Nevada entrance. According to its creator, Oskar Hansen, the sculpture symbolizes "the immutable calm of intellectual resolution, and the enormous power of trained physical strength, equally enthroned in placid triumph of scientific achievement."

The dam has become a major sightseeing attraction along with Lake Mead, America's largest artificial reservoir and a major Nevada recreation area.

Seven miles northwest of the dam on U.S. 93, you'll pass through **Boulder City,** which was built to house managerial and construction workers. Sweltering summer heat (many days it is 125°F) ruled out a campsite by the dam, whereas the higher elevation of Boulder City offered lower temperatures. The city emerged within a single year, turning a desert waste into a community of 6,000. By 1934, it was Nevada's third largest town.

TOURING THE DAM

The very nice **Hoover Dam Visitor Center,** a vast three-level circular concrete structure with a rooftop overlook, opened in 1995. You'll enter the Reception Lobby, where you can buy tickets; peruse informational exhibits, photographs, and memorabilia; and view three 12-minute video presentations (about the importance of water to life, the events leading up to the construction of Hoover Dam, and the construction itself as well as the many benefits it confers). Exhibits on the Plaza Level include interactive displays on the environment, habitation, and development of the Southwest, the people who built the dam, and related topics.

Yet another floor up, galleries on the Overlook Level demonstrate, via sculpted bronze panels, the benefits of Hoover Dam and Lake Mead to the states of Arizona, Nevada, and California. The Overlook Level additionally provides an unobstructed view of Lake Mead, the dam, the power plant, the Colorado River, and Black Canyon. (There are multiple photo opportunities throughout this trip.)

You can visit an exhibit center across the street where a 10-minute presentation in a small theater focuses on a topographical map of the 1,400-mile Colorado River. It also has a cafeteria. Notice, by the way, how the rest rooms in the center only have electric dryers, no paper towels. A tribute?

Thirty-minute tours of the dam depart from the Reception Lobby every 15 minutes or so daily, except Christmas. The Visitor Center opens at 8:30am, and the first tour departs soon after. The last tour leaves at 6pm, and the center closes at 6:30pm. Admission is $8 for adults, $7 for senior citizens, and $2 for children 6 to 16, free for children under 6. More extensive, and expensive, hard-hat tours are offered every half hour between 9:30am and 3:30pm; "survive the tour and you keep the hard hat!" Although it's not compulsory, it's not a bad idea to call in advance for the tour (☎ **702/294-3522**). Both tours, by the way, are "not recommended for claustrophobics or those persons with defibrillators."

The tour begins with a 561-foot elevator descent into the dam's interior, where an access tunnel leads to the Nevada wing of the power plant. (You only cross to Arizona on the hard-hat tour.) In the three stops on the regular tour, you see the massive turbines that generate the electricity using the water flow, go outside on the downriver side of the dam looking up at the towering structure (which is pretty awesome), and then go into one of the tunnels that contains a steel water diversion pipe that feeds the turbines. (It's one of the largest steel water pipes ever made—its interior could accommodate two lanes of automobile traffic.)

Some fun facts you might hear along the way: It took 6½ years to fill the lake. Though 96 workers were killed during the construction, contrary to popular myth, none were accidentally buried as the concrete was poured (it was poured only at a level of 8 inches at a time). Look for a monument to them outside— "they died to make the desert bloom"—along with one for their doggy mascot who was also killed, although after the dam was completed. Compare their wages of 50¢ an hour to their Depression-era peers, who made 5¢ to 30¢.

6

About Casino Gambling

What? You didn't come to Las Vegas for the Liberace Museum? We are shocked. *Shocked.*

Yes, there are gambling opportunities in Vegas. We've noticed this. You will, too. The tip-off will be the slot machines in the airport as soon as you step off the plane. Or the slot machines in the convenience stores as soon as you drive across the state line. Let's not kid ourselves, gambling is what Vegas is about. The bright lights, the shows, the showgirls, the food—it's all there just to lure you in and make you open your wallet. (The free drinks certainly help ease the latter as well.)

You can disappoint them if you want, but what would be the point? *This is Las Vegas.* You don't have to be a high roller. You would not believe how much fun you can have with a nickel slot machine. You won't get rich, but neither will most of those guys playing the $5 slots, either.

Of course, that's not going to stop anyone from trying. Almost everyone plays in Vegas with the hopes of winning The Big One. That only a few ever do win doesn't stop them from trying again and again and again. That's how the casinos make their money.

There is no system that's sure to help you win. Reading books and listening to others at the tables will help you pick up some tips, but if there were a surefire way to win, the casinos would have taken care of it (and we will leave you to imagine just what that might entail). Try to have the courage to walk away when your bankroll is up, not down. Remember, your children's college fund is just that, and not a gambling budget supplement.

1 The Games

As a rule of thumb, if you want to try a new game, we suggest you first read through these rules/explanations, and then go down and watch the game being played. Find an empty or near-empty table (daytime is better than night), preferably one with a very low minimum (Downtown may be your only hope these days) and ask the dealer to walk you through. Most are happy to do so. Then go back and read this section again—it will make a lot more sense at that point. And then, well, good luck!

BACCARAT

The ancient game of baccarat, or *chemin de fer,* is played with eight decks of cards. Firm rules apply, and there is no skill involved other than deciding whether to bet on the bank or the player. The dealer does all the other work.

Any beginner can play, but check the betting minimum before you sit down, as this tends to be a high-stakes game. The cards are shuffled by the croupier and then placed in a box that is called the "shoe." Players may wager on "bank" or "player" at any time. Two cards are dealt from the shoe and given to the player who has the largest wager against the bank, and two cards are dealt to the croupier acting as banker. If the rule calls for a third card (see rules on chart shown, below), the player or banker, or both, must take the third card. In the event of a tie, the hand is dealt over.

The object of the game is to come as close as possible to the number 9. To score the hands, the cards of each hand are totaled and the *last digit* is used. All cards have face value. For example: 10 plus 5 equals 15 (score is 5); 10 plus 4 plus 9 equals 23 (score is 3); 4 plus 3 plus 3 equals 10 (score is 0); and 4 plus 3 plus 2 equals 9 (score is 9). The closest hand to 9 wins.

Each player has a chance to deal the cards. The shoe passes to the player on the right each time the bank loses. If the player wishes, he or she may pass the shoe at any time.

Note: When you bet on the bank and the bank wins, you are charged a 5% commission. This must be paid at the start of a new game or when you leave the table.

BLACKJACK

The dealer starts the game by dealing each player two cards. In some casinos, they're dealt to the player face up, in others face down, but the dealer always gets one card up and one card down. Everybody plays against the dealer. The object is to get a total that is higher than that of the dealer without exceeding 21. All face cards count as 10; all other number cards except aces count as their number value. An ace may be counted as 1 or 11, whichever you choose it to be.

Starting at his or her left, the dealer gives additional cards to the players who wish to draw (be "hit") or none to a player who

Baccarat Rules

PLAYER'S HAND

Having

0-1-2-3-4-5	Must draw a third card.
6-7	Must stand.
8-9	Natural. Banker cannot draw.

BANKER'S HAND

Having	**Draws**	**Does Not Draw**
	When giving Player 3rd card of:	When giving Player 3rd card of:
3	1-2-3-4-5-6-7-8-9-10	8
4	2-3-4-5-6-7	1-8-9-10
5	4-5-6-7	1-8-9-10
6	6-7	1-2-3-4-5-8-9-10
7	*Must stand.*	
8-9	Natural. Player cannot draw.	

If the player takes no third card, the banker must stand on 6.
No one draws against a natural 8 or 9.

wishes to "stand" or "hold." If your count is nearer to 21 than the dealer's, you win. If it's under the dealer's, you lose. Ties are a push and nobody wins. After all the players are satisfied with their counts, the dealer exposes his or her facedown card. If his or her two cards total 16 or less, the dealer must "hit" (draw an additional card) until reaching 17 or over. If the dealer's total goes over 21, he or she must pay all the players whose hands have not gone "bust." It is important to note here that the blackjack dealer has no choice as to whether he or she should stay or draw. A dealer's decisions are predetermined and known to all the players at the table.

HOW TO PLAY

Here are eight "rules" for blackjack.

1. Place the number of chips that you want to bet on the betting space on your table.
2. Look at the first two cards the dealer starts you with. If your hand adds up to the total you prefer, place your cards *under*

your bet money, indicating that you don't wish any additional cards. If you elect to draw an additional card, you tell the dealer to "hit" you by making a sweeping motion with your cards, or point to your open hand (watch your fellow players).

3. If your count goes over 21, you go "bust" and lose, even if the dealer also goes "bust" afterward. Unless hands are dealt faceup, *you then turn your hand faceup on the table.*

4. If you make 21 in your first two cards (any picture card or 10 with an ace), you've got blackjack. *You expose your winning hand immediately,* and you collect 1½ times your bet, unless the dealer has blackjack, too, in which case it's a push and nobody wins.

5. If you find a "pair" in your first two cards (say, two 8s or two aces), you may "split" the pair into two hands and treat each card as the first card dealt in two separate hands. *Turn the pair faceup on the table,* place the original bet on one of these cards, then place an equal amount on the other card. *Split aces are limited to a one-card draw on each.*

6. You may double your original bet and make a one-card draw after receiving your initial two cards. *Turn your hand faceup* and you'll receive one more card facedown.

7. Anytime the dealer deals himself or herself an ace for the "up" card, you may insure your hand against the possibility that the hole card is a 10 or face card, which would give him or her an automatic blackjack. To insure, you place an amount up to one half of your bet on the "insurance" line. If the dealer does have a blackjack, you do not lose, even though he or she has your hand beat, and you keep your bet and your insurance money. If the dealer does not have a blackjack, he or she takes your insurance money and play continues in the normal fashion.

8. *Remember:* The dealer must stand on 17 or more and must hit a hand of 16 or less.

CRAPS

The most exciting casino action is always at the craps tables. Betting is frenetic, play fast-paced, and groups quickly bond yelling and screaming in response to the action.

THE POSSIBLE BETS

The craps table is divided into marked areas (Pass, Come, Field, Big 6, Big 8, and so on), where you place your chips to bet. The following are a few simple directions.

PASS LINE   A "Pass Line" bet pays even money. If the first roll of the dice adds up to 7 or 11, you win your bet; if the first roll adds up to 2, 3, or 12, you lose your bet. If any other number comes up, it's your "point." If you roll your point again, you win, but if a 7 comes up again before your point is rolled, you lose.

DON'T PASS LINE   Betting on the "Don't Pass" is the opposite of betting on the Pass Line. This time, you lose if a 7 or an 11 is thrown on the first roll, and you win if a 2 or a 3 is thrown on the first roll.

   If the first roll is 12, however, it's a push (standoff), and nobody wins. If none of these numbers are thrown and you have a point instead, in order to win, a 7 will have to be thrown before the point comes up again. A "Don't Pass" bet also pays even money.

COME   Betting on "Come" is the same as betting on the Pass Line, but you must bet *after* the first roll or on any following roll. Again, you'll win on 7 or 11 and lose on 2, 3, or 12. Any other number is your point, and you win if your point comes up again before a 7.

DON'T COME   This is the opposite of a "Come" bet. Again, you wait until after the first roll to bet. A 7 or an 11 means you lose; a 2 or a 3 means you win; 12 is a push, and nobody wins. You win if 7 comes up before the point. (The point, you'll recall, was the first number rolled if it was none of the above.)

FIELD   This is a bet for one roll only. The "Field" consists of seven numbers: 2, 3, 4, 9, 10, 11, and 12. If any of these numbers is thrown on the next roll, you win even money, except on 2 and 12, which pay to 2 to 1 (at some casinos 3 to 1).

BIG 6 AND 8   A "Big 6 and 8" bet pays even money. You win if either a 6 or an 8 is rolled before a 7.

ANY 7   An "Any 7" bet pays the winner 5 for 1. If a 7 is thrown on the first roll after you bet, you win.

"HARD WAY" BETS   In the middle of a craps table are pictures of several possible dice combinations together with the odds the casino will pay you if you bet and win on any of those combinations being thrown. For example, if 8 is thrown by having a 4 appear on each die, and you bet on it, the bank will pay 10 for 1; if 4 is thrown by having a 2 appear on each die, and you bet on it, the bank will pay 8 for 1; if 3 is thrown, the bank pays 15 for 1. You win at the odds quoted if the exact combination of numbers you bet on comes up. But you lose if either a 7 is rolled or if the number you bet on was rolled any way other than the "Hard Way" shown on the table. In-the-know gamblers tend to avoid "Hard Way" bets as an easy way to lose their money. And note that the odds quoted are not 3 to 1, 4 to 1, or 8 to 1; here the key word is *for*—that is, 3 for 1 or 8 for 1.

ANY CRAPS   Here you're lucky if the dice "crap out"—if they show 2, 3, or 12 on the first roll after you bet. If this happens, the bank pays 8 for 1. Any other number is a loser.

PLACE BETS   You can make a "Place Bet" on any of the following numbers: 4, 5, 6, 8, 9, and 10. You're betting that the number you choose will be thrown before a 7 is thrown. If you win, the payoff is as follows: 4 or 10 pays at the rate of 9 to 5; 5 or 9 pays at the rate of 7 to 5; 6 or 8 pays at the rate of 7 to 6. "Place Bets" can be removed at any time before a roll.

SOME PROBABILITIES

Because each die has six sides numbered from 1 to 6, and craps is played with a pair of dice, the probability of throwing certain numbers has been studied carefully. Professionals have employed complex mathematical formulas in searching for the answers. And computers have data-processed curves of probability.

Suffice it to say that 7 (a crucial number in craps) will be thrown more frequently than any other number over the long run, for there are six possible combinations that make 7 when you break down the 1 to 6 possibilities on each separate die. As to the total possible number of combinations on the dice, there are 36.

Comparing the 36 possible combinations, numbers, or point combinations, run as follows:

2 and 12 may be thrown in *1 way* only.

3 and 11 may be thrown in *2 ways.*

4 and 10 may be thrown in *3 ways.*

5 and 9 may be thrown in *4 ways.*

6 and 8 may be thrown in *5 ways.*

7 may be thrown in *6 ways.*

So 7 has an advantage over all other combinations, which, over the long run, is in favor of the casino. You can't beat the law of averages.

KENO

Easy to play, and offering a chance to sit down and converse between bets, keno is one of the most popular games in town—despite the fact that *the house percentage is greater than that of any other casino game!*

To play, you must first obtain a keno form, available at the counter in the keno lounge and in most Las Vegas coffee shops. In the latter, you'll usually find blank keno forms and thick black crayons on your table. Fill yours out, and a miniskirted keno runner will come and collect it. After the game is over, she'll return with your winning or losing ticket. If you've won, it's customary to offer a tip, depending on your winnings.

Looking at your keno ticket and the keno board, you'll see that it is divided horizontally into two rectangles. The upper half contains the numbers 1 through 40; the lower half contains the numbers 41 through 80. You can win a maximum of $50,000, even more on progressive games, though it's highly unlikely (the probability is less than a hundredth of a percent). Mark up to 15 out of the 80 numbers; bets range from about 70¢ on up. A one-number mark is known as a one-spot, a two-number selection is a two-spot, and so on. After you have selected the number of spots you wish to play, write the price of the ticket in the right-hand corner where indicated. The more you bet, the more you can win if your numbers come up. Before the game starts, you have to give the completed form to a keno runner or hand it in at the keno lounge desk, and pay for your bet. You'll get back a duplicate form with the number of the game you're playing on it. Then the game begins. As numbers appear on the keno board, compare them to the numbers you've marked on your ticket. After 20 numbers have appeared on the board, if you've won, turn in your ticket immediately for a payoff before the next game begins. Otherwise, you will forfeit your winnings, a frustrating experience to say the least.

On a straight ticket that is marked with one or two spots, all of your numbers must appear on the board for you to win anything. With a few exceptions, if you mark from 3 to 7 spots, three numbers must appear on the board for you to win anything. Similarly, if you mark 8 to 12 spots, usually at least five numbers must come up for you to win the minimum amount. And if you mark 13 to 15 spots, usually at least six numbers must come up for a winning ticket. To win the maximum amount ($50,000), which requires that all of your numbers come up, you must select at least 8 spots. The more numbers on the board matching the numbers on your ticket, the more you win. If you want to keep playing the same numbers over and over, you can replay a ticket by handing in your duplicate to the keno runner; you don't have to keep rewriting it.

In addition to the straight bets described above, you can split your ticket, betting various amounts on two or more groups of numbers. Helpful casino personnel in the keno lounge can assist you with combination betting.

POKER

There are lots of variations on the basic game, but one of the most popular is **Hold 'Em.** Five cards are dealt faceup in the center of the table, and two are dealt to each player. The player uses the best five of seven, and the best hand wins. The house dealer takes care of the shuffling and the dealing and moves a marker around the table to alternate the start of the deal. The house rakes 1% to 10% (it depends on the casino) from each pot. Most casinos include the usual seven-card stud, and a few have hi-lo split.

If you don't know how to play poker, don't attempt to learn at a table. Find a casino that teaches it in free gaming lessons.

Pai gow poker (a variation on poker) has become increasingly popular. The game is played with a traditional deck plus one joker. The joker is a wild card that can be used as an ace or to complete a straight, a flush, a straight flush, or a royal flush. Each player is dealt seven cards to arrange into two hands: a two-card hand and a five-card hand. As in standard poker, the highest two-card hand is two aces, and the highest five-card hand is a royal flush. The five-card hand *must* be higher than the two-card hand (if the two-card hand is a pair of sixes, for example, the five-card hand must be a pair of sevens or better). Any player's hand that is set incorrectly is an automatic loser. The object of the game is for both of the player's hands to rank higher than both of the banker's hands. Should one hand rank exactly the same as the banker's hand, this is a tie (called a "copy"), *and the banker wins all tie hands.* If the player wins one hand but loses the other, this is a "push," and no money changes hands. The house dealer or any player may be the banker. The bank is offered to each player, and each player may accept or pass. Winning hands are paid even money, less a 5% commission.

Caribbean stud poker is yet another variation on the basic game that is gaining in popularity. Players put in a single ante bet and are dealt five cards facedown from a single deck; they play solely against the dealer, who receives five cards, one of them faceup. Players are then given the option of folding, or may call by making an additional bet that is double their original ante. After all player bets have been made, the dealer's cards are revealed. If the dealer doesn't qualify with at least an ace/king combination, players are paid even money on their ante and their call bets are returned. If the dealer does qualify, each player's hand is compared to the dealer's. On winning hands, players receive even money on their ante bets, and call bets are paid out on a scale according to the value of their hands. The scale ranges from even money for a pair, to 100 to 1 on a royal flush, although there is usually a cap on the maximum payoff that varies from casino to casino.

An additional feature of Caribbean stud is the inclusion of a progressive jackpot. For an additional side bet of $1, a player may qualify for a payoff from a progressive jackpot. The jackpot bet only pays off on a flush or better, but you can win on this bet even if the dealer ends up with a better hand than you do. The odds of hitting a royal flush for the entire progressive jackpot are astronomical, but considering that Caribbean stud has a house advantage that is even larger than the one in roulette, if you're going to play, you might as well toss in the buck and pray.

ROULETTE

Roulette is an extremely easy game to play, and it's really quite colorful and exciting to watch. The wheel spins and the little ball bounces around, finally dropping into one of the slots, numbered 1 to 36, plus 0 and 00. You can bet on a single number, a combination of numbers, or red or black, odd or even. If you're lucky, you can win as much as 35 to 1 (see the table). The method of placing single-number bets, column bets, and others is fairly obvious. The dealer will be happy to show you how to "straddle" two or more numbers and make many other interesting betting combinations. Each player is given different-colored chips so that it's easy to follow the numbers you're on.

Some typical bets are indicated by means of letters on the roulette layout depicted here. The winning odds for each of these sample bets are listed. These bets can be made on any corresponding combinations of numbers.

SLOTS

You put the coin in the slot and pull the handle. What, you thought there was a trick to this?

The casinos make more from slots than from craps, blackjack, and roulette combined. There are 115,000 slot machines (not including video poker) in the county. Some of these are at the airport, steps from you as you deplane.

But in order to keep up with the increasing competition, the plain old machine, where reels just spin, has become nearly obsolete. The idea is still simple: Get three (sometimes four) cherries (clowns, sevens, dinosaurs, whatever) in a row and you win something. Each machine has its own combination. Some will pay you something with just one symbol showing; on most, the more combinations there are, the more opportunities for loot. Study each machine to learn what it does.

The **payback** goes up considerably if you bet the limit (from two to as many as 45 coins). But while the payoff can be much bigger, the odds *against* winning also go up when you put in the limit. (So if you hit something on a machine and realize your $25 win would have been $500 had you only put in more money, take a deep breath, stop kicking yourself, and remember you might not actually have hit that winning combination so easily had you bet the limit.)

Progressive slots are groups of machines where the jackpot gets bigger every few moments (just as lottery jackpots build up). Bigger and better games keep showing up; for example, there's Anchor Gaming's much-imitated **Wheel of Gold,** wherein if you get the right symbol, you get to spin a roulette wheel, which guarantees you a win of a serious number of coins. **Totem Pole** is the Godzilla of slot machines, a behemoth that allows you to spin up to three reels at once (provided you put in the limit).

Other gimmick machines include the popular **Wheel of Fortune** machines, slots that have a gorilla attempt to climb the Empire State Building, heading up as you win, and machines with themes like Elvis or the Three Stooges. And, of course, there are always those **Big Giant Slot** machines, gimmicky devices found in almost every casino. They may not win as often as regular slots (though there is no definite word on it one way or the other), but not only are they just plain fun to spin, they often turn into audience participation gambling, as watchers gather to cheer you on to victory.

Slot Clubs

If you play slots or video poker, it definitely pays to join a slot club. These so-called clubs are designed to attract and keep customers in a given casino by providing incentives: meals, shows, discounts on rooms, gifts, tournament invitations, discounts at hotel shops, VIP treatment, and (more and more) cash rebates. Join a slot club, and soon you too will be getting those great hotel rate offers—$20-a-night rooms, affordable rooms at the luxury resorts, even free rooms. (This is one way to beat the high hotel rates.) Of course, your rewards are greater if you play just in one casino, but your mobility is limited.

When you join a slot club (inquire at the casino desk), you're given something that looks like a credit card, which you must insert into an ATM-like device whenever you play. (Don't forget to retrieve your card when you leave the machine, as we sometimes do—though that may work in your favor if someone comes along and plays the machine without removing it.) The device tracks your play and computes bonus points.

Which slot club should you join? Actually, you join one at any casino where you play, since even the act of joining usually entitles you to some benefits. It's convenient to concentrate play where you're staying. It may also now factor into your airline choice—National Airlines is affiliated with both Harrah's and the Rio, and you can accumulate slot club points when you fly with them. Consider, though, particularly if you aren't a high roller, the slot clubs Downtown. You get more bang for your buck because you don't have to spend as much to start raking in the goodies.

If you want to compare the various slot clubs in depth, order a copy of Jeffrey Compton's *The Las Vegas Advisor Guide to Slot Clubs* ($9.95 plus shipping) at ☎ **800/244-2224**. Compton gives high ratings to the clubs at Caesars Palace, the Desert Inn, the Mirage, Treasure Island, The Flamingo Las Vegas, the Rio, the Sahara, Sam's Town, the Four Queens, the Golden Nugget, and Lady Luck.

Are there surefire ways to win on a slot machine? No. But you can lose more slowly. The slots are on computer timers, and there are times when they are hitting and times when they are not. A bank of empty slots probably (but not certainly) means they aren't hitting. Go find a line where lots of people are sitting around with trays full of money. A good rule of thumb is that if your slot doesn't hit something in four or five pulls, leave it and go find another.

SPORTS BOOKS

Most of the larger hotels in Las Vegas have sports book operations, which look a lot like commodities-futures trading boards. In some, almost as large as theaters, you can sit comfortably, occasionally in recliners and sometimes with your own video screen, and watch ball games, fights, and, at some casinos, horse races on huge TV screens. To add to your enjoyment, there's usually a deli/bar nearby that serves sandwiches, hot dogs, soft drinks, and beer. As a matter of fact, some of the best sandwiches in Las Vegas are served next to the sports books. Sports books take bets on virtually every sport (and not just who'll win, but what the final score will be, who'll be first to hit a home run, who'll be MVP, who'll wear red shoes, you name it). They are best during important playoff games or big horse races, when everyone in the place is watching the same event, shrieking, shouting, and moaning sometimes in unison. Joining in with a cheap bet (so you feel like you, too, have a personal stake in the matter) makes for bargain entertainment.

VIDEO POKER

Rapidly coming up on slots in popularity, video poker works the same way as regular poker, except you play against the machine. You are dealt a hand, you pick which cards to keep and which to discard, and then get your new hand. And, it is hoped, you collect your winnings. This is somewhat more of a challenge and more active than slots because you have some control (or at least illusion of control) over your fate, and it's easier than playing actual poker with a table full of folks who probably take it very seriously.

There are a number of varieties of this machine, with **Jacks Are Better, Deuces Wild,** and so forth. Be sure to study your machine before you sit down. (The best returns are offered on the **Jacks Are Wild** machines, when the payback for a pair of Jacks or better is two times your bet, and three times for three of a kind.) Some machines offer **Double Down:** After you have won, you get a chance to draw cards against the machine, with the higher card the winner. If you win, your money is doubled and you are offered a chance to go again. Your money can increase nicely during this time, and you can also lose it all very quickly, which is most annoying.

Technology is catching up with Video Poker, too. Now they even have touch screens, which offer a variety of different poker games, blackjack, and video slots—just touch your screen and choose your poison.

2 The Casinos

Everyone should casino-hop at least once to marvel at the spectacle and the sheer excess of it all. But beyond decoration, there isn't too much difference. You've got your slot machines, your gaming tables, and your big chandeliers.

Don't be a snob, and don't be overly dazzled by the fancy casinos. Sometimes you can have a better time at one of the older places Downtown, where stakes are lower, pretensions are nonexistent, and the clientele is often friendlier.

SOUTH STRIP

Excalibur. 3850 Las Vegas Blvd. S. ☎ **702/597-7777.**

As you might expect, the Excalibur casino is replete with suits of armor, stained-glass panels, knights, dragons, and heraldic banners, with gaming action taking place beneath vast iron-and-gold chandeliers fit for a medieval castle fortress. This all makes it fine for kitsch-seekers, but anyone who hates crowds or is sensitive to noise will hate it. The overall effect is less like a castle and more like a dungeon, albeit a dungeon of 100,000-plus square feet. A no-smoking area is a plus.

Luxor Las Vegas. 3900 Las Vegas Blvd. S. ☎ **702/262-4000.**

More accessible than ever thanks to the addition of the air-conditioned people-mover from Excalibur, the Luxor has been completely remodeled and, in our opinion, improved immeasurably. You enter through a giant temple gateway flanked by massive statues of Ramses. Gone is the space-wasting central area that used to contain the bathrooms, cashiers, and casino offices. This additional space gives the casino a much more airy feel, which gives it a low claustrophobia level—in parts, you can see all the way up the inside of the pyramid. King Tut heads and sphinxes adorn slot areas. Sports action unfolds on 17 large-screen TVs and 128 personalized monitors in Luxor's race and sports book.

We already felt inclined to like this casino thanks to a good run at blackjack, but the redesign has made it even more inviting.

Mandalay Bay. 3950 Las Vegas Blvd. S. ☎ **702/632-7777.**

"Elegant" gaming in a pre-fab, deliberate way, with a very high ceiling that produces a very low claustrophobia factor. Definitely the right place if you're looking for less hectic, less gimmick-intrusive play. Its layout makes it look airy, and it's marginally less confusing and certainly less overwhelming than many other casinos. Because it is so far off the Strip, there can be fewer walk-in players, but the presence of the House of Blues and the increasing popularity of rumjungle as a nightclub can mean a late-night influx of customers. There's also a big, ultra-comfortable sports book.

MGM Grand. 3799 Las Vegas Blvd. S. ☎ **702/891-7777.**

The world's largest casino at 171,500 square feet—we've been to countries that were smaller!—is divided into four themed areas, in a futile attempt to make it seem smaller. Many of the Wizard of Oz decorations have been removed, but spend an hour in here and you may feel like Dorothy after she got hit by the twister. One section features a high-roller slot area with machines that operate on coins valued at $100 and $500! The sports casino houses a big poker room, a state-of-the-art race and sports book, and the Turf Club Lounge. Carousels of progressive slots unique to the MGM Grand include the very popular Majestic Lions high-frequency $1 slot machines that pay out more than $1 million daily and Lion's Share $1 slots, which are capable of jackpots exceeding $1 million each at any time.

The Monte Carlo. 3770 Las Vegas Blvd. S. ☎ **702/730-7777.**

This place is all huge ceilings and white-light interiors: Obviously, they're trying to evoke gambling in Monaco. While the decor shows lots of attention, it perhaps had too much attention. Bulbs line the ceiling, and everywhere you look is some detail or other. It's busy on both your eyes and your ears. So despite the effort put in, it's not a pleasant place to gamble. There's a large and comfortable race and sports book area, with its own cocktail lounge.

✪ **New York–New York.** 3790 Las Vegas Blvd. S. ☎ **702/740-6969.**

Another theme-run-wild place: tuxes on the backs of gaming chairs, change carts that look like yellow cabs, and so forth, all set in a miniature New York City. It's all fabulous fun, but despite a low claustrophobia level (thanks to an unusually high ceiling), it is a major case of sensory overload. This may prove distracting. On the other hand, we won there, so we love it. Serious gamblers understandably may sniff at it all and prefer to take their business to a more seemly casino, but everyone else should have about the most Vegasy time they can.

Orleans. 4500 W. Tropicana Ave. ☎ **702/365-7111.**

This is not a particularly special gambling space, though it has a low claustrophobia level, but over the sound system they sometimes play Cajun and zydeco music, so you can two-step while you gamble, which can make losing somewhat less painful. It has all the needed tables, plus plenty of slots, including a Wheel of Fortune machine that works like those other roulette wheel slots, but in this case, actually plays the theme song from the TV show. It will even applaud for you if you win.

The Tropicana. 3801 Las Vegas Blvd. S. ☎ **702/739-2222.**

The Trop casino is quite good-looking, and, yes, highly tropical, with gaming tables situated beneath a massive stained-glass archway and art nouveau lighting fixtures. In summer, it offers something totally unique: swim-up blackjack tables located in the hotel's stunning 5-acre tropical garden and pool area. A luxurious high-end slot area has machines that take up to $100 on a single pull. Numerous tournaments take place here, and free gaming lessons are offered weekdays.

MID-STRIP

Bally's Las Vegas. 3645 Las Vegas Blvd. S. ☎ **702/739-4111.**

Bally's casino is large (the size of a football field), with lots of colorful signage. The big ceiling makes for a low claustrophobia level. The casino hosts frequent slot tournaments, and free gaming lessons are offered. There are also blackjack tables and slot/video-poker machines in Bally's Avenue Shoppes. There is not, however, a Big Giant Slot machine. For shame.

Barbary Coast. 3595 Las Vegas Blvd. S. ☎ **702/737-7111.**

The Barbary Coast is a 1890s-style casino ornately decorated with $2 million worth of gorgeous stained-glass skylights and signs, as well as immense crystal-dangling globe chandeliers over the gaming tables. It's kind of small, dark, and cluttered, but it's also old Las Vegas (and we mean "old" loosely) and small is rare on the Strip.

Bellagio. 3600 Las Vegas Blvd. S. ☎ **888/987-6667.**

The slot machines here are mostly encased in marble. How's that for upping the ante on classy? In all fairness, Bellagio comes the closest to re-creating the feel of gambling in Monte Carlo (the country, not the next-door casino), but its relentless good taste means this is one pretty forgettable casino. After all, we are suckers for a wacky theme, and European class just doesn't cut it. Sure, there are good touches—we always like a high ceiling to reduce the claustrophobia index, and the place is laid out in an easy-to-navigate grid with ultra-wide aisles, so walking through doesn't seem like such a crowded collision-course maze. (*Tip:* The main casino path is identified with black carpets.) And we won big here, so there's that. Anyway, the cozy sports book has individual TVs and entirely denlike leather chairs—quite, quite comfortable.

✪ **Caesars Palace.** 3570 Las Vegas Blvd. S. ☎ **702/731-7110.**

Caesars' casino is simultaneously the ultimate in gambling luxury and the ultimate in Vegas kitsch. Cocktail waitresses in togas parade about, as you gamble under the watchful gaze of faux-marble Roman statues. The very high ceiling makes for a very low claustrophobia level.

A notable facility is the state-of-the-art **Race and Sports Book,** with huge electronic display boards and giant video screens. (Caesars pioneered computer-generated wagering data that can be communicated in less than half a second, and has sophisticated satellite equipment that can pick up the broadcast of virtually any sporting event in the world.)

Most upscale of the Caesars gaming rooms is the intimate, European-style casino adjoining the **Palace Court** restaurant. It's a gorgeous and elegant place to gamble, but we've never won there, so we hate it.

The Flamingo Las Vegas. 3555 Las Vegas Blvd. S. ☎ **702/733-3111.**

If you've seen the movie *Bugsy,* you won't recognize this as Mr. Siegel's baby. We can't say for sure what their seemingly years-long casino renovation actually did. It all looks pretty much the same, but it might be marginally less confusing and tortuous a layout (trust us, anything is an improvement) with better, and most welcome, access to the street (before, you needed a trail of bread-crumbs and a lot of stamina to find your way out). We have to say that of all the casinos that qualify as older, this is the most pleasant one in which to play. Unfortunately, the gambler seems to be paying for it; no more daytime $3 blackjack. One of our favorite slot machines is here, but we won't tell you which one, to save it for ourselves. Sorry.

Gold Coast. 4000 W. Flamingo Rd. ☎ **702/367-7111.**

Adjacent to the Rio, this casino is not only well-lit but totally unique in Vegas: It has windows! It's a little thing, but it made us really excited. They also had a higher ratio of video-poker machines to slot machines, rather than the other way around.

Harrah's. 3475 Las Vegas Blvd. S. ☎ **702/369-5000.**

Confetti carpeting and fiber-optic fireworks overhead combine with murals and an overall Mardi Gras theme to make a festive environment. Does it help you win more? Who knows. But the different, better energy that has resulted from this recent, costly face-lift certainly couldn't hurt. Don't miss the "party pits," gaming-table areas where dealers are encouraged to wear funny hats, celebrate wins, and otherwise break the usual stern dealer facade. Singing, dancing, and the handing out of party favors have all been known to break out. (Gambling is supposed to be fun, so enjoy it!) There are no-smoking areas, and free gaming lessons are offered on weekdays.

The Imperial Palace. 3535 Las Vegas Blvd. S. ☎ **702/731-3311.**

The 75,000-square-foot casino here reflects the hotel's pagoda-roofed Asian exterior with a dragon-motif ceiling and giant wind-chime chandeliers. There is a no-smoking slot machine area separate from the main casino (as opposed to just another part of the room, at best, in other casinos), and a Breathalyzer for voluntary alcohol-limit checks on your way to the parking lot (useful, since there are nine bars on the casino premises). The Imperial Palace boasts an attractive 230-seat race and sports book; the room is tiered like a grandstand, and every seat has its own color monitor. One Big Giant Slot machine is red, white, and blue; try singing the National Anthem to it, and see if you win more money.

✪ **The Mirage.** 3400 Las Vegas Blvd. S. ☎ **702/791-7111.**

Gamble in a Polynesian village in one of the prettiest casinos in town. It has a meandering layout, and the low ceiling makes for a medium claustrophobia level, but neither of these things is overwhelming. This remains one of our favorite places to gamble. The elaborate race and sports book offers theater stereo sound and a movie-theater-size screen. It's one of the most pleasant, and popular, casinos in town, so it's crowded more often than not.

Paris–Las Vegas Casino. 3655 Las Vegas Blvd. S. ☎ **702/946-7000.**

Ringed by a rather Disney-esque ⅓-scale replica of the streets of Paris, this new casino is a very pleasant place to gamble, in that Vegas-gimmick kind of way. A tall ceiling adds to the illusion of trying to bust the bank while strolling outside; if nothing else, it has a much more airy, less stifling effect. It doesn't feel all that large, thanks to a meandering layout. It's also one of those gimmicky places real gamblers are appalled by. To heck with them, we say.

The Rio. 3700 W. Flamingo Rd. ☎ **702/252-7777.**

This Brazilian-themed resort's 85,000-square-foot casino is, despite the presence of plenty of glitter and neon, very dark. It has about the highest claustrophobia rating of the major casinos and seems very dated these days. Its sports book feels a little grimy. The waitresses wear scanty costumes (particularly in the back), probably in an effort to distract you and throw your game off. Do not let them. The part of the casino in the new Masquerade Village is considerably more pleasant (the very high ceilings help), though still crowded, plus the loud live show adds even more noise. There are no-smoking slot and gaming table areas.

Treasure Island. 3300 Las Vegas Blvd. S. ☎ **702/894-7111.**

Treasure Island's huge casino is highly themed. If you have ever been on Disney World's Pirates of the Caribbean and thought, "Gee, if only this were a casino," this is the place for you. Kids seem to be everywhere, because they are dazzled by the pirate stuff. Many people complain that they don't like the atmosphere here, possibly because that very theme backfires.

Throughout the casino, there's something called Slot 2000. Hit a button, and a video screen pops up showing a (female) casino worker, to whom you can talk. She will answer questions, send someone over with drinks, make reservations, and otherwise help make your time there better. If you win a jackpot, she'll come on and congratulate you. No, she can't see you, so don't try to flirt.

There are no-smoking gaming tables in each pit. A race and sports book boasts state-of-the-art electronic information boards and TV monitors at every seat as well as numerous large-screen monitors.

The Venetian. 3355 Las Vegas Blvd. S. ☎ **702/414-1000.**

"Tasteful" is the watchword in these days of classy Vegas gaming, and consequently, with the exception of more hand-painted Venetian art re-creations on parts of the ceiling, the Venetian's casino is interchangeable with those found at Mandalay Bay, the Monte Carlo, and to a certain extent, Bellagio. All that gleaming marble, columns, and such is very nice, but after a while, also a bit ho-hum. Besides, this is Vegas, and we want our tacky theme elements, by gosh. The lack thereof, combined with poor signage, may be why this casino is so hard to get around—every part looks exactly the same. It's not precisely claustrophobic, but it can be confusing. Plus, there is no (at this writing) Big Giant Slot machine. On the other hand, we made a killing at blackjack, so we love the place.

NORTH STRIP

Circus Circus. 2880 Las Vegas Blvd. S. ☎ **702/734-0410.**

This vast property has three full-size casinos that, combined, comprise one of the largest gaming operations in Nevada (more than 100,000 square feet). More importantly, they have an entire circus midway set up throughout, so you are literally gambling with trapeze stunts going on over your head. The other great gimmick is the slot machine carousel—yep, it turns while you spin the reels. Circus Bucks progressive slot machines here build from a jackpot base of $500,000, which players can win on a $2 pull. There's also a 10,000-square-foot race and sports book with 30 video monitors. Unfortunately, the casino is crowded and noisy, and there are lots of children passing through. That, plus some low ceilings (not in the Big Top, obviously), make for a very high claustrophobia rating

The Riviera. 2901 Las Vegas Blvd. S. ☎ **702/734-5110.**

The Riviera's 100,000-square-foot casino, one of the largest in the world, offers plenty of opportunities to get lost and cranky. A wall of windows lets daylight stream in (most unusual). Nickeltown is just that—nothin' but nickel slots and video poker. The race and sports book here offers individual monitors at each of its 250 seats, and this is one of the few places in town where you can play the ancient Chinese game of *sic bo.*

The Sahara. 2535 Las Vegas Blvd. S. ☎ **702/737-2111.**

This is one place where there seem to be more tables than slots and video-poker machines. It also has good deals like $1 craps, but with that comes the kind of people who are drawn by $1 craps—belligerent drunks and other fun-killing folks. When we were last there, they had a whole row of Piggy Bankin' machines that were all paying off, so we were happy. The Sahara runs frequent slot tournaments and other events.

The Stardust. 3000 Las Vegas Blvd. S. ☎ **702/732-6111.**

Always mobbed, this popular casino features 90,000 square feet of lively gaming action, including a 250-seat race and sports book with a sophisticated satellite system and more than 50 TV monitors airing sporting events and horse-racing results around the clock. If you're a novice, take advantage of the free gaming lessons. We usually do well there, so even though it's a little loud, we like it. Check out those $1 slots just inside the front door—they've been very good to us.

The Stratosphere. 2000 Las Vegas Blvd. S. ☎ **702/380-7777.**

Originally set up to evoke a world's fair but ending up more like a circus, the Stratosphere redid its whole casino area to make it more appealing for the many adults who were staying away in droves. The newly redone facility aims for class but doesn't necessarily achieve it. It's not that it fails—it just no longer has any identity at all. They heavily advertise their high payback on certain slots and video poker: 98% payback on dollar slots and 100% payback on quarter video poker (if you bet the maximum on each). We can't say we noticed a difference, but other people around us were winning like crazy. There's a test area for new slot games, a Harley slot area with motorcycle-seat stools, and a high-roller slot room ($5 minimum bet) where chairs move up and down and can vibrate to give you a back massage while you play.

Westward Ho Hotel & Casino. 2900 Las Vegas Blvd. S. ☎ **702/ 731-2900.**

This small but centrally located Strip casino hosts many slot tournaments.

EAST OF THE STRIP

✪ **Hard Rock Hotel & Casino.** 4455 Paradise Rd. ☎ **702/693-5000.**

Where Gen X goes to gamble. The Hard Rock has certainly taken casino decor to a whole new level. The attention to detail and the resulting playfulness is admirable, if not incredible. Gaming tables have piano keyboards at one end; some slots have Fender guitar fretboards as arms; gaming chips have band names and/or pictures on them; slot machines are similarly rock-themed (check out the Jimi Hendrix machine!); and so it goes. The whole thing is set in the middle of a circular room, around the outskirts of which are various rock memorabilia in glass cases. Rock blares over the sound system, allowing boomers to boogie while they gamble. All this is genuinely amazing, but the noise level is above even that of a normal casino and we just hated it. We are in the minority, though; most people love it (that's why we gave it a star anyway), so assume you will be one of them.

A bank of slots makes gambling an act of charity: Environmentally committed owner Peter Morton (the Hard Rock's motto is "Save the Planet") donates profits from specified slots to organizations dedicated to saving the rain forests. The race and sports book here provides comfortable seating in leather-upholstered reclining armchairs. Gaming facilities include selected no-smoking tables.

✪ **Las Vegas Hilton.** 3000 Paradise Rd. ☎ **702/732-7111.**

The casino has two parts, thanks to the space-themed portion adjacent to Star Trek: The Experience. In an area designed to look like a spaceport, you find space-themed slot machines, many of which have no handles—just pass your hand through a light beam to activate. You'll find other gimmicks throughout the casino (though already some have been dropped since the recent opening), including urinals that give you an instant "urinalysis"— usually suggesting this is your lucky day to gamble. We do like a well-designed space in which to lose our money.

Over in the original casino section, Austrian crystal chandeliers add a strong touch of class. The casino is actually medium-size, but it does have an enormous sports book—at 30,500 square feet, the world's largest race and sports book facility. It, too, is a luxurious precinct equipped with the most advanced audio, video, and computer technology available, including 46 TV monitors, some as large as 15 feet across. In fact, its video wall is second in size only to NASA's. The casino is adjacent to the lobby but is neither especially loud nor frantic.

Sam's Town. 5111 Boulder Hwy. (at Nellis Blvd.). ☎ **702/456-7777.**

In its three immense floors of gaming action (153,083 square feet, second only to the MGM Grand in size), Sam's Town maintains the friendly, just-folks ambience that characterizes the entire property. The casino is adorned with Old West paraphernalia and is looking a bit less dated thanks to some recent sprucing up. Sam's Town claims its friendliness extends to looser slots. Free gaming lessons are offered weekdays from 11am to 4pm, poker lessons at other times. Gaming facilities include a race and sports book with more than 60 monitors, and a no-smoking slot area.

DOWNTOWN

✪ **Binion's Horseshoe.** 128 E. Fremont St. (between Casino Center Blvd. and First St.). ☎ **702/ 382-1600.**

Professionals who know say that "for the serious player, the Binions are this town." Benny Binion could neither read nor write, but boy, did he know how to run a casino. His venerable establishment has been eclipsed over the years, but it claims the highest betting limits in Las Vegas on all games (probably in the entire world, according to a spokesperson). It offers single-deck blackjack and $2 minimums, 10-times odds on craps, and high progressive jackpots. Real gamblers won't consider going anywhere else.

We especially like the older part of the casino here, which looks like a turn-of-the-century Old West bordello, though it has a very high claustrophobia level. They have two Big Giant Slot machines, at least one of which has been very, very good to us.

The California Hotel/Casino. 12 Ogden Ave. (at 1st St.). ☎ **702/ 385-1222.**

The California is a festive place filled with Hawaiian shirts and balloons. This friendly facility actually provides sofas and armchairs in the casino area—an unheard-of luxury in this town. This is the first place we found our favorite Piggy Bankin' machines.

El Cortez. 600 Fremont St. (between 6th and 7th sts.). ☎ **702/385-5200.**

This casino is one of the last shreds of pre-1980s Las Vegas, which is either wonderful or horrible depending on your view. Features frequent big-prize drawings (up to $50,000) based on your Social Security number. It's also popular for low limits (10¢ roulette and 25¢ craps).

Fitzgeralds. 301 Fremont St. (at 3rd St.). ☎ **702/388-2400.**

Fitzgeralds recently redid its casino in greens and golds, and the overall effect is not quite as tacky as you might expect. In fact, it's rather friendly and with a medium to low claustrophobia level. The casino actually has two levels: From the upstairs part, you can access a balcony from which you get an up-close view of the Fremont Street Experience. Their mascot, Mr. O'Lucky (a costumed leprechaun), roams the casino. You don't have to be nice to him.

Blackjack, craps, and keno tournaments are frequent events here. Slot machines that paid back over 100% the previous week are marked with a Mr. Lucky sign. Several slot machines have cars as prizes, fun books provide two-for-one gaming coupons, and there are $1-minimum blackjack tables. They have dollar Piggy Bankin' machines.

The Four Queens. 202 Fremont St. (at Casino Center Blvd.). ☎ **702/ 385-4011.**

The Four Queens is New Orleans–themed, with turn-of-the-century-style globe chandeliers, which make for good lighting and a low claustrophobia level. It's small, but the dealers are helpful, which is one of the pluses of gambling in the more manageably sized casinos.

The facility boasts the world's largest slot machine. It's more than 9 feet high and almost 20 feet long; six people can play it at one time! It's the Mother of all Big Giant Slot machines, and frankly, it intimidates even us. Here is also the world's largest blackjack table (it seats 12 players). Slot, blackjack, and craps tournaments are frequent events, and there are major poker tournaments every January and September. The casino also offers exciting multiple-action blackjack (it's like playing three hands at once with separate wagers on each).

Fremont Hotel & Casino. 200 E. Fremont St. (between Casino Center Blvd. and 3rd St.). ☎ **702/385-3232.**

This 32,000-square-foot casino offers a relaxed atmosphere and low gambling limits ($2 blackjack, 25¢ roulette). It's also surprisingly open and bright for a Downtown casino. Just 50¢ could win you a Cadillac or Ford Mustang here, plus a progressive cash jackpot. No Big Giant Slot machine, though.

✪ **The Gold Spike.** 400 Ogden Ave. (at Las Vegas Blvd.). ☎ **702/ 384-8444.**

Okay, we usually criticize dingy, time-forgotten Downtown spaces, and the Gold Spike certainly lands in that category. So what? Here, everyone is equal, and everyone is having a good time, or at least they can sincerely join you in your misery. Think 1970s shag carpeting, faux-wood paneling, and best-not-thought-too-hard-about 49¢ shrimp cocktails. Best of all, they have penny slots! (Not very many, to be sure, and getting a seat at one can require patience.) Hey tightwads, take a buck and spend a few hours.

The Golden Gate. 1 Fremont St. ☎ **702/382-3510.**

This is one of the oldest casinos Downtown, and though its age is showing, it's still fun to go there. As you might expect from the name, old San Francisco artifacts and decor abound. At one end of the narrow casino is the bar, where a piano player performs ragtime jazz, which is better than the homogenized pop offered in most casino lounges. Unfortunately, the low ceiling, dark period wallpaper, and small dimensions give this a high claustrophobia level.

The Golden Nugget. 129 E. Fremont St. (at Casino Center Blvd.). ☎ **702/385-7111.**

Frankly, this is not the standout that other casino properties owned by Steve Wynn are. It goes for luxury, of course, but there's too much crammed into too little space. That's not to say we didn't like it, because we won a lot of money here. And compared to most other Downtown properties, this is the most like the Strip. Despite the overcrowding, it has a much cleaner and fresher feeling than many of the dingy, time-forgotten spaces Downtown. There are blackjack tables with $1 minimum bets.

Jackie Gaughan's Plaza Hotel/Casino. 1 Main St. (at Fremont St.). ☎ **702/386-2110.**

This is old Vegas, with an attempt at '60s glamour (think women in white go-go boots). Now it's a little worn. Cautious bettors will appreciate the $1 blackjack tables and penny slots here.

Lady Luck. 206 N. 3rd St. (at Ogden Ave.). ☎ **702/477-3000.**

Even though Lady Luck is an older casino with the anticipated drop in glamour, it's surprisingly cheerful and with a low to medium claustrophobia level. Decorations give it a festive quality, and cocktail waitresses push drink carts to mix you up something right on the spot. Liberal game rules are attractive to gamblers. You can play "fast-action hold 'em" here—a combination of 21, poker, and pai gow poker.

○ **Main Street Station.** 200 N. Main St. (between Fremont St. and I-95). ☎ **702/387-1896.**

Part of an old hotel that has been recently renovated and reopened to great success, this is the best of the Downtown casinos, at least in terms of comfort and a pleasant environment. Even the Golden Nugget, nice as it is, has more noise and distractions. The decor here is, again, classic Vegas/Victorian-era San Francisco, but with extra touches (check out the old-fashioned fans above the truly beautiful bar) that make it work much better than other attempts at same. Strangely, it seems just about smoke-free, perhaps thanks in part to a very high ceiling. The claustrophobia level is zero.

Showboat. 2800 Fremont St. (between Charleston Blvd. and Mojave Rd.). ☎ **702/385-9123.**

The Showboat's casino, recently renovated, has a Mardi Gras/Bourbon Street theme. It's not the most elaborate in town, but it is certainly clean, friendly, and comfortable. At night, a jazz band plays from an open pavilion. The Showboat's enormous 24-hour bingo parlor is a facility also noted for high payouts. If you're traveling with kids ages 2 to 7, you can leave them at an in-house baby-sitting facility free for 3 hours while you gamble. Older kids can be dropped at the Showboat's 106-lane bowling center.

7

Shopping

*U*nless you're looking for souvenir decks of cards, Styrofoam dice, and miniature slot machines, Las Vegas is not exactly a shopping mecca. It does, however, have several noteworthy malls that can amply supply the basics. And many hotels also offer comprehensive, and sometimes highly themed, shopping arcades, most notably Caesars Palace and the Venetian (details below).

You might consider driving **Maryland Parkway,** which runs parallel to the Strip on the east and has just about one of everything: Target, Toys 'R' Us, several major department stores, Tower Records, major drugstores (in case you forgot your shampoo and don't want to spend $8 on a new one in your hotel sundry shop), some alternative-culture stores (tattoo parlors and hip clothing stores), and so forth. It goes on for blocks.

1 The Malls

Boulevard Mall. 3528 S. Maryland Pkwy. (between Twain Ave. and Desert Inn Rd.). ☎ **702/732-8949.** Mon–Fri 10am–9pm, Sat 10am–8pm, Sun 11am–6pm.

The Boulevard is the largest mall in Las Vegas. Its 144-plus stores and restaurants are arranged in arcade fashion on a single floor occupying 1.2 million square feet. Geared to the average consumer (not the carriage trade), it has anchors like Sears, JCPenney, Macy's, Dillard's, and Marshalls. Other notables include The Disney Store, The Nature Company, a 23,000-square-foot Good Guys (electronics), Gap, Gap Kids, The Limited, Victoria's Secret, Colorado (for outdoor clothing and gear), and African and World Imports. You can find just about anything you need here. There's free valet parking.

DFS Galleria. 3057 Las Vegas Blvd. S. (just north of the Desert Inn). ☎ **702/731-6446.** Daily 10:30am–midnight.

If the words *duty-free shopping* are sacred to you, then come here for a collection that includes Estée Lauder, Burberry, Cartier, Bulgari, Dendi, Bally, Ferragamo, Coach, Le Sport, and Christian

Dior. Note that it's contained in a mall that caters to an Asian clientele, so there are some interesting import stores plus a very good dim sum restaurant.

Fashion Show Mall. 3200 Las Vegas Blvd. S. (at the corner of Spring Mountain Rd.). ☎ **702/369-0704.** Mon–Fri 10am–9pm, Sat 10am–7pm, Sun noon–6pm.

This luxurious and centrally located mall, one of the city's largest, is about to become even bigger, thanks to an expansion that will include the city's first Nordstrom's. The mall presently comprises more than 130 shops, restaurants, and services. It is anchored by Neiman Marcus, Saks Fifth Avenue, Macy's, Robinsons-May, and Dillard's. There are several card and book shops, a wide selection of apparel stores for the whole family, jewelers, shoe stores, and gift and specialty shops. There are dozens of eating places. Valet parking is available, and you can even arrange to have your car hand-washed while you shop.

The Galleria at Sunset. In nearby Henderson, 1300 W. Sunset Rd. (at Stephanie St., just off I-515). ☎ **702/434-0202.** Mon–Sat 10am–9pm, Sun 11am–6pm.

This is a 1-million-square-foot Southwestern-themed shopping center, 9 miles southeast of Downtown Las Vegas. Anchored by four department stores (Dillard's, JCPenney, Mervyn's California, and Robinsons-May), the Galleria has 110 of the usual mall suspects. Dining facilities include an extensive food court and two restaurants.

The Meadows. 4300 Meadows Lane (at the intersection of Valley View and U.S. 95). ☎ **702/878-4849.** Mon–Fri 10am–9pm, Sat–Sun 10am–7pm.

Another immense mall, The Meadows comprises 144 shops, services, and eateries, anchored by four department stores: Macy's, Dillard's, Sears, and JCPenney. In addition, there are 15 shoe stores, a full array of apparel for the entire family (including maternity wear, petites, and large sizes), and an extensive food court. Fountains and trees enhance the Meadows's ultramodern, high-ceilinged interior, and there are a few comfortable conversation/seating areas for resting your feet a moment.

2 Factory Outlets

Las Vegas has a big factory-outlet center just a few miles past the southern end of the Strip (see below). If you don't have a car, you

can take a no. 301 CAT bus from anywhere on the S,
change at Vacation Village to a no. 303.

Dedicated bargain hunters may want to make the roug
40-minute drive along I-15 (there's also a $10 shuttle from Nev
York–New York) to the **Fashion Outlet at Primm** (☎ **888/
424-6898**), right on the border of California and Nevada. On
your left is a large factory outlet with some designer names
prominent enough to make that drive well worthwhile—
Kenneth Cole, Donna Karan, even Prada, among several others.
Why so far out of town? Our guess is because all these designers
have full-price boutiques in various hotels, and they don't want
you ignoring those in favor of discounted items.

Belz Factory Outlet World. 7400 Las Vegas Blvd. S. (at Warm Springs Rd.).
☎ **702/896-5599.** Mon–Sat 10am–9pm, Sun 10am–6pm.

Belz houses 145 air-conditioned outlets, including a few dozen
clothing stores and shoe stores. It offers an immense range of
merchandise at savings up to 75% off retail prices. Among other
emporia, you'll find Adolfo II, Casual Corner, Levi's, Nike, Dress
Barn, Oshkosh B'Gosh, Leggs/Hanes/Bali, Esprit, Aileen, Bugle
Boy, Carters, Reebok, Spiegel, Guess Classics, Oneida, Spring-
maid, We're Entertainment (Disney and Warner Bros.), Bose
(electronics), Danskin, Van Heusen, Burlington, Royal Doulton,
Lennox (china), Waterford (crystal), and Geoffrey Beene here.
There is also a carousel.

3 Hotel Shopping Arcades

Just about every Las Vegas hotel offers some shopping opportunities. The following have the most extensive arcades. The physical spaces of these shopping arcades are always open, but
individual stores keep unpredictable hours.

Note: The Forum Shops at Caesars and the Grand Canal shops
at the Venetian—as much sightseeing attractions as shopping
arcades—are in the must-see category.

BELLAGIO   The Via Bellagio collection of stores isn't as big as
some of the other mega-hotel shopping arcades, but here it's
definitely quality over quantity. It's a veritable roll call of glossy
magazine ads: Armani, Prada, Chanel, Tiffany, Hermès, Fre
Leighton, Gucci, and Moschino. That's it. You need anything
else? Well, yes—money. A nice touch is a parking lot by the far
entrance to Via Bellagio, so you need not navigate the great

gio's main parking structure, but can simply
rself up a little something.

ACE   Since 1978, Caesars has had an
...hops called the **Appian Way.** Highlighted
....cnse white Carrara-marble replica of Michelangelo's
~avid standing more than 18 feet high, its shops include the
aptly named Galerie Michelangelo (original and limited-edition
artworks), jewelers (including branches of Ciro and Cartier), a
logo merchandise shop, and several shops for upscale men's and
women's clothing. All in all, a respectable grouping of hotel
shops, and an expansion is in the works.

But in the hotel's tradition of constantly surpassing itself, in
1992 Caesars inaugurated the fabulous ✪ **Forum Shops,**
an independently operated 250,000-square-foot Rodeo-Drive-
meets-the-Roman-Empire affair complete with a 48-foot triumphal arch entranceway, a painted Mediterranean sky that
changes as the day progresses from rosy-tinted dawn to twinkling
evening stars, acres of marble, lofty scagliola Corinthian columns
with gold capitals, and a welcoming goddess of fortune under
a central dome. And at the Festival Fountain, seemingly immov-
able "marble" Animatronic statues of Bacchus (slightly in his
cups), a lyre-playing Apollo, Plutus, and Venus come to life for a
7-minute revel with dancing waters and high-tech laser-light
effects. The shows take place every hour on the hour. The whole
thing is pretty incredible, but also very Vegas—particularly the
Bacchus show, which is truly frightening and bizarre. Even if you
don't like shopping, it's worth the stroll just to giggle.

More than 70 prestigious emporia here include Louis Vuitton,
Plaza Escada, Bernini, Christian Dior, A/X Armani Exchange,
bebe, Caché, Gucci, Ann Taylor, and Gianni Versace, along with
many other clothing, shoe, and accessory shops. Other notables
include a Warner Brothers Studio Store (a sign at the exit reads
THATIUS FINITUS FOLKUS), The Disney Store, Kids Kastle (beautiful children's clothing and toys), Rose of Sharon (classy styles for
large-size women), Sports Logo (buy a basketball signed by
Michael Jordan for $695!), Museum Company (reproductions
ranging from 16th-century hand-painted Turkish boxes to ancient
Egyptian scarab necklaces), West of Santa Fe (Western wear and
Native American jewelry and crafts), Antiquities (neon Shell gas
signs, 1950s malt machines, Americana; sometimes "Elvis" is on
hand), and the Endangered Species Store (ecology-themed

merchandise). There's much more, including jewelry shops and art galleries.

And as if that weren't enough, in 1998, the Forum Shops added an extension. The centerpiece is a giant **Roman Hall,** featuring a 50,000-gallon circular aquarium and another fountain that also comes to life with a show of fire (don't stand too close—it gets really hot), dancing waters, and Animatronic figures as the mythical continent of Atlantis rises and falls every hour. The production values are much higher than the Bacchus extravaganza, but it takes itself more seriously, so the giggle factor remains. The hall is also the entrance to the **Race for Atlantis IMAX 3-D ride** (see chapter 5).

In this shopping area, you'll find a number of significant stores, including a DKNY, Emporio Armani, Niketown, Fendi, Polo for Ralph Lauren, Guess, Virgin Megastore, and FAO Schwarz. Do go see the latter, as it is fronted by a gigantic Trojan horse, in which you can clamber around, while its head moves and smoke comes out its nostrils. We love it. Also in the shops is Wolfgang Puck's Chinois, a Cheesecake Factory, and a Caviartorium, where you can sample all varieties of the high-priced fish eggs.

And if that weren't all still enough, yet another expansion is underway as you read this!

The shops are open Sunday to Thursday 10am to 11pm, Friday and Saturday 10am to midnight.

EXCALIBUR   The shops of **"The Realm"** for the most part reflect the hotel's medieval theme. Dragon's Lair, for example, features items ranging from pewter swords and shields to full suits of armor, and Merlin's Mystic Shop carries crystals, luck charms, and gargoyles. Other shops carry more conventional wares. At Fantasy Faire, you can have your photo taken in Renaissance attire. And most important, they have a branch of Krispy Kreme donuts!

HARRAH'S   Harrah's has finished up a massive new renovation that includes a new shopping center called **Carnivale Court.** It's a small outdoor shopping promenade and among the store highlights is a Ghirardelli Chocolate store, a branch of the famous San Francisco–based chocolate company. Other stores include On Stage (a CD and video store) and Carnival Corner (gourmet foods and cigars). You might also swing into the hotel and examine the artwork found in **The Art of Gaming,** which is all gambling-related.

THE MGM GRAND   The hotel's **Star Lane Shops** include more than a dozen upscale emporia lining the corridors en route from the monorail entrance. The Knot Shop carries designer ties by Calvin Klein, Gianni Versace, and others. El Portal features luggage and handbags—Coach, Dior, Fendi, Polo Ralph Lauren, and other exclusive lines. Grand 50's carries Route 66 jackets, Elvis T-shirts, photos of James Dean, and other mementos of the 1950s. MGM Grand Sports sells signed athletic uniforms, base-balls autographed by Michael Jordan, and the like; it is the scene of occasional appearances by sports stars such as Floyd Patterson and Stan Musial. You can choose an oyster and have its pearl set in jewelry at The Pearl Factory. Other Star Lane Shops specialize in movie memorabilia, Betty Boop merchandise, *EFX* wares, chil-dren's clothing, decorative magnets, MGM Grand logo items and Las Vegas souvenirs, seashells and coral, candy, and sunglasses.

THE MONTE CARLO   An arcade of retail shops here includes Bon Vivant (resort wear for the whole family, dress wear for men), Crown Jewels (jewelry, leather bags, crystal, Fabergé eggs, and gift items), a florist, logo shop, jeweler, food market, dessert store, and Lance Burton magic paraphernalia shop.

THE RIO   The new 60,000-square-foot **Masquerade Village** is a nicely done addition to the Rio. It's done as a European vil-lage, and is two stories, featuring a wide variety of shops includ-ing the nation's largest Nicole Miller, Speedo, and the N'awlins store, which includes "authentic" voodoo items, Mardi Gras masks, and so forth.

THE STRATOSPHERE   Shopping is no afterthought here. The internationally themed second-floor **Tower Shops** prome-nade, which will soon house 40 stores, is entered via an escalator from the casino. Some shops are in "Paris," along the Rue Lafayette and Avenue de l'Opéra (there are replicas of the Eiffel Tower and Arc de Triomphe in this section). Others occupy Hong Kong and New York City streetscapes.

TREASURE ISLAND   Treasure Island's shopping promenade has wooden ship figureheads and battling pirates suspended from its ceiling. Emporia here include the Treasure Island Store (your basic hotel gift/sundry shop, also offering much pirate-themed merchandise, plus a section devoted to Calvin Klein clothing), Loot 'n' Booty, Candy Reef, Captain Kid's (children's clothing), and Damsels in Dis'Dress (women's sportswear and accessories).

The Mutiny Bay Shop, in the video-game arcade, carries logo items and stuffed animals. In the casino are the Buccaneer Bay Shoppe (logo merchandise) and the Treasure Chest (a jewelry store; spend those winnings right on the spot). And the Crow's Nest, en route to the Mirage monorail, carries Cirque du Soleil logo items. Cirque du Soleil and *Mystère* logo wares are also sold in a shop near the ticket office.

✪ **THE VENETIAN**   The **Grand Canal Shoppes** are a direct challenge to Caesars. As in the Forum Shops, you stroll through a re-created Italian village—in this case, more or less Renaissance-era Venice, complete with a painted, cloud-studded blue sky overhead, and a canal right down the center on which gondoliers float and sing. Pay them ($12) and you can take a lazy float down and back, serenaded by your boatsman (actors hired especially for this purpose and with accents perfect enough to fool Roberto Begnini). As you pass by, under and over bridges, flower girls will serenade you and courtesans will flirt with you, and you may have an encounter with a famous Venetian or two, as Marco Polo discusses his travels, and Casanova exerts his famous charm. The stroll (or float) ends at a miniature (though not by all that much) version of St. Mark's Square, the central landmark of Venice. Here, plans are to have more opera singers, strolling musicians, glass blowers, and other bustling marketplace activity. It's all most ambitious and beats the heck out of Animatronic statues.

The Shoppes are accessible directly from outside (so you don't have to navigate miles of casino and other clutter), via a grand staircase whose ceiling features more of those impressive hand-painted art re-creations. It's quite smashing. The Venetian's "Phase Two" hotel addition will some day adjoin the Shoppes at the far end of St. Mark's Square.

Oh, the shops themselves? The usual high- and medium-end brand names: Jimmy Choo, Mikimoto, Movado, Davidoff, Lana Marks, Kieselstein-Cord, Donna Karan, Oliver & Col, Ludwig Reiter, Kenneth Cole, Ann Taylor, BCBG, bebe, Banana Republic, Rockport, and more, plus Venetian glass and paper makers. Our favorite store here, hands down, is ✪ **Sephora** (☎ **702/ 735-3896;** open daily 10am–midnight), the ultimate girly store, offering just about every high-end department-store cosmetic and perfume line on earth.

At the entrance is a 55,000-square-foot Warner Bros. complex that will include a restaurant along with retail shops and screening rooms. Madame Tussaud's waxworks is also located here, and so is the Canyon Ranch Spa Club.

4 Vintage Clothing

The Attic. 1018 S. Main St. ☎ **702/388-4088.** Daily 10am–6pm.

The Attic shares a large space with **Cafe Neon,** a coffeehouse that also serves Greek-influenced cafe food, and a comedy club stage; it's also upstairs from an attempt at a weekly club (as of this writing, the Saturday-night Underworld). The store itself, former star of a Visa commercial, has plenty of clothing choices on many racks. During a recent visit, a man came in asking for a poodle skirt for his 8-year-old. They had one.

Buffalo Exchange. 4110 S. Maryland Pkwy. (at Flamingo, near Tower Records). ☎ **702/791-3960.** Mon–Sat 11am–7pm, Sun noon–6pm.

This is actually part of a chain of such stores spread out across the western United States. If the chain part worries you, don't let it—this merchandise doesn't feel processed. Staffed by plenty of incredibly hip alt-culture kids (ask them what's happening in town during your visit), it is stuffed with dresses, shirts, pants, and so forth. Like any vintage shop, the contents are hit or miss. You can easily go in one day and come out with 12 fabulous new outfits, but you can just as easily go in and come up dry. But it's still probably the most reliable of the local vintage shops.

5 Souvenirs

Now, you'd think Vegas would be THE place for kitschy souvenirs—the town itself is such a bastion of good taste, after all. But alas, even by generous standards, most of the crap sold is, well, crap. But there are a few places for some of your snow globe and fuzzy dice needs.

The **Arts Factory Complex,** 103 E. Charleston Blvd. (☎ 702/382-3886), has a gift shop full of pink flamingos and Vegas-specific items. There should be something here for every camp fancy.

But if you prefer your souvenirs to be less deliberately iconic, head over to the **Bonanza Gift and Souvenir Shop,** 2460 Las Vegas Blvd. S. (☎ 702/384-0005). We looked, and we felt the tackiest item available was the pair of earrings made out of poker chips.

For reverent camp, encrusted with sequins, do take a peek at the **Liberace Museum gift store,** 1775 E. Tropicana Ave. (☎ **702/ 798-5595**). Encourage them to get even more out there (don't you think they should add Liberace mouse pads and screen savers?).

If you like your souvenirs with more style (spoil sports), **Cirque de Soliel's "O"** has a gift shop in the Bellagio, 3600 Las Vegas Blvd. S. (☎ **702/693-7444**), with Cirque-specific articles, but also fanciful pottery, masks, and other curiosities.

6 Candy

M&M World. In the Showcase Mall, 3785 Las Vegas Blvd. S. ☎ **702/ 736-7611.** Sun–Thurs 10am–midnight, Fri–Sat 10am–1am.

Everybody needs one vice and for us, it's chocolate, by gosh. Its lure is so powerful it overwhelms our usual snooty stance against anything even remotely resembling a tourist trap and leads us right to M&M World. What can one do when faced with a wall of M&M's in colors never before seen by man (black! hot pink! turquoise!)? Overpriced? Hell, yeah! Who cares? There are doo-dads galore, replete with the M&M logo, and a surprisingly enjoyable short film and comedy routine, ostensibly about the "history" of the candy, but really just a cute little adventure with a decent budget behind it, and well worth the $3 admission.

7 Antiques

Antiques in Vegas? You mean really old slot machines, or the people playing the really old slot machines?

Actually, Vegas has quite a few antiques stores—nearly two dozen, of consistent quality and price, nearly all located within a few blocks of each other. We have one friend, someone who takes interior design very seriously, who comes straight to Vegas for most of her best finds (you should see her antique chandelier collection!).

To get there, start in the middle of the **1600 block of East Charleston Boulevard** and keep driving east. The little stores, nearly all in old houses dating from the '30s, line each side of the street. Or you can stop in at **Silver Horse Antiques,** 1651 E. Charleston Blvd. (☎ **702/385-2700**), and pick up a map to almost all the locations, with phone numbers and hours of operation.

Sampler Shops Antique Mall. 6115 W. Tropicana Ave. ☎ **702/368-1170.**
Mon–Sat 10am–6pm, Sun noon–6pm.

Head here for everything under one roof. More than 200 small
antiques shops sell their wares in this mall, which offers a diversity
of antiques ranging from exquisite Indian birdcages to *Star Wars*
memorabilia (let's not call those sorts of items "antiques" but
rather "nostalgia"). Changing selections of course mean you can
never guarantee what will be available, but you can probably
count on antique clothing and shoes, lamps, silver, decorative
plates and china, old sewing machines, antique furniture, and
'50s prom dresses. The displays are well labeled and well laid out,
making it easy to take in all the antiques. The oldest antiques are
from the mid-1800s and range in price from $100 to $4,000.

8

Las Vegas After Dark

*T*his is a town that truly comes alive only after dark. Don't believe us? Just look at the difference between the Strip during the day, when it's kind of dingy and nothing special, and at night when the lights hit and the place glows in all its glory. Night is when it's happening in this 24-hour town. In fact, most bars and clubs don't even get going until close to midnight.

But you also won't lack for things to do before 11pm. There are shows all over town, ranging from traditional magic shows to cutting-edge acts like *Mystère*. The showgirls remain, topless and otherwise; Las Vegas revues are what happened to vaudeville, by the way, as chorus girls do their thing in between jugglers, comics, magicians, singers, and specialty acts of dubious category.

Every hotel has at least one lounge, usually offering live music. But the days of fabulous Vegas lounge entertainment, when the lounge acts were sometimes of better quality than the headliners (and headliners like Sinatra would join the lounge acts on stage between their own sets), are gone. Most of what remains is homogeneous and bland, and serves best as a brief respite or background noise. On the other hand, finding the most awful lounge act in town can be a rewarding pursuit of its own.

Vegas still does attract some dazzling headliner entertainment in its showrooms and arenas. Bruce Springsteen played his first Vegas show ever in early 2000, while Bette Midler did a millennium show at Mandalay Bay, the Rolling Stones played both the MGM Grand and the Hard Rock Hotel's Joint, Pavarotti inaugurated Mandalay Bay's Arena, with Bob Dylan doing the same for the House of Blues, and Cher opened up the Venetian with a rare live performance. It is still a badge of honor for comedians to play Vegas, and there is almost always someone of marquee value playing one showroom or the other.

Admission to shows runs the gamut, from about $28 for *An Evening at La Cage* (a female impersonator show at the Riviera) to $90 and more for top headliners or *Siegfried and Roy.* Prices usually include two drinks or, in rare instances, dinner.

To find out who'll be performing during your stay and for up-to-date listings of shows (prices change, shows close), you can call the various hotels, using their toll-free numbers. Or call the **Las Vegas Convention and Visitors Authority** (☎ 702/892-0711) and ask them to send you a free copy of *Showguide* or *What's On in Las Vegas* (one or both of which will probably be in your hotel room). You can also check out what's playing at **www.lasvegas24hours.com**. It's best to plan well ahead if you have your heart set on seeing one of the most popular shows, or catching a major headliner.

More rock bands are coming to town, attracted to the House of Blues, the Hard Rock Hotel's Joint, or the Huntridge Theater, so that means you can actually see folks like Marilyn Manson and Beck in Vegas. But otherwise, the alternative club scene in town is no great shakes. If you want to know what's playing during your stay, consult the local free alternative papers: the *Las Vegas Weekly* (actually biweekly, with great club and bar descriptions in their listings) and *City Life* (weekly, with no descriptions but comprehensive listings of what's playing where all over town). Both can be picked up at restaurants, bars, record and music stores, and hip retail stores.

In addition to the listings below, consider the **Fremont Street Experience,** described in chapter 5.

1 What's Playing Where

The big resort hotels, in keeping with their general over-the-top tendencies, are pouring mountains of money into high-spectacle extravaganzas, luring big-name acts into decades-long residencies and surrounding them with special effects that would put some Hollywood movies to shame. Which is not to say the results are Broadway quality—they're big, cheesy fun. Still, with the exception of the astonishing work done by both Cirque du Soleil productions, most of what passes for a "show" in Vegas is just a flashier revue, with a predictable lineup of production number/magic act/production number/acrobatics/production number.

Unfortunately, along with big budgets and big goals come big-ticket prices. Sure, you can still take the whole family of four to a show for under $100, but you're not going to see the same production values that you'd get by splurging on *EFX*. Which is not to say you always get what you pay for: There are some reasonably priced shows that are considerably better values than their more expensive counterparts.

Note: Although every effort has been made to keep up with the volatile Las Vegas show scene, keep in mind that the following reviews may not be indicative of the actual show you'll see, but the basic concept and idea will be the same.

The following section will describe each of the major production shows currently playing in Las Vegas, arranged alphabetically by the title of the production. But first, here's a handy list arranged by hotel:

- **Bally's:** ✪ *Jubilee!* (Las Vegas–style revue)
- **Bellagio:** ✪ Cirque du Soleil's *O* (unique circus-meets-performance-art theatrical experience)
- **Excalibur:** *Tournament of Kings* (medieval-themed revue)
- **Flamingo Las Vegas:** *Forever Plaid* (off-Broadway revue featuring '60s music) and *The Great Radio City Spectacular* (Las Vegas–style revue featuring the Radio City Music Hall Rockettes)
- **Harrah's:** Harrah's always has a show or revue, but their 2001 offering was still unannounced at press time.
- **Imperial Palace:** *Legends in Concert* (musical impersonators)
- **Jackie Gaughan's Plaza:** *Kenny Kerr's Boylesque* (female impersonators)
- **The Luxor:** ✪ *Blue Man Group: Live at Luxor* (hilarious performance art)
- **MGM Grand:** ✪ *EFX* (special-effects revue featuring Tommy Tune)
- **The Mirage:** ✪ *Siegfried and Roy* (magical extravaganza); *Danny Gans* (impressions)
- **Monte Carlo:** ✪ *Lance Burton: Master Magician* (magic show and revue)
- **Rio Suites:** *At the Copa* (production show starring David Cassidy)
- **Riviera Hotel:** *An Evening at La Cage* (female impersonators), *Crazy Girls* (sexy Las Vegas–style revue), and *Splash* (aquatic revue)
- **Stratosphere Tower:** *American Superstars* (an impression-filled production show) and *Viva Las Vegas* (Las Vegas–style revue)

- **Treasure Island:** ✪ Cirque du Soleil's *Mystère* (unique circus performance)
- **Tropicana:** *Folies Bergère* (Las Vegas–style revue)

2 The Major Production Shows

American Superstars. In the Stratosphere Las Vegas, 2000 Las Vegas Blvd. S. ☎ **800/99-TOWER** or 702/380-7711.

One of an increasing number of celebrity impersonator shows (well, it's cheaper than getting the real headliners), *American Superstars* is one of the few in which said impersonators actually sing live. Five performers do their thing; the celebs impersonated vary depending on the evening.

A typical Friday night featured Gloria Estefan, Charlie Daniels, Madonna, Michael Jackson, and Diana Ross and the Supremes. (And recently they added the Spice Girls—the catty among us will notice the impersonators have better figures than the real Girls.) The performers won't be putting the originals out of work anytime soon, but they aren't bad. The youngish crowd (by Vegas standards) included a healthy smattering of children and seemed to find no faults with the production.

Showroom Policies: No smoking; maître d' seating.

Price: $22.95, including tax.

Show Times: Sun–Tues at 7pm; Wed and Fri–Sat at 7 and 10pm; dark Thurs.

Reservations: Up to 3 days in advance.

At the Copa. In the Rio Suites, 3700 W. Flamingo Rd. ☎ **702/252-7777.**

"Well, I'm completely in love with David Cassidy now," said one otherwise naturally jaded audience member, and that sums up the appeal of this show. The one-time teen heartthrob has matured into a wholly likable, all-around entertainer—not overwhelmingly talented in any one area, but more than capable and charismatic in all of them. He seems like he's having a whale of a good time, and his enthusiasm rubs off.

Oh, the show? Well, it's the story of nightclub performers Johnny Flamingo (Cassidy) and Ruby Bombay (as of this writing, Sheena Easton) and their tragic love story. In other words, it's a showcase for Cassidy and whoever ends up being his co-star. The songs run the gamut from standards to weird choices to the leads' respective hits, making for a confusing mix. Alas, though Ms.

Easton has the vocal chops, she's a lox of a performer. The story-line, staging, costume choices, and Fosse-esque choreography are all "borrowed," rather shamelessly, straight from the hit revival of *Chicago,* but at least they tried. And the 18-piece live orchestra is a treat in this town. If you really care about the staging, try to get seats either close up or in second or third tiers of the showroom for better sightlines. Also, the production is just a bit too racy for younger children.

Showroom Policy: No smoking; pre-assigned seating.

Price: $58 (includes one drink, tax, and gratuity).

Show Times: Tues and Sat 7 and 9:30pm; Sun and Wed–Fri 8pm; dark Mon.

Reservations: Taken 45 days in advance.

⭐ **Blue Man Group: Live at Luxor.** In the Luxor Las Vegas, 3900 Las Vegas Blvd. S. ☎ **702/262-4000.**

Are they blue? Indeed they are—three hairless, non-speaking men dipped in azure paint, doing decidedly odd stunts with marshmallows, art supplies, audience members, tons of paper, and an amazing array of percussion instruments fashioned fancifully from PVC piping. If that doesn't sound very Vegas, well, it's not. It's the latest franchise of a New York–originated performance-art troupe that seems to have slipped into town through a side door opened by Cirque de Soleil's groundbreaking successes. Don't get the wrong idea; this is no Cirque clone. There's no acrobatics or flowing choreography, no attempt to create an alternate universe, just a series of unconnected bits. But even if the whole is no greater than the sum of the parts, the parts are pretty great themselves.

Showroom Policy: No-smoking; pre-assigned seating.

Price: $71.50 and $60.50 (includes tax and gratuity).

Show Times: Sun–Mon 7pm; Wed–Sat 7pm and 10pm; dark Tues.

Reservations: Taken 3 months in advance.

⭐ **Cirque du Soleil's *Mystère*.** In Treasure Island, 3300 Las Vegas Blvd. S. ☎ **800/392-1999** or 702/796-9999. www.cirquedusoleil.com.

The in-house ads for *Mystère* (say miss-*tair*) say "Words don't do it justice," and for once, that's not just hype. The show is so visual that trying to describe it is a losing proposition. And simply calling it a circus is like calling the Hope Diamond a gem, or the Taj Mahal a building. It's accurate but doesn't begin to do it justice.

Cirque du Soleil began in Montréal as a unique circus experience, not only shunning the traditional animal acts in favor of gorgeous feats of human strength and agility, but also adding elements of the surreal and the absurd. The result seems like a collaboration between Salvador Dalí and Luis Buñuel, with a few touches by Magritte and choreography by Twyla Tharp. Mirage Resorts has built the troupe its own theater, an incredible space with an enormous dome and super-hydraulics that allow for the Cirque performers to fly in space. Or so it seems.

While part of the fun of the early Cirque was seeing what amazing stuff they could do on a shoestring, seeing what they can do with virtually unlimited funds is spectacular. Cirque took full advantage of this new largesse, and their art only rose with their budget. The show features one simply unbelievable act after another (seemingly boneless contortionists and acrobats, breathtakingly beautiful aerial maneuvers), interspersed with Dadaist/Commedia dell'Arte clowns, and everyone clad in costumes like nothing you've ever seen before. All this and a giant snail.

The show is dreamlike, suspenseful, funny, erotic, mesmerizing, and just lovely. However, for some children, it might be a bit too sophisticated and arty. Even if you've seen Cirque before, it's worth coming to check out, thanks to the large production values. It's a world-class show, no matter where it's playing. That this is playing in Vegas is astonishing.

Showroom Policies: No smoking; pre-assigned seating.

Price: $68 per person (tax and drinks extra).

Show Times: Wed–Sun at 7:30 and 10:30pm; dark Mon–Tues.

Reservations: You can reserve by phone via credit card up to 7 days in advance (make sure to reserve early, since it often sells out).

✪ **Cirque du Soleil's O.** In Bellagio, 3600 Las Vegas Blvd. S. ☎ **888/488-7111** or 702/693-7722.

How to describe the indescribable wonder and artistry of Cirque du Soleil's latest and most dazzling display? An Esther Williams–Busby Berkeley spectacular on peyote? A Salvador Dalí painting come to life? A stage show by Fellini? The French troupe has topped itself with this production—and not simply because

> ## ⓘ Family-Friendly Shows
>
> Appropriate shows for kids, all described in this chapter, include the following:
>
> - **Tournament of Kings** at Excalibur *(see p. 180)*
> - **Siegfried and Roy** at the Mirage *(see p. 178)*
> - **Lance Burton** at the Monte Carlo *(see p. 176)*
> - **EFX** at the MGM Grand *(see p. 172)*
> - **Cirque du Soleil's** *Mystère* at Treasure Island *(see p. 169)*

it's situated its breathtaking acrobatics in, on, around, and above a 1½-million-gallon pool (*eau*—pronounced O—is French for water). Even without those impossible feats, this might be worth the price just to see the presentation, a constantly shifting dreamscape tableau that's a marvel of imagination and staging. If you've seen *Mystère* at Treasure Island or other Cirque productions, you'll be amazed that they've once again raised the bar to new heights without losing any of the humor or stylistic trademarks, including the sensuous music. If you've never seen a Cirque show, prepare to have your brain turned inside out.

Showroom Policies: No smoking; pre-assigned seating. No tank tops, shorts, or sneakers. Attendees are asked to be seated half an hour before show time. Please do—you will be tremendously annoyed and distracted by those who come late.

Price: $90 and $100 (tax included).

Show Times: Fri–Tues at 7:30 and 11pm; dark Wed–Thurs.

Reservations: Tickets may be purchased by the general public 28 days in advance, 90 days in advance for guests of Mirage Resorts. Do reserve them early, as this is a very popular show.

Crazy Girls. In the Riviera Hotel & Casino, 2901 Las Vegas Blvd. S. ☎ **800/ 634-3420** or 702/734-9301.

Crazy Girls, presented in an intimate theater, is probably the raciest revue on the Strip. It features sexy showgirls with perfect bodies in erotic song-and-dance numbers enhanced by innovative lighting effects. Think of *Penthouse* poses coming to life. Perhaps it was best summed up by one older man from Kentucky: "It's okay if you like boobs and butt. But most of the girls can't even dance."

Showroom Policies: No smoking; maître d' seating.

Price: General admission $24.80, VIP admission $33 (includes two drinks; gratuity extra).

Show Times: Fri–Wed at 8:30 and 10:30pm, with an extra midnight show Sat; dark Thurs.

Reservations: Tickets can be purchased at the box office and over the phone, in advance if you wish.

✪ **Danny Gans:** *The Man of Many Voices.* In The Mirage, 3400 Las Vegas Blvd. S. ☎ **800/963-9634** or 702/791-7111.

In a town where the consistent sellouts are costly, elaborate extravaganzas, it's a tribute to Danny Gans's charisma and appeal that his one-man variety act can draw the same crowds with nothing more than a back-up band and a few props. Gans is "the man of many voices"—more than 400 of them—and his show features impressions of 80 different celebrities, usually a different mix each night depending on audience demographics.

The emphasis is on musical impressions (everyone from Sinatra to Springsteen), with some movie scenes (Hepburn and Fonda from *On Golden Pond,* Tom Hanks in *Forrest Gump*) and weird, fun duets (Michael Bolton and Dr. Ruth) thrown in. A standout is "The Twelve Months of Christmas" sung by 12 different celebrities (Paul Lynde, Clint Eastwood, Woody Allen, and so on). Gans's vocal flexibility is impressive, though his impersonations are hit or miss. Truth be told, he's better than his current material (particularly if the mood strikes and he improvises), which has a weakness for obvious jokes and mawkish sentimentality. Still, he's a consistent crowd-pleaser, and the lack of bombast can be a refreshing change of pace.

Showroom Policies: No smoking; maître d' seating.

Price: $67.50 (tax, drinks, and gratuities all extra).

Show Times: Tues–Thurs and Sat–Sun at 8pm; dark Mon and Fri.

Reservations: Tickets can be ordered up to 30 days in advance.

✪ **EFX.** In the MGM Grand, 3799 Las Vegas Blvd. S. ☎ **800/929-1111** or 702/891-7777.

EFX's $40-million makeover (initially retailored to fit David Cassidy during his lengthy starring run) was a case of money being used wisely, updating the classic Vegas revue into a live-action version. It's not just cheese anymore; it's expensive and occasionally jaw-dropping cheese.

Which is not to say it's bad—quite the opposite. It probably worked best under Cassidy's tutelage, when the loose narrative was at its most coherent, and some real semblance of an actual story played out. As we write this (but possibly not by the time you read this), the show stars Broadway musical perennial Tommy Tune, billed as "the tallest dreamer of them all" (6-foot-7 in case you're counting), and has reverted to a revue nominally linked around "Tommy's dreams," which conveniently dovetail with already existing production numbers involving King Arthur and Merlin, Houdini, H.G. Wells, and P.T. Barnum. This implies that no matter what star takes over the lead in the future, it will remain roughly the same, delivering set pieces of better-than-usual dancing, magic, singing, acrobatics, and illusion. And, of course, special effects (*EFX* is the movie industry term for same).

The sets are lavish, beyond belief; the costumes and some of the acting show the Cirque influence; and the choreography is considerably more imaginative and fresh than any other such show in town. The songs are somewhat bland but sung almost totally live, and some prove surprisingly hummable. And the effects (flying saucers and cast members, fire-breathing dragons, 3-D time travel, lots of explosions) show where the money is. Cranks may occasionally spot wires, and sometimes said effects are a little painful on the eyes and ears (and they overdo it on the fog machine). The ticket price isn't cheap, so it might be worth taking the less-expensive seats in the mezzanine, as the view is just as good from there.

Showroom Policies: No smoking; pre-assigned seating.

Price: $51.50–$72 adults; $37 for children ages 5–12.

Show Times: Tues–Sat at 7:30 and 10:30pm; dark Sun–Mon.

Reservations: You can reserve by phone any time in advance.

An Evening at La Cage. In the Riviera Hotel & Casino, 2901 Las Vegas Blvd. S. ☎ **800/634-3420** or 702/734-9301.

No, it wasn't inspired by the French movie or the recent American remake, or even the Broadway musical. Actually, it's more like the stage show from *Priscilla, Queen of the Desert.* Female impersonators dress up as various entertainers (with varying degrees of success) to lip-synch to said performers' greatest hits (with varying degrees of success). A Joan Rivers impersonator, looking not unlike the original but sounding not at all like her, is the hostess, delivering scatological phrases and stale jokes. They do make the most of a tiny stage with some pretty stunning lighting, though the choreography is bland. Still, it's a crowd pleaser.

Showroom Policies: No smoking; maître d' seating.

Price: $28.10 and $36.35 (includes one drink; gratuity extra).

Show Times: Wed–Mon at 7:30 and 9:30pm, with an extra show at 11:15pm Wed and Sat; dark Tues.

Reservations: Tickets can be purchased at the box office only, in advance if you wish.

Folies Bergère. In The Tropicana Resort & Casino, 3801 Las Vegas Blvd. S. ☎ **800/829-9034** or 702/739-2411.

The longest-running production show in town has recently undergone a "sexier than ever" facelift, but the result is far from that. It's more like tamed-down burlesque, as done by a college drama department. Bare breasts pop up (sorry) at odd moments (late shows only): not during the can-can line, but rather during a fashion show and an en-pointe ballet sequence. The effect is not erotic or titillating, suggesting only that absent-minded dancers simply forgot to put their shirts on. The dance sequences (more acrobatics than true dance) range from the aforementioned ballet and can-can to jazz and hoedown, and are only occasionally well-costumed. A coyly cute '50s striptease number on a "Hollywood Squares"–type set is more successful, as is a clever and funny juggling act (don't miss his finale with the vest and hat).

Showroom Policies: No smoking; pre-assigned seating.

Price: $44.95 for a table seat, $54.95 for a booth seat at the early show, $39.95 and $49.95 for the late show.

Show Times: Fri–Wed at 7:30 and 10:30pm; dark Thurs.

Reservations: You can charge tickets in advance via credit card.

Forever Plaid. In the Flamingo Las Vegas, 3555 Las Vegas Blvd. S. ☎ **800/221-7299** or 702/733-3333.

The Flamingo presents the off-Broadway hit *Forever Plaid* in its Bugsy's Celebrity Theatre. The plot line is bizarre, to say the least, and is just an excuse for a zany musical stroll down memory lane consisting of 29 oldies: songs like "Rags to Riches," "Sixteen Tons," "Love Is a Many-Splendored Thing," and "Three Coins in the Fountain." The performers' voices range from solid to darn close to outstanding, though the bits between songs are lengthy and unnecessary. If you're sentimental about the '50s and early '60s, you'll love it. And if you aren't, you probably won't.

Showroom Policies: No smoking; maître d' seating.
Price: $24.95 (includes tax).
Show Times: Tues–Sun 7:30 and 10pm; dark Mon.
Reservations: Tickets can be reserved a week in advance.

✪ **Jubilee!** In Bally's Las Vegas, 3645 Las Vegas Blvd. S. ☎ **800/237-7469** or 702/739-4567.

A classic Vegas spectacular, crammed with singing, dancing, magic, acrobats, elaborate costumes and sets, and, of course, bare breasts. It's a basic revue, with production numbers featuring homogenized versions of standards (Gershwin, Cole Porter, some Fred Astaire numbers) sometimes sung live, sometimes lip-synched, and always accompanied by lavishly costumed and frequently topless showgirls. Humorous set pieces about Samson and Delilah and the sinking of the *Titanic* (!) show off some pretty awesome sets. The finale features aerodynamically impossible feathered and bejeweled costumes and headpieces designed by Bob Mackie. So what if the dancers are occasionally out of step, and the action sometimes veers into the dubious (a Vegas-style revue about a disaster that took more than 1,000 lives?) or even the inexplicable (a finale praising beautiful and bare-breasted girls suddenly stops for three lines of "Somewhere Over the Rainbow"?).

With plenty of rhinestones and nipples on display, this is archetypal Vegas entertainment and the best of those presently offered.

Showroom Policies: No smoking; pre-assigned seating.
Price: $49.50 and up (tax included, drinks extra).
Show Times: Wed–Mon at 7:30 and 10:30pm; dark Tues.
Reservations: You can reserve up to 6 weeks in advance.

Kenny Kerr's *Boylesque.* In Jackie Gaughan's Plaza Hotel/Casino, 1 Main St. ☎ **800/634-6575** or 702/386-2444.

Kenny Kerr has been a headliner on the Strip for over 20 years and is as comfortable in a dress as he is with the crowd. This female impersonator/comedian sings (live—no lip-synching, unlike the other performers in the show), does patter, and chats with the audience in a question-and-answer session that is funny in a crude way and informative only if you've never had contact with a drag queen before. (And some of you, quite possibly, have not.) In between Kenny's schtick are other impersonators, none as memorable as Kenny's outstanding Barbra Streisand, but more than adequate, though perhaps not having as much fun as they ought. The most notable act (we do so hope he is still part of the show) is the hefty clown who paints a face on his torso and can somehow make his stomach fold over to give the impression that the mouth is speaking. Weird, but pretty incredible.

Showroom Policies: No smoking; maître d' seating.
Price: $28.95 (includes one drink).
Show Times: Tues–Sat at 8 and 10pm; dark Sun–Mon.
Reservations: Can be made in advance.

✪ *Lance Burton: Master Magician.* In the Monte Carlo Resort & Casino, 3770 Las Vegas Blvd. S. ☎ **800/311-8999** or 702/730-7000.

Magic acts are a dime a dozen in Vegas of late. So when someone pops up who is original—not to mention charming and, yes, actually good at his job—it comes as a relief. The Monte Carlo dumped a lot of money into building the lush Victorian music hall–style Lance Burton Theater for their star, and it was worth it. Handsome and folksy, Burton is talented and engaging, for the most part shunning the big-ticket special effects that seem to have swamped most other shows in town. Instead, he offers an extremely appealing production that starts small, with "close-up" magic. These rather lovely tricks are truly extraordinary. (We swear that he tossed a bird up in the air, and the darn thing turned into confetti in front of our eyes. Really.) Burton doesn't have patter, per se, but his dry, laconic, low-key delivery is plenty amusing and contrasts nicely to other performers in town, who seem as if they have been spending way too much time at Starbucks. He does eventually move to bigger illusions, but his manner follows him—he knows the stuff is good, but he also knows the whole thing is a bit silly, so why not have fun with it?

Accompanying him are some perky showgirls, who border on the wholesome, and talented comic juggler Michael Goudeau. The latter is a likable goofball who instantly wins you over (or should) when he juggles three beanbag chairs.

All this and extremely comfortable movie-theater-style plush seats with cup holders. And for a most reasonable price.

Showroom Policies: No smoking; pre-assigned seating.
Price: $44.95 and $49.95 (includes tax; drinks are extra).
Show Times: Tues–Sat at 7 and 10pm; dark Sun–Mon.
Reservations: Tickets can be purchased 60 days in advance.

Legends in Concert. In the Imperial Palace, 3535 Las Vegas Blvd. S. ☎ **702/ 794-3261.**

This is a crowd pleaser, which is probably why it's been running since May 1983. Arguably the best of the Vegas impersonator shows (though it's hard to quantify such things), *Legends* does feature performers singing live, rather than lip-synching. And the performers look remarkably like the originals; free use of video cutting between action on stage and the real performer generally shows what a good simulation the former is. Acts vary from night to night (in a showroom that could use a facelift) on a nice, large stage with modern hydraulics but twinkle lighting that is stuck in a *Flip Wilson Show* time warp. The personal touches here include scantily clad (but well-choreographed) male and female dancers, and an utterly useless green laser. When we went, the performers included a carbon copy (at least in looks) of the early Little Richard, a crowd-pleasing Shania Twain, an energetic Prince, an appropriately flamboyant Liberace, a striking Bette Midler, and one helluva Elvis impersonator.

Showroom Policies: No smoking; maître d' seating.

Price: $34.50 (includes tax and two drinks or one Polynesian cocktail, such as a mai tai or zombie; gratuity extra).

Show Times: Mon–Sat at 7:30 and 10:30pm; dark Sun.

Reservations: You can make reservations by phone up to 2 weeks in advance.

Lord of the Dance. In New York–New York, 3790 Las Vegas Blvd. S. ☎ **702/ 740-6815.**

No, Celtic tap-meister Michael Flatley (arrogant ham or genuine talent? You decide!) is not starring in this production, even though he originally created it as a showcase for himself. He's off with other projects, but his show works without him—and it actually is an excellent production. No, really—surprised us, too. Essentially, it's a Celtic dance revue; the dancing is truly fabulous and most impressive, while the set is simply but perfectly designed, movable yet unobtrusive.

There is a vague storyline. Punched-up Celtic melodies are shown off to their full advantage, thanks to an excellent sound system, while taps ring clear as miked heels punch them out. Unfortunately, the show is about half again as long as it should be, because frankly, there are only so many steps.

Even beyond the skills of the dancers, it is worth going to see for the two women who do violin duets, rather like Dueling Banjos but with a different sort of stringed instrument. Marvelous musicians and quite cute, they are the real stars of the show (presumably since Flatley's not around to jerk attention back to himself).

This is enjoyable even if you aren't a fan of All Things Celtic—though non-admirers may think the 90-minute show a few minutes too long.

Showroom Policies: No smoking; pre-assigned seats.

Price: $52–$60 (includes tax).

Show Times: Tues–Wed and Sat at 7:30 and 10:30pm, Thurs–Fri at 9pm; dark Sun–Mon.

Reservations: Tickets can be purchased about 45 days in advance.

★ **Siegfried & Roy.** In The Mirage, 3400 Las Vegas Blvd. S. ☎ **800/ 963-9634** or 702/792-7777.

A Vegas institution for more than 2 decades, illusionists Siegfried and Roy started as an opening act, became headliners at the Frontier, and finally were given their own $30-million show and $25-million theater in the Mirage. They (and their extensive exotic animal menagerie) have amply repaid this enormous investment by selling out every show since. No wonder The Mirage has them booked "until the end of time."

But while the spectacle is undeniable, the result is overproduced. From the get go, there's too much light, sound, smoke, and fire; too many dancing girls, fire-breathing dragons, robots, and other often completely superfluous effects, not to mention an original (and forgettable) Michael Jackson song. It almost overwhelms the point of the whole thing. Or maybe it's *become* the point of the whole thing. The magic, which was the Austrian duo's original act, after all, seems to have gotten lost. Sometimes literally. The tricks are at a minimum, allowing the flash pots, lasers, and whatnot to fill out the nearly 2-hour show. More often than not, when a trick is actually being performed, our attention was elsewhere, gawking at an effect, a showgirl, or something. Only the gasps from the audience members who actually happened to be looking in the right place let us know we missed something really neat.

Tellingly, the best part of the show is when all that stuff is switched off, and Siegfried and Roy take the stage to perform smaller magic and chat with the audience. The charm that helped get them so far shines through, and spontaneity is allowed to sneak in. The white tigers are certainly magnificent, but they don't do much other than get cuddled (charmingly) by Roy and badly lip-synch to pretaped roars. The duo is clearly doing something right, judging from the heartfelt standing ovations they receive night after night. But more than one couple was heard to say it was not the best show they had seen, and also to express a feeling that it was overpriced. And those ticket prices (over $90 *per person!*) are indeed sky-high. Go if you can't live without seeing a true, modern Vegas legend, but you can find better entertainment values in town.

Showroom Policies: No smoking; pre-assigned seating.

Price: $95 (includes tax, two drinks, gratuity, and souvenir brochure).

Show Times: Fri–Tues at 7:30 and 11pm, except during occasional dark periods; dark Wed–Thurs.

Reservations: Tickets can be purchased 3 days in advance.

Splash. In the Riviera Hotel & Casino, 2901 Las Vegas Blvd. S. ☎ **800/ 634-3420** or 702/734-9301.

They took out the mermaids and water tank that gave this show its name, froze the water, and added ice skaters and some increased production values. If the show is now the one in town that most closely resembles the guffaw-inducing extravaganza in *Showgirls,* it's nonetheless a considerable improvement over its previous incarnations. That may be because we are partial to ice skaters in any form, even if they are performing to the music from *Titanic* while topless dancers preen on a small version of the deck of same. The weird lip-synching numbers still remain, though they've been improved and more ambitious choreography has been added. Expect up-close looks at bare breasts as the flashy and not-terribly competent dancers parade through the crowd. Some "comedy gauchos" crack whips and insensitive jokes, and there's a truly talented trio of juggling brothers. Pass the time wondering if it's uncomfortable skating in a butt thong. *Seating warnings:* Seats on the sides are so bad that fully three-quarters of the stage might be obscured.

Showroom Policies: No smoking; pre-assigned seating.

Price: $39.50–$49.50, the latter for best seats in the house (includes tax; drinks and gratuity extra).

Show Times: Nightly at 7:30 and 10:30pm (10:30pm show is topless).

Reservations: You can reserve by phone up to a month in advance.

Tournament of Kings. In Excalibur, 3850 Las Vegas Blvd. S. ☎ **800/ 933-1334** or 702/597-7600.

If you've seen the Jim Carrey movie *The Cable Guy,* you probably laughed at the scene in which the two protagonists went to a medieval dinner and tournament. Perhaps you thought it was satire, created just for the movie. You would be wrong. It's actually part of a chain, and something very like it can be found right here in Vegas.

For a fixed price, you get a dinner that's better than you might expect (Cornish game hen, very fine baked potato, and more), which you eat with your hands (in keeping with the theme), while Merlin (or someone like him) spends too much time trying to work the crowd up with a sing-a-long. This gives way to a competition between the kings of various medieval countries, competing for titles in knightly contests (jousting, horse races, and such) that are every bit as unrehearsed and spontaneous as a professional wrestling match. Eventually, good triumphs over evil and all that.

Each section of the arena is given a king to be the subject of and to root for, and the audience is encouraged to hoot, holler, and pound on the tables, which kids love, but teens will be too jaded for (though we know some from whom a spontaneous "way cool" slipped out a few times unchecked). Many adults might find it tiresome, particularly when they insist you shout "huzzah!" and other period slang. Acrobatics are terrific, and certain buff performers make for a different sort of enjoyment.

Showroom Policies: No smoking; pre-assigned seating.

Price: $36.95 (including tax, drink, gratuity, and dinner).

Show Times: "Knightly" at 6 and 8:30pm.

Reservations: You can reserve up to 6 days in advance by phone.

Viva Las Vegas. In the Stratosphere Las Vegas, 2000 Las Vegas Blvd. S. ☎ **800/99-TOWER** or 702/380-7777.

An everything-but-the-kitchen-sink Vegas variety show, good only if you really need an hour's respite in the afternoon from the slots. Which isn't a bad idea, since the pre-show warm-up comic's "funny" gaming tips actually prove useful, if not all that funny. A lead singer and a small troupe of dancers perform numbers, including the now-ubiquitous "My Heart Will Go On." A comedian delivers some very adult humor (fat jokes, gay jokes, breast jokes, and so on) given the time of day and the number of kids in the audience. Another comedian does a manly-man routine ripped off from Tim Allen. One bright point was when the white female dancers donned Jackson Five outfits and lip-synched "ABC," fully aware of the giggles this sight engendered (unlike, unfortunately, the Elvis impersonator who closed the show).

Note: Discount coupons are often found in those free magazines in your hotel room. Sometimes the discount gets you in free, with just the price of a drink.

Showroom Policies: No smoking; maître d' seating.
Price: $11.50.
Show Times: Mon–Sat at 2 and 4pm; dark Sun.
Reservations: Not accepted.

3 The Bar Scene

In addition to the venues listed below, consider hanging out, as the locals quickly began doing, at **Aureole, Red Square,** and **the House of Blues,** all in **Mandalay Bay** (see chapter 3). You might also check out the incredible nighttime view at the bar atop the **Stratosphere**—nothing beats it. There's also the **Viva Las Vegas Lounge** at the Hard Rock Hotel, where every rock-connected person in Vegas will eventually pass through.

The Bar at Times Square. In New York–New York, 3790 Las Vegas Blvd. S. ☎ **702/740-6969.** Cover $5 Sun–Thurs, $10 Fri–Sat.

If you're looking for a quiet piano bar, this is not the place for you. It's smack in the middle of the Central Park part of the New York–New York casino. Two pianos are going strong every night, and the young hipster, cigar-smoking crowd overflows out the doors. It always seems to be packed with a singing, swaying, drinking throng full of camaraderie and good cheer—or at least, full of booze. Hugely fun, provided you can get a foot in the door. And yes, every night, right outside, the ball on top drops at midnight, for a little auld lang syne. Open daily from 8pm to 2am.

Holy Cow. 2432 Las Vegas Blvd. S. (at Sahara Ave.). ☎ **702/732-COWS.**

Okay, so maybe you go to serious bars for serious drinking, but anyplace with a giant bovine on the roof and an extensive cow theme on the inside can't be all bad. Cows are everywhere—cow paintings, cow-motif lighting fixtures, a "sidewalk of fame" of cow hoof prints outside, even slot machines called (irresistibly) "Moolah." The microbrew pub upstairs offers a free tour, or you can taste its four hand-crafted microbrews. Pub grub is also offered, which they assure us requires only one stomach to consume. Frankly, once you get past giggling at all the cow-related puns around (which can take a while), you notice it's a bit busy on the eyes and aggressive with gambling devices. Indeed, this is more casino than bar.

✪ **Triple 7 Brew Pub.** In Main Street Station, 200 Main St. ☎ **702/ 387-1896.**

Stepping into this microbrew pub feels like stepping out of Vegas. Well, maybe, except for the dueling piano entertainment. It has a partial modern warehouse look, but a hammered tin ceiling continues the hotel's Victorian decor; the overall effect seems straight out of San Francisco's North Beach. It's a bit yuppified but escapes being pretentious. And frankly, it's a much-needed modern touch for the Downtown area. This place has its own brewmaster, a number of microbrews ready to try, and if you want a quick bite, there's also an oyster and sushi bar, plus fancy burgers and pizzas. It can get noisy during the aforementioned piano duel act, but otherwise casino noise stays out.

✪ **Peppermill's Fireside Lounge.** 2985 Las Vegas Blvd. S. ☎ **702/ 735-7635.**

Walk through the classic Peppermill's coffee shop (not a bad place to eat, by the way) on the Strip, and you land in its dark, plush, cozy lounge. A fabulously dated view of hip, it has low, circular banquette seats, fake floral foliage, low neon, and electric candles. But best of all is the water and fire pit as the centerpiece—a piece of kitsch thought long vanished from the earth, and attracting nostalgia buffs like moths to a flame. It all adds up to a cozy, womblike place, perfect for unwinding a bit after some time spent on the hectic Strip. The enormous, exotic froufrou tropical drinks (including the signature bathtub-size margaritas) will ensure that you sink into that level of comfortable stupor.

Pink E's. 3695 W. Flamingo Rd. ☎ **702/252-4666.**

Sick of the attitude at Club Rio? (And well you should be.) Escape directly across the street to Pink E's, where the theme is pink. (You were expecting maybe seafoam?) Anyway, at least one regular described this as "the only place to go if you are over 25 and have a brain." And like pink. Because everything here is: the many pool tables, the Ping-Pong tables, the booths, the lighting, the lava lamp on the bar, and even the people. In its own way, it's as gimmick-ridden as The Beach dance club (see below), but surely no one would put out a pink pool table in all seriousness? Yeah, it's a ludicrous heresy, but don't you want to play on one? Anyway, Pink E's offers retro diner food and a DJ on weekends. The dress code basically translates to "no gangsta wannabe wear." Go, but wear all black just to be ornery.

Sand Dollar Blues Lounge. 3355 Spring Mountain Rd. (at Polaris Ave.). ☎ **702/871-6651.**

Here's a funky, no-decor, atmosphere-intensive, slightly grimy, friendly bar. Just up the road from Treasure Island, this is a great antidote to artificial Vegas. Attracting a solid mix of locals and tourists, the Sand Dollar features live blues (both electric and acoustic, with a little Cajun and zydeco thrown in) every night. The dance floor is tiny and often full. The minimal cover always goes to the band. Depending on your desires, it's either refreshingly not Las Vegas, or just the kind of place you came to Vegas to escape. Go before someone has the idea to build a theme hotel based on it.

Sky Lounge. At the Polo Towers, 3745 Las Vegas Blvd. S. ☎ **702/261-1000.**

It may not quite be the view offered by the Stratosphere's bar, but it's pretty darn good and a lot easier to get to. You see too much of the Holiday Inn Boardwalk directly across the street and not quite enough of the MGM Grand to the left, but otherwise there are no complaints. The decor is too modern (heavy on '80s black and purple), but overall the place is quiet (especially during the day) and civil. A jazz vocal/piano act performs at night, when the views are naturally best. The atmosphere produced by all this is classic Vegas in the best sense (with only a slight touch of necessary kitsch). Worth a trip for an escape from the mob, though you won't be the only tourist fighting for window seats. Open 8am until whenever they feel like closing.

Tom & Jerry's. 4550 S. Maryland Pkwy. (at Harmon Ave.). ☎ **702/736-8550.**

The dull exterior belies what's inside: a lively bar with three different rooms, each with its own entirely different feel and atmosphere. Decidedly catering to the UNLV crowd (it's right across the street, after all), it prides itself on being ethnically diverse and holding no pretensions. "Drink cheap, be loose, have fun" is the owner's motto, and the result is more enjoyable than the words "college bar" might make you think. Each room has its own ambience; the first is indeed a basic college bar, with a mural homage to UNLV wrapping its walls. The next room serves as the dance area, where cover bands and reggae groups play every night but Sunday and Monday. The back room is a pool hall with 20 tables. Most nights feature some kind of $1-drink specials, plus weekly beer busts and other such tempting offers. There's a moderate cover that changes week to week.

Tommy Rocker's. 4275 Industrial Blvd. (at Flamingo Rd.). ☎ **702/ 261-6688.**

Tommy Rocker is the owner—surely he wasn't born with that name—and he plays his club every Friday and Saturday nights, mixing bar band standards with '80s and '90s hits. It's a one-man show, with Strip musicians dropping by after their own shifts are done. (Occasionally, local bands are permitted to play as well.) Sort of like the inside of a Quonset hut painted black, his vaguely beach-frat-party-themed club has become the home for local and out-of-town Parrot Heads (Jimmy Buffet fans, for those not in the know), with the result that the crowd is 5 to 10 years past their heavy college drinking days. The large bar dominates the middle of the room; there are two pool tables and a grill for ordering food, plus an espresso machine.

4 Dance Clubs

In addition to the options listed below, country music fans might want to wander on over to **Dylan's,** 4660 Boulder Hwy. (☎ **702/451-4006**), and **Rockabilly's,** 3785 Boulder Hwy. (☎ **702/641-5800**). Not far from each other, both offer country music (live and otherwise) and line dancing, with free dance lessons. Dylan's is more casual and basic, whereas Rockabilly's is a bit more posh—the kind of place where you might squeeze a Manhattan in between your beer and line dancing.

✪ **The Beach.** 365 S. Convention Center Dr. (at Paradise Rd.). ☎ **702/ 731-1925.** Cover $10 and up on Fri–Sat and for special events.

If you're a fan of loud, crowded, 24-hour party bars filled with tons of good-looking fun-seekers, then bow in this direction, for you have found Mecca. This huge tropical-themed nightclub is right across the street from the Convention Center and is, according to just about anyone you ask, the hottest club in the city. It's a two-story affair with five separate bars downstairs and another three up.

Just in case walking the 20 feet to the closest bar is too much of an effort, they also have bikini-clad women serving beer out of steel tubs full of ice (they also roam the floor with shot belts). The drinks are on the pricey side, but the unfailingly gorgeous bartenders (both men and women) are friendly and offer rotating drink specials.

Downstairs is the large two-story dance floor. The sound system is top-of-the-line, as is the lighting design, and there wasn't one square inch of space available on a recent Friday night. Upstairs, there are balconies overlooking the dance floor, pool tables, darts, foosball, pinball, and various other arcade games plus slot machines, video poker, and a sports book. Other neat touches include tarot-card readings by the stairs and hot-pizza vendors. And let's not forget those Jell-O shot contests where club-goers try to eat shaky cubes of alcohol-spiked gelatin off each other's partially bared bodies.

The crowd is aggressively young and pretty, more men than women (70/30 split), and about 60% tourist, which is probably why the place can get away with charging a $10 cover. Party people look no further. There's free valet parking, and if you've driven here and become intoxicated, they'll drive you back home at no charge.

Club Rio. In the Rio Suites, 3700 W. Flamingo Rd. ☎ **702/252-7777.** Wed–Sat 10:30pm until 4am or later. Advertised cover $10 for men, local women free, out-of-state women $5 (but frequently when we went by on a weekend night, the cover was $20 for everyone).

This is one of the hottest nightspots in Vegas as of this writing, but apparently made so by people who don't mind long lines, restrictive dress codes, attitudinal door people, hefty cover charges, and bland dance music. Waits can be interminable and admittance denied thanks to the wrong footwear or shirt. The dress code (no sneakers and shirts must have a collar) is supposed to make the clientele look more sophisticated than grungy; the effect is the opposite, as most of the men end up in combinations of chinos and button-down shirts. Of course, it's so dark you can't tell if someone is wearing sneakers.

Once inside, you find a large, circular room, with a spacious dance floor taking up much of the space. Giant video screens line the upper parts of the walls, showing anything from shots of the action down below to catwalk footage. Comfy circular booths fill out the next couple of concentric circles; these seem mostly reserved, and when empty, they leave the impression that the place isn't very full—so why the wait? Music on a recent visit included a Madonna medley and the perennial "Celebration," not the most au courant of tunes. The total effect is of a grown-up, not terribly drunken, frat and sorority mixer.

✪ **Drink.** 200 E. Harmon Ave. (at Koval Lane). ☎ **702/796-5519.** Cover $10 ($15–$25 when major artists are performing); no minimum.

Where Gen X Vegas hangs out. The decor is hip, which in this case means an odd mix of industrial warehouse, peeling plaster, and brick country cottage exterior; somehow, it works. The rooms are all good-looking (all are candle-lit, and at least one rope hammock swings in case you need to relax), though much of the detail is lost in the obligatory dark nightclub lighting. Soundproofing is impressive; you can literally pass from the hard-rock room to the dance room with only a second's worth of the two overlapping into each other. (Of course, getting there can be a problem—the hallways from room to room are narrow and bottlenecks are frequent. Be patient.) A recent stroll through the hard-rock room heard a mix of retro and more current rock.

The different sounds mean different appeals for different rooms—thus something for everyone. If you're traveling in a group, you don't need to have a consensus on musical tastes. Despite a young, fashion-conscious crowd, this place is friendlier than you'd imagine, and surprisingly enough, there's virtually no attitude. Jay Leno, Matthew Perry, Dennis Rodman, and Charles Barkley have apparently been spotted there, but don't hold that against the place. They serve food, too. Self-parking is free, valet parking $3. Open Thursday through Saturday from 10pm till 4am or later.

Ra. In the Luxor Las Vegas, 3900 Las Vegas Blvd. S. ☎ **702/262-4000.** Cover $10 for men, $5 for women; higher for concerts and special events.

The futuristic Egyptian-themed Ra is part of the new generation of Vegas hotspots. It has that Vegas "we're a show and an attraction" vibe, but is still not overly pretentious. The staff is friendly, which is a rare thing for a hot club. It might be worth it to go just to gawk at the heavy gilt decor. You can also find a major light show, cigar lounges off the disco, draped VIP booths, and plenty of little nooks and crannies. Current dance music (mostly techno) is on the soundtrack. The later you go, the more likely the mid- to upper 20s clientele will be entirely local. Ra is supposed to stay open until 6am but can close earlier if it's slow—and, surprisingly, on a recent Friday night, it was. (That may be deceptive; on other nights, there was a line to get in.)

✪ **rumjungle.** In Mandalay Bay, 3950 Las Vegas Blvd. S. ☎ **702/ 632-7408.** Cover $15 Thurs, $20 Fri–Sat.

Now, normally our delicate sensibilities wince at such overkill, and we tend to write off efforts such as just trying a bit too hard. But surprisingly, rumjungle really delivers the great fun it promises. The fire-wall entrance that gives way to a wall of water; a two-story bar is full of the largest collection of rum varieties anywhere, each bottle illuminated with a laser beam of light; go-go girls dance and prance between bottles of wine, to dueling congas; and the food all comes skewered on swords. It's all a bit much, but it works, really it does. A great deal of thought went into the various clever designs and schemes, and it's paid off. Almost instantly, rumjungle became the hottest club in Vegas, with lines out the door every night, ready to dance to live world beat music. Get there early (before 10pm) to avoid lines/guest lists/the cover charge, and consider having dinner (served till 11pm); it's costly, but it's a multicourse, all-you-can-eat feast of flame-pit-cooked Brazilian food. For the amount of food and the waiving of the cover charge, dinner is a good deal. Then dance it all off all night long (the club is open till 2am on weeknights, till 4am Thursday through Saturday nights).

Studio 54. In the MGM Grand, 3799 Las Vegas Blvd. S. ☎ **702/891-1111.** Cover $10 for men Sun–Thurs, $20 Fri–Sat; free for women.

The legendary Studio 54 has been resurrected here in Las Vegas, but with all the bad elements and none of the good ones. Forget Truman, Halston, and Liza doing illegal (or at least immoral) things in the bathroom stalls; that part of Studio 54 remains but a fond memory. However, the snooty, exclusive door attitude has been retained. Hooray. Red-rope policies are all well and good if you're trying to build a mystique in a regular club, but for a tourist attraction, where guests are likely to be one-time-only (or at best, once a year), it's obnoxious. Oddly, this doesn't lead to a high-class clientele; of all the new clubs, this is the most touristy and trashy (though apparently the hot night for locals is Tuesday, so if you do go, go then). The large dance floor has a balcony overlooking it, the decor is industrial, the music is hip hop and electronic, and there is nothing to do other than dance. If the real Studio 54 were this boring, no one would remember it today. Open Tuesday through Saturday from 10pm until 3am or later.

✪ **Utopia.** In the Epicenter, 3765 Las Vegas Blvd. S. ☎ **702/736-3105.** Cover varies.

According to the old *Scope* magazine, Utopia was "less a discotheque and more a revolution"—which is an apt description, considering that in Las Vegas, underground once-a-week nightclubs usually disappear in a matter of weeks. (And for that matter, the underground itself is a shaky, hard-to-find thing.) Utopia is still going strong, despite the death (in a car accident) of its founder, Aaron Britt. The music is progressive house, tribal, trance, techno, and rave. The atmosphere is industrial, foggy, and heavy with lasers and other dazzling visuals. A cool and outrageous crowd fills three rooms with fun, peace, and love, in a heart-pounding, techno way. It's for the tragically hip, but isn't it good to know they are out there in Vegas? Internationally known DJs spin and live rave acts play. It's open Wednesday to Saturday 10pm to 3am (or so).

5　Gay Bars & Clubs

Hip and happening Vegas locals know that some of the best scenes and dance action can actually be found in the city's gay bars. And no, they don't ask for sexuality ID at the door. All are welcome at any of the following establishments—as long as you don't have a problem with the people inside, they aren't going to have a problem with you. For women, this can be a fun way to dance and not get hassled by overeager lotharios. (Lesbians, by the way, are just as welcome at any of the gay bars.)

If you want to know what's going on in gay Las Vegas during your visit, pick up a copy of the ***Las Vegas Bugle,*** a free gay-oriented newspaper that's available at any of the places described below. Or call them at ☎ **702/369-6260.** You can also find gay nightlife listings on the Web at **www.gayvegas.com**.

Angles/Lace. 4633 Paradise Rd. (at Naples St.). ☎ **702/791-0100.** No cover or minimum.

This 24-hour gay bar (Lace is the lesbian bar attached to it), though among the most upscale in Las Vegas, is a casual neighborhood hangout compared to gay bars in other cities. The clientele is mostly local, about 85% men (including drag queens) in their mid-20s to early 30s. There are special promotions that vary from week to week, including occasional drag shows and go-go boys. There's a dance floor (the music's pretty loud), a small outdoor courtyard, and a game room with pool tables, darts, and pinball machines.

The Buffalo. 4640 Paradise Rd. (at Naples St.). ☎ **702/733-8355.** No cover or minimum.

Close to both Angles and Gipsy, this is a leather/Levi's bar popular with motorcycle clubs. It features beer busts (all the beer you can drink for $5) Friday night from 9pm to midnight. Pool tables, darts, and music videos play in an otherwise not-striking environment. It's very cheap, however, with long necks going for $1.75, and it gets very, very busy very late (3 or 4am). Open 24 hours.

The Eagle. 3430 E. Tropicana Ave. (at Pecos Rd.). ☎ **702/458-8662.** No cover.

Off the beaten track in just about every sense of the phrase, The Eagle is the place to go if well-lit bars make you nervous. It's dark and slightly seedy but in that great '70s gay bar kind of way. All in all, it's a refreshing change from the overprocessed slickness that is Las Vegas. The crowd, tending toward middle age, is mostly male and is of the Levi's/leather group. There is a small dance area (calling it a dance floor would be generous), a pool table, and a nice-size bar. Drinks are inexpensive, and special events make them even more so. For instance, The Eagle is rapidly becoming famous for its twice-weekly underwear parties (if you check your pants, you receive draft beer and well drinks for free). That's right: free. The 20-minute drive from the strip makes it a questionable option, but if you've got a sense of adventure go see for yourself. Open 24 hours.

Gipsy. 4605 Paradise Rd. (at Naples St.). ☎ **702/731-1919.** Cover varies, but is usually $5 and up on weekends, less or even free on weekdays.

For years, Gipsy reigned supreme as the best gay dance place in the city, and for good reason: great location (Paradise Road near the Hard Rock), excellent layout (sunken dance floor and two bars), and very little competition. A few years ago, some fierce competition stole some of its spotlight, along with a good portion of the clientele, and so the Gipsy fought back with a $750,000 renovation. The changes seemed to have paid off, because this is, once again, the hottest gay spot in Las Vegas. The new look includes a marble and etched-glass interior, an upgraded sound-and-light system, and a quiet bar area that is glassed-off. With broken columns, vines hanging down, and archaeological-type pits, it all comes off as a gay version of *Indiana Jones and the Temple of Doom*. Really. The separate bar area makes the enlarged space actually look smaller, and the prices have gone up to pay for it all. Drink specials along with special events, shows, male dancers, and theme nights have always made this place a good party bar. Open daily 10pm to 6am.

Good Times. In the Liberace Plaza, 1775 E. Tropicana Ave. (at Spencer St.). ☎ **702/736-9494.** No cover.

This quiet neighborhood bar is located (for those of you with a taste for subtle irony) in the same complex as the Liberace Museum, a few miles due east of the MGM Grand. There's a small dance floor, but on a recent Friday night, nobody was using it, the crowd preferring instead to take advantage of the cozy bar area. A small conversation pit is a perfect spot for an intimate chat. Of course, there's the omnipresent pool and video poker if you're not interested in witty repartee. We remember this place as being a lot more crowded than it was during our most recent visit (but perhaps we were there on an off night). It makes a nice respite after the Liberace Museum (after which you may very well need a stiff drink). Open 24 hours.

6 Strip Clubs

An essential part of the Vegas allure is decadence, and naked flesh would certainly qualify, as does the thrill of trying something new and daring. Of course, by and large, the nicer bars aren't particularly daring, and if you go to more than one in an evening, the thrill wears off, and the breasts don't look quite so bare.

Cheetah's. 2112 Western Ave. ☎ **702/384-0074.** $10 cover. Topless.

This is the strip club used in the movie *Showgirls*, but thanks to the magic of Hollywood and later renovations by the club, only the main stage will look vaguely familiar to those few looking for Nomi Malone. There's also a smaller stage, plus three tiny "tip stages" so that you can really get close to (and give much money to) the woman of your choice—and it gets them closer to the bar. Eight TVs line the walls; the club does a brisk business during major sporting events. The management believes, "If you treat people right, they will keep coming back," so the atmosphere is friendlier than at other clubs. They "encourage couples—people who want to party—to come here. We get a 21- to 40-aged party kind of crowd," the manager told us. And indeed there is a sporty, frat-bar feel to the place. (Though on a crowded Saturday night, some unescorted women were turned away, despite policy.) Table dances are $10, couch dances are $20. Open 24 hours.

Club Paradise. 4416 Paradise Rd. ☎ **702/734-7990.** $10 cover, 2-drink minimum (drinks are $4.50 and up). Unescorted women allowed. Topless.

This is possibly the nicest of the strip clubs. The outside looks a lot like the Golden Nugget; the interior and atmosphere are rather like that of a hot nightclub where most of the women happen to be topless. The glitzy stage looks like something from a miniature showroom: The lights flash and the dance music pounds, there are two big video screens (one featuring soft porn, the other showing sports!), the chairs are plush and comfortable, the place is relatively bright by strip-club standards, and they offer champagne and cigars. Not too surprisingly, they get a very white-collar crowd here. The result is not terribly sleazy, which may please some and turn off others. The girls ("actual centerfolds") are heavy (and we do mean heavy) on the silicone. They don't so much dance as pose and prance, after which they don skimpy evening dresses and come down to solicit lap dances, which eventually fills the place up with writhing girls in thongs. The club says it is "women-friendly," and indeed there were a few couples, including one woman who was receiving a lap dance herself—and didn't seem too uncomfortable. Occasionally the action stops for a minirevue, which ends up being more like seminaked cheerleading than a show. Lap dances are $20. Open Monday to Friday 4pm to 6am and Saturday and Sunday 6pm to 6am.

Glitter Gulch. 20 Fremont St. ☎ **702/385-4774.** No cover, 2-drink minimum (drinks $6.75–$7.75). Topless.

Right there in the middle of the Fremont Street Experience, Glitter Gulch is either an eyesore or the last bastion of Old Las Vegas, depending on your point of view. The inside is modern enough: black light and bubble fountains, arranged around a runway strip.

The shows are basic—the women take off sequined gowns to reveal G-strings. Customers sit in comfortable booths, and the dancers then come around and offer up-close-and-personal table dances, often chatting merrily away while they expose themselves. As you enter, you are assigned your own (overly clothed) waitress who escorts you to your table. They also offer limo service to the hotels and even a line of souvenir clothing. Given such services and its convenient location, this is the perfect place for the merely curious—you can easily pop in, check things out, goggle and ogle, and then hit the road, personal dignity intact. Table dances are $20. Open daily noon to 4am.

Olympic Gardens Topless Cabaret. 1531 Las Vegas S. Blvd. ☎ **702/ 385-8987.** Cover $20 (includes 2 drinks). Unescorted women allowed. Topless.

Possibly the largest of the strip clubs, this almost feels like a family operation, thanks to the middle-aged women handling the door. They also have a boutique selling lingerie and naughty outfits. (Since they get a lot of couples coming in, perhaps this is in case someone gets inspired and wants to try out what they learned here at home.) There are two rooms: one with large padded tables for the women to dance on, the other featuring a more classic strip runway. The girls all seemed really cute—perhaps the best-looking of the major clubs. The crowd is a mix of 20s to 30s blue-collar guys and techno geeks. As the place fills up and the chairs are crammed in next to each other, it's hard to see how enjoyable, or intimate, a lap dance can be when the guy next to you is getting one as well. That didn't seem to stop all the guys there, who seemed appropriately blissed out. Table dances are $20, more in VIP room. Open Monday to Sunday 2pm to 6am.

Index

See also Accommodations, Restaurant, and Buffet indexes below.

BUFFETS

NOTES

FROMMER'S® COMPLETE TRAVEL GUIDES

Alaska
Amsterdam
Arizona
Atlanta
Australia
Austria
Bahamas
Barcelona, Madrid &
  Seville
Beijing
Belgium, Holland &
  Luxembourg
Bermuda
Boston
British Columbia & the
  Canadian Rockies
Budapest & the Best of
  Hungary
California
Canada
Cancún, Cozumel &
  the Yucatán
Cape Cod, Nantucket &
  Martha's Vineyard
Caribbean
Caribbean Cruises & Ports
  of Call
Caribbean Ports of Call
Carolinas & Georgia
Chicago
China
Colorado
Costa Rica
Denmark
Denver, Boulder & Colorado
  Springs
England
Europe

European Cruises & Ports
  of Call
Florida
France
Germany
Greece
Greek Islands
Hawaii
Hong Kong
Honolulu, Waikiki & Oahu
Ireland
Israel
Italy
Jamaica
Japan
Las Vegas
London
Los Angeles
Maryland & Delaware
Maui
Mexico
Montana & Wyoming
Montréal & Québec City
Munich & the Bavarian
  Alps
Nashville & Memphis
Nepal
New England
New Mexico
New Orleans
New York City
New Zealand
Nova Scotia, New Brunswick
  & Prince Edward Island
Oregon
Paris
Philadelphia & the
  Amish Country

Portugal
Prague & the Best of the
  Czech Republic
Provence & the Riviera
Puerto Rico
Rome
San Antonio & Austin
San Diego
San Francisco
Santa Fe, Taos & Albuquerque
Scandinavia
Scotland
Seattle & Portland
Shanghai
Singapore & Malaysia
South Africa
Southeast Asia
South Florida
South Pacific
Spain
Sweden
Switzerland
Thailand
Tokyo
Toronto
Tuscany & Umbria
USA
Utah
Vancouver & Victoria
Vermont, New Hampshire
  & Maine
Vienna & the Danube Valley
Virgin Islands
Virginia
Walt Disney World &
  Orlando
Washington, D.C.
Washington State

FROMMER'S® DOLLAR-A-DAY GUIDES

Australia from $50 a Day
California from $60 a Day
Caribbean from $70 a Day
England from $70 a Day
Europe from $70 a Day

Florida from $70 a Day
Hawaii from $70 a Day
Ireland from $60 a Day
Italy from $70 a Day
London from $85 a Day

New York from $80 a Day
Paris from $80 a Day
San Francisco from $60 a Day
Washington, D.C.,
  from $70 a Day

FROMMER'S® PORTABLE GUIDES

Acapulco, Ixtapa &
  Zihuatanejo
Alaska Cruises & Ports of Call
Bahamas
Baja & Los Cabos
Berlin
California Wine Country
Charleston & Savannah
Chicago
Dublin

Hawaii: The Big Island
Las Vegas
London
Los Angeles
Maine Coast
Maui
Miami
New Orleans
New York City
Paris

Puerto Vallarta, Manzanillo
  & Guadalajara
San Diego
San Francisco
Sydney
Tampa & St. Petersburg
Venice
Washington, D.C.

FROMMER'S® NATIONAL PARK GUIDES

Family Vacations in the
  National Parks
Grand Canyon

National Parks of the
  American West
Rocky Mountain

Yellowstone & Grand Teton
Yosemite & Sequoia/
  Kings Canyon
Zion & Bryce Canyon

FROMMER'S® MEMORABLE WALKS

Chicago
London

New York
Paris

San Francisco
Washington, D.C.

FROMMER'S® GREAT OUTDOOR GUIDES

New England
Northern California

Southern California & Baja
Southern New England

Washington & Oregon

FROMMER'S® BORN TO SHOP GUIDES

Born to Shop: France
Born to Shop: Italy

Born to Shop: London
Born to Shop: New York

Born to Shop: Paris

FROMMER'S® IRREVERENT GUIDES

Amsterdam
Boston
Chicago
Las Vegas

London
Los Angeles
Manhattan
New Orleans

Paris
San Francisco
Seattle & Portland
Vancouver

Walt Disney World
Washington, D.C.

FROMMER'S® BEST-LOVED DRIVING TOURS

America
Britain
California

Florida
France
Germany

Ireland
Italy
New England

Scotland
Spain
Western Europe

THE UNOFFICIAL GUIDES®

Bed & Breakfasts in
  California
Bed & Breakfasts in
  New England
Bed & Breakfasts in
  the Northwest
Bed & Breakfasts in
  Southeast
Beyond Disney
Branson, Missouri

California with Kids
Chicago
Cruises
Disneyland
Florida with Kids
Golf Vacations in the
  Eastern U.S.
The Great Smoky &
  Blue Ridge
  Mountains

Inside Disney
Hawaii
Las Vegas
London
Miami & the Keys
Mini Las Vegas
Mini-Mickey
New Orleans
New York City
Paris

San Francisco
Skiing in the West
Southeast with Kids
Walt Disney World
Walt Disney World
  for Grown-ups
Walt Disney World
  for Kids
Washington, D.C.

SPECIAL-INTEREST TITLES

Frommer's Britain's Best Bed & Breakfasts and
  Country Inns
Frommer's Britain's Best Bike Rides
The Civil War Trust's Official Guide
  to the Civil War Discovery Trail
Frommer's Caribbean Hideaways
Frommer's Adventure Guide to Central America
Frommer's Adventure Guide to South America
Frommer's Adventure Guide to Southeast Asia
Frommer's Food Lover's Companion to France
Frommer's Gay & Lesbian Europe
Frommer's Exploring America by RV
Hanging Out in Europe

Israel Past & Present
Mad Monks' Guide to California
Mad Monks' Guide to New York City
Frommer's The Moon
Frommer's New York City with Kids
The New York Times' Unforgettable
  Weekends
Places Rated Almanac
Retirement Places Rated
Frommer's Road Atlas Britain
Frommer's Road Atlas Europe
Frommer's Washington, D.C., with Kids
Frommer's What the Airlines Never Tell You